Specialist Aircrew

by
Squadron Leader David Berry

By the same author:

'*Tales from the Crewroom*'

'*The Motorcaravan Handbook*'

'*The Whispering Giant in Uniform*'

'*RV in UK*'

Specialist Aircrew

The life and times of a 1951 to 1991 RAF pilot

by

Squadron Leader David Berry

Keyham Books

First published in 1999
by
Keyham Books
Startley
Chippenham SN15 5HG

Tel: 01249 720239
Fax: 01249 720557

http://www.keyhambooks.freeserve.co.uk

ISBN 0 9527715 2 7

Set in 10pt Times New Roman by Keyham Books
Printed and bound by The Cromwell Press, Trowbridge

Contents

Chapter 1
Naivety

'The bints round 'ere look as if they don't know whot it's for!'

This coarse comment, sanitised here for your eyes, was made by one of my fellow new recruits into the Royal Air Force, on the service coach that met us at Bedford railway station. It marked my transition from being a rather naive schoolboy to being a rather naive member of His Majesty's Armed Forces.

The bus was taking us to RAF Cardington, home of the bygone military dalliance with airships; huge hangars are a memorial to those days. In 1951, the station had the lesser role of being the attestation centre for new RAF recruits. Here we were to swear allegiance to His Majesty King George VI and put our mark that meant that we were 'signed up' and subject to military law - there was no turning back now. I was relieved to see that the companion of the rude remark was herded into a different group to me; the first mark of the elitism of being *aircrew*!

I had signed on the dotted line as a potential pilot - I say potential as there was a long and difficult obstacle course ahead. I had arrived at this point in my life thanks to Biggles! The creation of Captain W E Johns, Captain James Bigglesworth had been my childhood hero. I was quite young when I discovered the treasure trove that was contained in our local library. Within the walls of a rather

1

The year of this magazine was 1939, so it must have been a very early stimulus to my interest in flying.

2

small and mean looking building, in one of the not too salubrious districts of Plymouth, was contained a world in print that widened the horizons of this council house boy. I read avidly and Biggles gave me an early compelling interest in aviation. In much later years, Biggles was the subject of much analysis and it was pointed out that women did not feature in his life. I am pleased to report that this element of his fictional existence did not affect mine!

Like all young boys I thirsted after knowledge of 'it', without being really sure what 'it' was; there was no discussion of the subject in our family. I tried to fill this gap with reading but there was little available; certainly our local library was totally deficient in this area. A rich source was a family set of Everyman's Encyclopaedia, which had been acquired at a discounted price using coupons from the '*John Bull*' magazine. If each of our copies of these twelve small volumes - 'Everyman's' quest for knowledge was obviously deemed to be limited - were examined then it would have been found that one fell open at a particular page. This gave a cross-section of 'a woman with child'. There was no textual information on how this particular state had come about but, at least, it was some evidence that there was something mysterious that was being kept from me. My attempts to uncover this secret were to continue.

But there was plenty to satisfy my curiosity and increasing enthusiasm for flying. My father bought, without fail, a monthly called '*Practical Mechanics*'. This covered every aspect of the increasing wave of technology of the 1930s that was to become tidal in later years. The range of subjects was vast. The wonders of an electric machine that could toast bread would represent one end of the spectrum with, say, a discussion on the possibility of space flight at the other. One series that appealed to me covered the construction of a 'Flying Flea', a minuscule biplane for one person, which could be built by the home constructor. Unfortunately, its ingenuity was not matched by its airworthiness; it proved to be dangerously unstable in flight and it was banned from flying by the powers-that-be. But it was a wonder to a ten year-old.

My father's main interest in the magazine was the radio content. He grew to manhood in the days of 2LO, the 'cat's whisker' radio and the like. Progress to a wireless with valves was a wonder. He built, for its day, a magnificent radio for our living room, the internals of which I was unable to appreciate - I do remember that it had two, pint size, lead acid accumulators that had to be regularly charged. But it was the cabinet that I could wonder at; it was a tribute to fretwork - the cutting of intricate shapes in thin plywood. This art form was shown in all its glory with the 2ft x 2ft covering for the loudspeaker. It was a lighthouse with its beams radiating to all sides. But there was a down side to this wonder for my brother and I - and this brings me to soldering!

Father wore a wing collar long after they became unfashionable.

My father, Henry, started his working life as an apprentice in HM Dockyard, Devonport and his trade was shipwright. An element of this was welding and his knowledge of this subject had to be pretty comprehensive. It perhaps was a natural progression that he should carry over some of this experience to the home scene in the form of soldering - although there seemed to be something lost is this transference; totally unsuitable demands were made on the durability of the soldered joint. Which brings me back to the radio. The doors and various flaps had handles which were diamond shaped pieces of what passed for plastic in those days. These were pivoted on their attachment to the woodwork. My brother and I only had to look at these - from the other side of the room - and they would break off! After a few harsh words - and possibly a clip round the ear - out would come the soldering iron; the smell of flux would fill the air and the handle would be repaired - only to fail again when, a few days later, we took another glance.

This soldering mania seemed to continually enter our lives. Later I shall tell the story of 'The bike I was given for passing 'The Scholarship''; suffice for now to say that I rode this bike to and from school - four times a day. The distance, each way, was not inconsiderable - a good three miles. One day, when descending one of Plymouth's hills, the front brake cable failed - the nipple had pulled off the end.

It was with some dread that I reported this for it would be made clear that I could not have been applying the brakes properly for such a thing to happen. That over, it was time for the repair - and, yes, out came the soldering iron. It will come as no surprise to you that, a couple of weeks later, the soldered joint failed. Again, I would be held to blame as the soldering iron heated up. This went on for years - in fact it may have a contributory factor to me leaving home to join the Royal Air Force!

Before leaving the soldering topic, one of Henry's major construction projects is reported - an automatic, 'teaspoonful of tea' dispenser. My father did not so much as lift a finger in the house to help my mother but, clearly, he had some sympathy for her domestic plight which would be alleviated if she did not have to spoon the tea leaves into the teapot. The dispenser worked rather on the principle of a spirit optic in a pub - put the teapot under it, push up on a rod and a spoonful of tea would be released - repeat, as required. The device was constructed from tins that had contained government subsidised powdered baby milk for my baby sister - a 1945, 'home from the war', product which caused me, as that ill-informed 12 year-old, some wonderment and intrigue. The tins were tailored to shape - and soldered - successfully, one has to say; after all, this is the intended use of solder. And the success of the dispenser? Well, there has to be the admission that it did dispense one teaspoonful of tea when required - and a sporadic supply, on to the kitchen top, when not. This would always be associated with some alleged totally unreasonable behaviour of Brother John or I. Nowadays, I cannot see a silvery solder joint without being reminded of radio cabinet handles, bike brakes and tea leaves.

Henry dabbled with photography and this seems to be a night study

I muse on what brought my mother and father together - but as I am now sexually mature and well informed, it really should not be a mystery; my mother was a good looking young woman - and there is evidence that my father, perhaps not in keeping with his age and era (the 1920s), was also sexually mature and well informed. But they really were not psychologically suited to each other. One thing they did have in common, and without it they would never have met, is that they both lost their mothers at a relatively young age. Alice May Devereux's mother died in childbirth - as did the twin girl babies - when May was 16 years old. She was sent from her home town of Stockton-on-Tees to Plymouth to live with a distant aunt. Henry's father, Percy, had moved to Plymouth in pursuit of work. Henry's mother, Anna Maria, died shortly after at the acceptable age, in those days, of 52. Percy and Henry sorted themselves out in a very basic flat in an appropriately named Stone Hall. For more reasons than one, a woman was required.

It seemed that Alice May sought some independence and found it by becoming a waitress at 'The Criterion' restaurant outside the gates of the Devonport Dockyard and taking a part-time domestic service job that offered accommodation. Henry met Alice at the former and visited her at the latter. The consequence was a small informal wedding and a Peter Berry. All of this is revealed in very touching letters from May to Henry during their courting days. Strangely, he kept these to his dying day, when the truth was revealed to John and I about the, infrequently referred to, 'prematurely born', sickly brother that preceded us. Peter died when he was ten months old. The sadness of this is revealed in those letters. Even though Mum and Dad were now married, her letters continued to him when he was at sea. This was something that Henry had to endure as part of his Dockyard employ. 'Sea Trials' were the culmination of the job and representatives of the technical staff were obliged to be aboard. Poor Henry - a strong stomach was not one of his assets. I well remember him, the years later, coming home from work with a face as grey as Plymouth granite - and then spending the evening regularly departing to the toilet.

'Daddy's got one of his bilious attacks,' Mum would explain.

So, on these sea trials, he was furiously seasick - a condition for which my mother could express sympathy, whilst writing, almost as an aside, that baby Peter was dying.

It must have been a strange and strained situation at Stone Hall - Percy, son Henry and new wife, Alice May plus sad baby Peter. Perhaps it was a breakaway from this that, after the death of the baby, they moved to a better environment - a new council house, 53 North Down Crescent, Keyham, Devonport, Plymouth. Was Percy the power behind this move?

He is a character worth examining more closely.

Lance Corporal Percy Berry, No. 2458, 1st East Surrey.
His Discharge Certificate described his conduct as, 'Good - a sober man'.

Chapter 2
Grandad Percy

Percy de Rippe Berry - there is a story attached to the de Rippe - was born in 1870 of farming stock, which is not a distinguishing feature of those years - the vast majority of Englishmen of that time worked on the land. He was to exchange the tyranny of an agricultural life for the no less restrictive one of the Army. He joined the East Surrey Regiment at the age of 18 and was promptly posted to India - for eight years! Yes, eight unbroken years! This completed his engagement and he returned home and was demobilised. He must have found life very strange and it is perhaps natural that he should fall back on his upbringing and take up gardening work. He obviously cast his eye about for some female company and there is a charming note preserved in the family archives that reads:

Haling Grove, South Croydon, Surrey

Dear Mr Berry

Excuse me writing I should like to know if you got back safe & hope Mr & Mrs Hornely were not waiting Mr Berry I shall be out tomorrow Tuesday & I should like the pleasure of your company if you care to meet me at half past six at the Red deer where the tram starts Tuesday night an answer will greatly obidge

Yours Sincere   *A Drane*

PS I hope you will come

The letter was from Annie Maria Drane, who was to become Percy's wife. But this love match was to be temporarily thwarted - the Boer War broke out and poor Percy, hardly back from India, was called up from the Reserves and found himself in South Africa. This would not have been a happy time, undoubtedly shared by others; an archive newspaper cutting reports the hint of a mutiny amongst troops being transported to the war. Percy served long enough in the war zone to receive, along with every soldier at the front, a tin box of chocolates from Queen Victoria, (still in existence - unopened!) and a bullet in the leg - also preserved! This was his ticket home and a medical discharge. Although the wound was to trouble him for the rest of his life, it was probably a blessing in disguise. Firstly, he was out of South Africa and, secondly, it excused him from World War I service and the associated high probability of death.

He was reunited with Anna Maria and they married, Henry was born - and Percy kept on gardening for the more privileged. This undoubtedly was a thorn in his flesh as he constantly smarted under an injustice which robbed him of a more comfortable life-style. When he was born, an aunt with no heirs, asked that he be christened a 'de Rippe' to continue a family name. The promise was that he would then inherit the family property - 'The de Rippe Villas'. But he was robbed by a 'scoundrel' - his own father who had gone off the rails, somewhat. The villas were not to be his. This was a story that constantly came into family conversations - conversations which I was to regularly hear as, with the death of his wife and the marriage of Henry and Alice May, Percy was to live with us for the rest of his days. So, my grandfather was very much a feature of my childhood.

He was unconventional in many ways; one of his enthusiasms was writing poetry. A dog-eared foolscap book would appear from time to time and we would be treated to a reading; we listened in respectful silence:

All those who read my poetry
Will they kindly understand
That I was never educated
But brought up on the land

To work and earn my living
With no time for school or play
So please excuse my errors
In what I write or say.

For the latter part of his working life he was a lighthouse keeper - but a land-locked one. Over the years, four lighthouses have been built on the Eddystone Rocks in the approaches to Plymouth Sound - these were built by Winstanley, Rudyerd, Smeaton and Douglass - yes, with two s's - why do I remember these names? They were the titles of our houses at Plymouth's Sutton High School! When the Smeaton lighthouse was replaced, the upper portion was dismantled, stone by stone, and rebuilt on Plymouth Hoe, where it stands to this day. Percy was its guardian and ticket seller - with, no doubt, the odd tale to tell the visitors. There was plenty of time to write his poems - and study chess.

He was the archetypal grandfather ... for instance, often repeating himself:

'I've only ever read one book - '*THE First and THE Last Love*' - not '*First and Last Love*' but '*THE First and THE Last Love*'.'

'The officer said to me, 'Do you know, Private, that the heels of your boots are dirty?!''

I replied, 'No Sir - a good soldier never looks behind!'

'How old are you, Grandad?'

'As old as my tongue and a little older than my teeth!'

We were continually reminded that, 'A little knowledge is a dangerous thing.'

Sadly we saw him slip into senility. He always washed the dishes and peeled the potatoes. As old age took its grip, poor Mother would have to hunt, high and low, for the hidden saucepan of peeled potatoes. To her undying shame she had to admit, towards his end, that she could no longer cope and he was taken to the geriatric hospital - what was so shameful? Well, it was the old workhouse and still carried that stigma.

Having a parent permanently living-in can be a considerable strain on a marriage but that aspect didn't show, perhaps largely because Percy kept himself to himself for much of the day. He was an inveterate cinema-goer - front row of the stalls every afternoon. Obviously, he had his own room which was 'out of bounds' to John and I. This meant that the occasional visit filled us with wonder - the

12

huge brass bedstead with its feather mattress, bulky furniture was crammed into the room - there were intriguing objects - a brass telescope, a chess set, a picture of Anna Maria - and a smell - of moth balls. There is probably a square mile of Plymouth that intrigues etymologists as being devoid of moths; it is the legacy of Percy's war against that species.

But there *were* strains on the marriage and, unfortunately it was we two kids - Father was not really cut out for parenthood. We were a nuisance that had to be contained - poor Mother had to continually stick up for us. Father adopted various discipline tactics which, basically, verged on mental cruelty. One that can be laughed at now but wasn't funny at the time was the 'Points Competition'. Below the high mantlepiece in the living room was a six foot long wooden rod for airing clothes. One day Father is engaged in carefully marking off

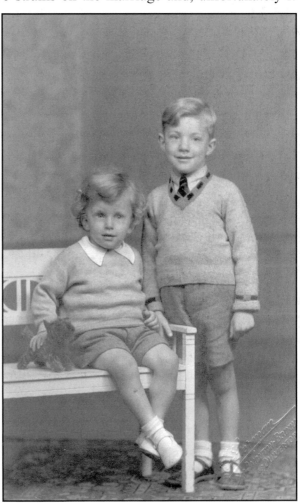

the pole at half inch intervals; that done, two long pins are provided with different coloured flags - mine red, John's blue. Why? Both flags were solemnly placed at the bolder centre mark. It was then carefully explained to us that if we did something 'good' then our flag would be moved one mark to the right - 'bad', one left. I don't think we were old enough to scheme and turn this into a pointless exercise; just the 'Law of Averages' of boys' behaviour ensured that the flags moved inexorably towards the left end - together. Perhaps part of the futility of the scheme was that Mum was not a fully participating member. And that was the pattern; I think I took after my mother and in adulthood was able to let minor, or even semi-major, irritants wash over me - but save myself for the big issues.

It is interesting to contemplate this 'big deal' council house that we lived in. No doubt it was quite something after Stone Hall but it had its shortcomings. In common with a lot of building in Plymouth, it was carved into sloping ground. The front garden never recovered from the slate that was revealed in this process - privet ruled, OK.

The back garden showed signs of early enthusiasm: a small lawn partitioned off with trellis work, a wire framework for a huge loganberry bush, a flower portion and vegetable patch. But the dominating feature was the shed. My childhood impression was that it was quite large but its unique property was that it leaned back at an angle of at least 15°. There was obviously some underlying assembly fault but it was never corrected; that early enthusiasm had faded.

Grandfather, with his gardener background, did his bit until old age seized up the essential horticultural muscles. I showed an interest but it was a forlorn battle with poor soil and little nutrient. There was also the matter of old ceiling material. Although it was before my time I feel that, totally non-gardening, Father must have applied his scientific mind to a problem with the soil and decided that, when some old ceilings were being pulled down in the house, the debris should be spread on the garden to counteract the acidity of the soil. Plant life didn't seem to care too much for broken lumps of ceiling plaster.

There were, in those days, still quite a number of horse drawn vehicles - in our road came the milklady, baker, rag and bone man. If one of these horses deposited a pile of 'dooh dah' in the road outside the house then Grandad would be out with a shovel and bucket. Diluted with water, the contents would water the roses or whatever.

'Dooh dah', 'dooh dah' - what sort of words are these? We lived with euphemisms - we had euphemisms for euphemisms. These would be mainly required in the urination and defecation area - it might be thought that the sexual one would also qualify but, as this was never referred to in any way whatsoever, then such cushioning was not needed. Clearly, urinating was once a 'Number One' (but for us 'spending a penny') as defecation was a 'Number Two'.

'The way you are fidgeting in that chair, it seems to me you need a Number Two.'

One fantastic feature of the garden was blackberry bushes - not your wild sort - these were 'American Blackberries' and produced fruit one inch across and full of juice. One of these bushes spread over the top of the Andersen Shelter - and there is a story to tell about that.

It is the outbreak of World War II and the civilian population is under threat of annihilation by the Luftwaffe. I have to presume that the countermeasure to this was the project of a Mr Andersen, for a shelter was named after him. Whatever, each household was delivered a heap of corrugated iron, some angle iron, nuts and bolts and an instruction sheet. The latter detailed the method of turning this ironmongery into a family air raid shelter with a semi-circular roof, to be half buried in a hole in the ground with the removed soil then placed over the top.

Receiving such directions was anathema to my father, as was digging a 4 foot deep, 8 x 4 feet hole. A bit of lateral thinking was required - or any sort of thinking to get out digging that damn hole. Solution: erect the shelter in the front room - which is just what he did!

Poor Mother was in despair; it has to be said that our front room was not a 'front room' in the Victorian sense, but it *was* our dining room and now it was three parts occupied by this corrugated iron monstrosity. I don't know what happened to persuade Father to

15

This was the Penzance house overlooking the ornamental gardens.

take it down; it must have been something pretty formidable for his mind was not easily changed, particularly when it concerned his more outlandish ideas. But it was dismantled and the hole in the garden dug.

We did go into the shelter one night, during an air raid, and that was enough to convince us not to repeat the exercise. This decision was reinforced by the fact that a shelter, complete with family, only a few doors away from ours, received a direct bomb hit. So, we stayed indoors; a bed for John and I was brought downstairs and the dining table top rigged up over it - poor Mother had lost her dining facility again. The shelter was used to store coal; this was not ideal as the top of the coal was below ground level - and the shelter flooded! But the blackberries that grew on top were delicious.

I was six years old when the war started so I have some vivid memories of the Home Front. What is amazing is that I do not recall any sense of danger, in fact it was all a bit of a good game. My father was sent from the Devonport Dockyard to Penzance to oversee the war effort work of a small shipbuilder. Mother, John and I followed.

Initially we stayed in a Guest House. Our young ears used to pick up snippets of adult conversation. I remember one topic being that the German-born landlord of the establishment had been interred - could it mean that he'd been buried alive? I know that we were being bombarded with anti-German propaganda but, surely, this was a bit strong?

I am reminded of another overheard remark, albeit at a different location. There had been some sort of road accident at a junction near our house and I heard Mother telling a friend:

'Well, the sailor came round the corner on his motorcycle and lost his head ...'

I can remember this mental picture I conjured up, in my young mind, of this matelot's head, complete with round hat, rolling along the road! I had a problem though, creating a picture in my mind to illustrate another overheard remark:

'He broke her heart.'

But, back to Penzance. We moved to what seemed a huge house right by the beach and spent a lot of time on the sand. One day we heard an aircraft and looked up to see swastikas and then as the aircraft passed overhead, bombs fell out. They landed in the sea at what seemed a very close distance; certainly dead fish from the explosion were thrown up on the rocks. What excitement - not fear!

There were several night raids on Penzance and we would spend the night in the basement. Our stay in Cornwall lasted nine months and we returned to Plymouth in time for more excitement - the Blitz. It was all a wonder for a small boy, the explosions, the searchlights, the deafening pom-pom of the anti-aircraft guns. A barrage balloon unit was established in our local park. For what more could a young lad wish?

Yet danger was close at hand. One piece of Air Raid Precautions (ARP) advice was to open windows and doors to lessen the damage from bomb blast. The air raid siren had sounded and Father had opened the front door and windows and was going to the back when a bomb fell, obviously alarmingly close. The blast blew out the fixed centre portion of our back room window. There was obviously then some reverse of air flow because the window was

17

blown back into its slot. This might seem unbelievable but the proof it happened was the trapped curtains.

Boys always collect things - and we had shrapnel; the bigger and more jagged it was the better. There were dangerous items; I find it unbelievable now but I know that memory is not deceiving me - Grandfather found an unexploded incendiary bomb and he kept it in his room. We were shown this treasure on our rare visits.

School went on - and didn't. Word had got about so we knew that our walk one morning, with Mother to Johnston Terrace, was a waste of time but we went to see the smouldering ruin of our school. Places were soon found for us at Camels Head - that was the name of the district; I know not why! This was to remain our junior school. We progressed through the classes: Big Miss Smith, Little Miss Smith, Miss Mar (who was dishy even to our young eyes) and the 'top' class, Mr Petherick.

True to the roots of his name, 'Pethy' lived in Cornwall and had to catch the train to Saltash. One of us would be posted at the classroom window at about quarter to four to see whether the Saltash train went past on the bridge over Camels Head Creek. If it didn't then it would be a rushed end to the day and 'Pethy' would dash off, able to catch the delayed train. The bad news was when the train was on time; there then was no rush to finish.

Discipline was pretty rigid:

'You're wandering about like the lost sheep in the House of Israel!'

This must have been said a thousand times to still be in my memory. Desks in rows was, obviously, the order of the day, with the brightest pupils trusted to be at the back and progress forward marking descending ability. In the very top corner were the brightest pair, Colin Baskerville and Valerie Hughes. Brains did not attract me, as I sat in the 'middle ground', close to Margaret G. She lived only a few doors from us and we used to play in the park behind our houses. Things became a bit 'heavy' there for a couple of ten year-olds, with a touch of, 'You can see mine if I can see yours.'

I was somewhat disappointed, a feeling no doubt reciprocated by Margaret.

But this clearly illustrates my determination to pursue knowledge of 'it'.

Our junior school was dominated by one aim, passing 'The Scholarship'. In later years it was called the 11+ and it really was the make or break of the rest of your life; it determined whether or not you went to 'THE Grammar School'. To say that it *did* decide your destiny is no exaggeration and yet we might have been blissfully relaxed

One of our better chair sitting days.

about it had it not been for considerable parental pressure; but then there was that about not eating with your mouth open, not sitting on the arms of the settee and the like. So the importance of the exam might have been lost on us had it not been for a promise if we passed - a bike! Clearly this put passing 'The Scholarship' above correction of our eating and sitting habits. Owning a bike was the peak of our ambitions. We lived in a car-less strata of society, the bike ruled, OK?

It was generally understood that this would be a new bike; they stood outside the bicycle shop beckoning anxious parents. But it wasn't going to be new for me. It must have been in their couple of childless years after the death of baby Peter and before my arrival that Mum and Dad pursued cycling. I can picture that Father was the force behind this. The purchase of two bikes must have been a con-siderable outlay for those 1930s' years.

Father's bike was a 'sit up and beg' roadster; Mother's was quite sporty - a green Royal Enfield with slightly dropped handle-bars. Children put paid to Mother's cycling and the bicycle lan-guished in the leaning shed. So, not for me a gleaming new machine, like my contemporaries, but a refurbished one - and one with NO CROSSBAR. Amazingly, this remained my steed for all my secondary school years - and I used to clean it and take pride in it. This would not be in front of my fellows; how can one be proud of a 12 year-old bike with NO CROSSBAR?! I had a Sturmey Archer 3-speed; they had Dérailleur gears - and metal pedals WITH toe straps; drop handlebars were *de rigueur* - with honking rubbers. Honking did not have its vomit connotation in those days; honking was standing up off the pedals for uphill work. The natural place for the hands was on the brake levers' handlebar mounting where the 'V' of the thumb and first finger were the body support. This could be painful against metal so rubber shrouds could be purchased - honking rubbers. One fashion I could join in on was having leather loops around the front and rear axles which cleaned these as the wheels rotated. Bikes were definitely 'the thing'.

Brother John was 'one year and ten months' younger than me - the interval was always precisely stated thus by Mother. So, how was he to fare in this bicycle business when his turn for 'The Scholarship' came? The shed stock was used up; buying new was not on - so one was assembled from scrap parts collected from various sources. Poor John - this humble pedigree was constantly revealed by mechanical failures. The final one came when the frame snapped - did I see Father reaching for his soldering iron?

I have mentioned my enthusiasm for reading; everything and anything was soaked up. One day it was an old book on cycling from Father's enthusiastic days. Now, I had been coached very carefully on the correct position of one's foot on the pedals; the ball of the foot not the instep. But, I read in this book that if you were really struggling uphill then a bit of instep work was OK. I happened to mention this at the tea table.

'Never,' says Dad, 'you are completely wrong. That would never be in a cycling book.'

'But I'm not - it does say that.'

'I'll give you all the money in my pocket if you can find it.'

This was from someone who never gambled a penny in his life. To give Father his due, he paid up - but I bet he felt sore!

Perhaps you get the impression that my childhood was a bit of an emotional turmoil; I think this was so - and it left its mark.

Chapter 3
More of the early years

The poet Philip Larkin wrote:

They fuck you up, your mum and dad.
They may not mean to, but they do.
They fill you with the faults they had
And add some extra, just for you.

I can endorse this! As my small child's lack of inhibitions were being shed, the full awkwardness and shyness of impending adolescence were taking over. This is nothing unusual for a child but I was also being 'fucked up' by my father who, perhaps unwittingly, did everything to undermine my confidence.

It may seem trivial but one outstanding embarrassment for me was short trousers! My adult height finished off at 6 feet 2 inches and there were clear signs of this elevation as I started the growth spurt of the ten year old. At age eleven I had long spindly legs which seemed more related to a donkey than a human being. But long trousers were not to be for another two years. I can remember, in order to cover my embarrassment, walking in public with a stance reminiscent of that Marx Brother with a cigar. It seemed worse when I wore the traditional navy blue raincoat. If I glanced down at my shoes they seemed almost out of sight - in spite of the fact that my feet were growing to the size of dinner plates. But this physical self-consciousness was only an outer sign of internal psychological mayhem. All this was not helped by the passage to the Grammar School.

Sutton High School - so called because it was located in the Sutton district of Plymouth - was a forbidding looking place dating from Victorian times. Elsewhere in the UK the uninviting granite construction would have drawn comment but not in Plymouth as all the public buildings and the like were constructed of this stone; it is a wonder that there was anything of Dartmoor left. This towering grey building was set amongst old terraced housing, right on the roadside of Regent Street. Its three storeys sat on a basement which necessitated a 'moat' all the way round. By this was a small playground containing ghastly outside toilets. The whole setting contained not a single blade of grass - granite, concrete, iron railings. Surprisingly, it survived as a school until 1986 - and the building still stands. Also, perhaps more surprisingly, some exceptional academic results were produced from within this ugly environment; even the results of Schoolboy Average were commendable.

The old term 'Grammar School', used above, might convey an impression of some élitist gentility, but such a quality had not penetrated to our part of the West Country. I had some very rough diamonds as compatriots.

A very basic example of the behaviour came when the bell was tolled for us to enter the school from the playground. The door was through an archway, up some steps - and all 600 pupils would attempt to pass through this entrance at the same time. Commonsense dictated that one held back until the hooligans had had their way - but this was 'not allowed'. A rearguard of the idiot contingent swept any shrinking violets into the mêlée. This meaningless exercise was repeated four times a day. The masters ignored it; I suppose their reasoning was that if they put a stop to this then the opposite effect would have been to have half the school loitering in the playground delaying the start of lessons.

I say masters but they were a bit thin on the ground for my first year - the War was still on. So we had the rather ancient males and a few females. My schooldays were haunted by a complete inability to learn French and I swear that this was due to my very first lesson from one of these mistresses.

'Guess what the French for window is,' says she.

It is possible that some of my compatriots didn't know what the **English** for window was! That was the start of five years of agony *à la Français* culminating in taking the School Certificate exam. GCEs were around the corner and we were one of the last of the School Cert, Matriculation brigade. In a written exam, it is one thing to stare blankly at a test paper and inadequately pen some small thing in response. But French had its final torture - an oral test. For this one optimistically learnt, parrot fashion, some sentences hoping that they could be moulded into a reply to the questions of the examiner.

'Pardonez moi, Monsieur, s'il vous plait, je n'est pas answer your question - mais voules vous ... observe out of la fenêtre that the weather est très bien/indifferent/bloody awful (delete as applicable).'

I was incapable of even carrying off this subterfuge and failed miserably. Perhaps if my success had rested upon knowing what was the French for window, that first lesson may have been my rescue.

As we moved upwards through the school, the War was left behind and the male staff increased. I realise now that the early

23

returners must have been qualified, pre-war. I remember a moment of hero worship when one of these appeared in his RAF pilot's uniform. A year later the 'emergency trained' teachers joined. It would be natural for me, as a young lad possessed with the arrogance of that development stage's judgement, to think that the staff were an odd lot. Although ours was not the behaviour chaos of many present day comprehensives, it did show early signs of this development. So a lid was kept on us. This was led by the sternest of men; Dr C F Jones was the headmaster. He held us in awe. Every now and then there would be an occasion which would present him in his full dominance. The whole school would be summoned to a special assembly in the middle of the day. Dr Jones would enter the hall, his black gown flowing behind him, and mount the stage. Tall, gaunt, he would glare down on his audience, stunned into total silence. We would learn that we had been called together because some invidious act had been committed - typically the theft of money from a cloakroom coat pocket. His tirade would always end with these words:

'Ye are the salt of the earth and if the salt have lost its savour, wherewith shall it be salted?'

I suppose we could have taken this as some sort of compliment but that aspect of the message was lost in the circumstance of its delivery.

An annual occasion when Doc Jones would hold the school in a spell was the Armistice Day Remembrance Service. This would culminate with him reading, slowly and solemnly, in a voice that would break from time to time, the names of 'Old Boys' who had died in the two World Wars. The, not over large, assembly hall contained 500-600 boys and you could have heard a pin drop. It is only recently that I discovered that Dr Jones was a holder of the Military Medal, so he must have been a soldier (not an officer) in World War I - and a brave one at that. No wonder he was so moved on the occasion that remembered that bloody and senseless war.

I did reasonably well in my first year, which I put down to the fact that, compared with my contemporaries, I was a bit of a swot. This totally turned to worms in Year 2 and I think that this was because of cabbage. Our classroom was in the basement with little light or air; it doubled up as the dining room for the 'school dinners'. In the morning we could smell the cabbage being cooked in the kitchen next door - pm there was the after-smell. Perhaps another cause of my downfall was sex. This was still pressing on my mind. It has been mentioned that Sutton High School stood in a far from salubrious Regent Street. The initial part of this was some humble shops. (One of them was a 'Gent's Outfitters' and the son was a classmate. His father's occupation was advertised by the fact that Butler wore a SPORTS JACKET! The rest of us were blazer-clad.) Another one of these shops was a newsagent and the owner used to display, in his window, the latest copy of the magazine 'Health and Efficiency'. This was supposedly, the organ, if you'll pardon the expression, of the naturist movement. It would be interesting to know what percentage of the sales were in the, nearest one could get to it in those days, soft porn market. Such philosophical thoughts did not occupy our schoolboy minds as we took furtive looks in the newsagent's window to try increase, from the latest front cover of the periodical, our knowledge of the female body form. On an information scale of 1 to 10, it might register a one but, as our knowledge was almost zero, it was a powerful intelligence source.

I think my pre-occupation with all this stopped me concentrating on why, or indeed remembering that, the square on the hypotenuse of a right angle triangle is equal to the sum of the squares on the other two sides.

Appreciating why Pythagoras leapt out of his bath shouting 'Eureka!' - no, ignore that, that was Archie somebody - was not helped by the demeanour of our mathematics teacher. Mr Perkins was the archetypal Victorian, in this 1940s' setting; bald, bespectacled, he ploughed through the lesson regardless of our understanding. Being able to accomplish this was aided by the fact that he would conduct the whole lesson chalking on the blackboard with his back to the class. But woe betide any boy who started 'mucking about'. There would be a black whirl as the begowned 'Polly' Perkins swung around from the blackboard and the chalk would speed towards the culprit with deadly accuracy. It was quite amazing; it had to be done with total precision; getting the wrong boy, or missing altogether, would have brought derision. 'Polly' never failed. It did cross my mind that he should take up darts but that demeanour would not have lent itself to this boozy sport.

Why should darts cross the mind of this 12 year old? Well, we used to play at home. For all his starchiness, in so many ways, Father was a great encourager of 'home' games - whilst holding the outdoor variety in total contempt; his comment on the football match in progress in the park behind our house:

'Look at those 22 idiots chasing after one ball!'

But, in our living room, out would come bagatelle with nails for the traps etc and ball bearings for the - well - balls. There was a skittles game where the skittles could fall over when hit by a ball on a string swung around a pole, to be re-erected with a pull of a knob which tugged on the string at the base of each skittle - and shove ha'penny. For the latter one had to have total respect for the shiny, worn flat, side of the Irish coins used - and for the french-chalked playing surface. No sweaty fingers had to contaminate either. We have seen that Mother's dining room and table were a fairly flexible facility. On the games' front they doubled up for 'ping pong'!

But it was darts that wore the crown of our indoor games. The approach to acquiring a dart board was somewhat laborious. Most people buy one - I suppose the odd entrepreneur uses a suitable tree cross-section. Always one for using material available, Father set about making a dart board ... from wallpaper! How? Take a three inch strip of said wallpaper and start rolling it up, applying adhesive made of flour - flour paste - as you go. When you have wound up about 200 yards of this strip then you will have a hard coil some three or four inches across. Don't despair - only another 20 or so inches to go. You might have gathered that one characteristic of my father was bloody mindedness; the strength of the trait would be increased in direct proportion to the amount of opposition/derision, whatever, that his latest project/opinion was receiving. With determination, the dart board grew. When it reached 18 inches, after weeks of effort, the flour paste soaked object became quite a slippery customer to handle - but Mother would clean up.

But, he finished it. He had to swallow his 'something from

nothing' principle and buy the metal grill to indicate the numbers, segments etc. A portion of the living room wall was covered with some rubber material and the first game of darts could commence. It wasn't long before one of the darts struck one of the metal parts, to ricochet off and stick into the adjacent round table - something of a family heirloom. Undoubtedly it was John or I who first accomplished this feat and there would be remonstration:

'It's the way you are throwing the darts!'

Anyone familiar with this pastime will know that a dart bouncing off the metal is not an unusual occurrence and very soon the table and other items of furniture, in the line of fire, were getting quite peppered. This was not quite as serious as it might seem as all the wood in our house was quite well endowed with woodworm holes, anyway.

I always associate my Uncle Ern with playing darts. Aunty Lily and Uncle Ern were not really related to us - Lily used to work with Mum at the 'Cri' - The Criterion Restaurant previously mentioned. Being somewhat short of real uncles and aunts, we did collect a number of pseudo ones. Uncle Ern was a Plymouth Corporation bus driver, a position with some status in our young eyes. His bus routes, in a red double decker, were Nos.1 and 2. We were constantly on the lookout for him and if we managed to get a wave before an audience of our compatriots then this was a real 'one up'. Ern rolled his own cigarettes. You will probably know that these do not have the property of the ready tailored variety of staying alight. So, most of the time this dead fag would hang from his bottom lip as he talked, bobbing up and down with each syllable. This would not be the only activity in this area; the top set of his false teeth would frequently drop down and collide with the bottom one. None of this stopped him being a great talker.

One was aware of social divisions but these were very finely delineated. As a youngster, I always considered Lil and Ern to be on a level above us. How could this be when comparing the social standing of a bus driver and that of my father who was a fairly senior draughtsman in HM Dockyard? The answer lies in house ownership. Lil and Ern lived in their own house; we were in a Council one. I had

27

a similar feeling about school peers of mine. It is strange to reflect on this as I now know that their semi-detached estate or terraced houses were not that grand - but they were not a 'Council House'. My father endured this state for long after I left home and then only bought the most modest of terraced houses. Why? With the wisdom of later years I put this down to 'The Depression'. The 1930s were hard times and particularly so in the South West - and for a young married couple with children. Father was one of the lucky ones and retained his dockyard job but had to take a drop in pay to do so. Such an experience leaves its scar and I think that my parents lived in the shadow of 'The Depression' for the rest of their lives, always being careful to have something 'put away' and not taking on financial commitments - such as a dreaded mortgage. So, in our Council House we stayed.

Returning to Lil and Ern, another thing to set them apart was that they had no children - and they had a car! It is difficult to imagine now how car-less those post-war years were. I didn't have a ride in a car until I was 12 years old - and that was a few hundred yards. Our vicar stopped and gave us a lift! Father was not to pass his test until he was 50; he then bought a new Austin A30 - the nest egg must have grown to a sufficiently comforting amount for him to splash out. For the rest of his years he became an expert on driving! With cars travelling in a column:

'The second driver should be stopped and fined - either overtake or drop right back.'

Seat belts:

'They give people a false sense of security and make them drive faster.'

Roundabouts, gear changing - there was an opinion on them all. Overtaking - his judgement was horrendous. It is perhaps unkind, but illuminating, to relate two of his motoring experiences. In the first he was 'done' for parking. When clearing out his personal effects after his death, I came across around 20 letters to the Chief Constable downwards outlining the injustice of this. The second 'trouble' was heralded by an evening visit to the house of a police constable - which would have completely mortified my mother.

They had been 'into town' that day and, whilst manoeuvring, Father was aware that he had 'touched' the car behind but it was so slight as to be of no consequence and certainly not worthy of investigation - the sad thought is that to have taken a look would have been an admission that a driving mistake had possibly been made. The policeman had called because the car that had been 'touched' was badly damaged; a bystander had made a note of the culprit's number. We will leave all the sordid detail of what ensued except to quote Father on his, often voiced, explanation of this event:

'During its construction, this car's structure had been put 'under tension'.'

No doubt he was transferring his shipwright's knowledge from the nautical scene to the automotive one. So, it had left the assembly line in this stressed state and had been waiting for some unsuspecting motorist to just give it a 'touch' for the transformation into a car that gave every appearance of having had someone back heavily into it!!

It might be gathered that Father was something of an obstinate person. So what of his attitudes towards 'indulgences'?

Sex did not exist - well it must have for me to be writing these words. But it was kept well under covers - pun intended! Drink was almost a total non-event in our household. The remains of the Christmas bottle of sweet sherry sat on what passed as a sideboard, in what passed as a decanter, for the rest of the year. With hindsight I would judge this was not because of lack of finance but complete lack of desire. Perhaps my life's enjoyment of the pleasures of alcohol cloud my judgement of the good sense of this state. Before moving away from the dreaded 'drink' to the, now low regarded, pleasures of nicotine, I do recall that Father did intermittently brush with the drink thing in typical style - something for nothing.

'Why are all those idiots spending money when you can make something perfectly acceptable yourself?'

The awfulness of his product was only really appreciated by me after I had left home and developed a taste for the real thing! In spite of warnings to the contrary, he persisted in using normal screw top bottles to contain his concoctions. From time to time these would explode, fortunately with only damage to property rather than person.

Strangely, smoking featured. Mother used to carry a packet of 'Craven A' in her handbag. The smell lingered with me to the time I, foolishly, took up smoking myself in my early RAF days, under the influence of peer pressure. The only time I recall Mother actually smoking these cigarettes was on her weekly meeting with Aunty Vi (another one of our pseudo relations) at Spooners' Tea Rooms. I had to sit through what seemed endless hours, salivating at the unconsumed fancy cakes on the plate on our table - the ration was one. There are photographs of a young Henry creating a raffish image with a cigarette in a holder. I only recall him smoking a pipe. Buying tobacco obviously began to niggle and Henry applied his mind, in this area, to the 'something for nothing' principle. It would seem that he studied photographs of tobacco plant leaves drying and concluded that they bore a close resemblance to the weeds that grow on verges - the sort with a single plate size leaf that looked like a coarse rhubarb one. These were harvested and hung to dry in the sloping shed. They then needed transforming into some appearance of being 'tobacco'; firstly, they were sliced but then some compression was required. A vital part of the clothes washing routine was a cast iron mangle, in the kitchen, with its big wooden rollers. The pressure that they exerted was adjusted by a large screw thread. Father adapted this to put pressure on a box containing his 'tobacco'. How this placed Mother and her weekly wash I am not sure - any inconvenience would have been brushed to one side.

After a suitable interval the box was removed and the product tested. You can well imagine that the resulting 'burn' bore a distinct resemblance to a garden bonfire! In fact, I am quite sure that the same effect could have been achieved by taking a smouldering spoonful of such a bonfire and placing that in the pipe. Father must have been suffering from the symptoms of smoke inhalation but obstinacy rules - the bizarre activity continued for some time. Did I hear you proclaim, 'What a nutter!'? How unkind - but how true.

To balance out some of this lack of charity, Father's ability with 'mending things' is described. Give him a clock that had ceased functioning and he would apply painstaking analysis to the problem.

Dismantling would be the first step and this would be executed with meticulous care. It was done on a tray; arranged along the back would be the 'trays' of used matchboxes. Into these, in order of taking apart, would be placed each screw, gear wheel, whatever. For reassembly the contents of the boxes would be used in reverse. A by-product of this mending activity was a tinful of 'spares' - those screws, gear wheels, whatever. One day, Father was engaged in some clock repair. Brother John - it wasn't me, honest - chose a moment, mid-repair, when Father's attention was diverted, to slip a cog wheel from the 'spares' tin into one of the trays. The frustration that this created was unbelievable - to the point where we could not reveal 'the joke'. This was an early indication of John's sense of humour which developed through the years.

Some photographs of the story so far ...

The girl Alice May with two of her brothers.

May and Henry in childless years?

.... when the childless years were over, it was double trouble.

Holidays were always an important ingredient of Henry and May's life.

A 'Valerie' is going to feature in these pages, Here, her brother, Nick, marries Cynthia. The smallest bridesmaid is Valerie. and her mother and father are on the left.

Chapter 4
The ATC Cadet

With my passage into the third form, and removal from the smell of cabbage, my academic standard improved and I achieved a satisfactory enough standard for the rest of my school years. I put this down to two things: the first is that I seemed to be able to cope with examinations - which tended to dominate the education scene. The second reason for success was fear - fear of the wrath of the teachers - and Father. Undoubtedly homework was a contributor to this but it was also a form of torture. On completion, I had to show it to Father. If I couldn't do a particular question then I was shown a 'similar one' and then left to solve the required one. Very sensible, but what a pain in the ass! Such 'help' was confined to the 'Sciences'; 'The Arts' were not a concern which, of course, affected my attitude - viz previous references to French - and sport.

With my attitude problem I was 'no good' at things physical. The weekly 'Physical Training' session was an agony, not the least part was having to change into PT shorts in the company of my peers. I developed a feeling that I was somewhat under-endowed in the kit-size area. I formed this impression from the glimpses that I had of some fellow genitalia. Undoubtedly I saw that belonging to the over-endowed who were quite proud to show off their physical attribute. I also had a more serious problem - mine was deformed. It was some relief for me to later discover what circumcision was, and that my parents had visited on me this strange operation. With the change into PT kit complete, it was into the gym for some fairly regimented exercising; then there was this terrifying wood and leather contraption over which one was expected to vault. There seemed to be constant danger that the little 'kit' one had stood at risk of being made even smaller. At the end of the session came 'relaxation' - a game of crab football. This followed the pattern of normal football which had to be constrained because of the limited indoor space. This was achieved by the rule that you could only move about with your feet and hands on the floor - hands behind your back. But it was amazing how agile some of my compatriots were in this configuration - and how powerful their kick was - another risk for the 'kit'. Looking back at school photographs, I realise that some of my companions were men when they were boys. I was tall but unbelievably thin - and a wimp!

My height did find me a place in the school Rugby 1st XV - when they were a bit short. I came to realise that I had quite an advantage in the line-outs and would be taking quite a few of the balls; that would be until one of the opposition 'took me out', in full stretch. My efforts would become somewhat subdued for the rest of the game and I would be running around the field, trying to give the impression of being totally involved but actually concentrating on not getting hurt. This was obviously not 100% convincing and, combined with the fact that I didn't really understand the off-side rules, would see me not re-selected for a number of weeks until memories had faded. I did get into the 1st XV annual photograph - because they were a bit short of people on the day!

The occasional photograph of the whole school was quite a major event not the least part being the arrangement of seating etc so that everyone was in the picture. With 500 - 600 boys plus staff, the picture was wide and was taken with a camera which started on the left and swivelled to the right taking a continuous picture as it went. A legend was that a small boy arranged to be on the extreme left and as the camera moved away from him, he dashed around the back to reappear on the right and thus was in the photograph twice. In the school photo I have, it does appear that I am the youthful school

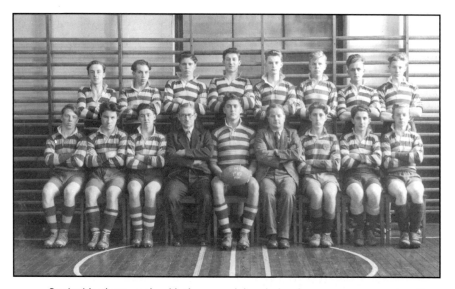

Study this photograph with the remark in mind ... 'some were men when they were boys'. The boyish looking chap, back row, last right, is the author. The Headmaster, Dr C F Jones, is on the captain's right.

chaplain, but the 'dog collar' was a bandage; one of the plagues of my youth was carbuncles and boils - which didn't contribute to the strength of my self-image.

Old school photographs remind one of the 'heroes' that existed, fellow pupils who attracted the right sort of attention - the head boy, the *victor ludorum*, house captains. It has been mentioned that we had four houses named after the lighthouses that stood guard on the Eddystone Rocks which were a hazard to shipping entering Plymouth Sound. The names, those of the builders, were Winstanley, Rudyerd, Smeaton and Douglass. The latter still stands; it replaced Smeaton which, as has been mentioned, was disassembled and re-erected on Plymouth Hoe - where it too still stands. Moving back, lighthouse construction was somewhat primitive but Rudyerd's lasted 47 years and then was destroyed by fire. My house was Winstanley and I think we suffered something of an image problem. Henry Winstanley built his lighthouse entirely of wood and it was destroyed in a severe storm after just five years. It did seem that our performances in various competitive activities reflected this inauspicious life.

The attainment of 14 years of age saw me in the 4th Form and entry into an organisation that was to determine my adult life. For all these secondary school years to date I had been longing to be old enough to join the Air Training Corps. We had a School Flight and the CO was Mr King, a chemistry teacher. It was amazing that there was appeal. We wore horrible, high necked, hairy blue uniforms. It meant staying on after school, not normally a voluntary activity. A large amount of our programme was drill where we were in the charge of older boys, elevated to the ranks of corporal, sergeant and flight sergeant, who had seen too many military movies and imagined themselves as Sgt Hardcase, or whatever. Take a bunch of adolescent lads and many of them, almost literally, cannot tell their left from their right - so drill always developed into something of a farce with the NCO i/c only marginally retaining control.

On reflection I think there must have been some difficulty occupying our time. Inevitably, we ended up in a classroom. I remember some instruction on navigation but I think there was some lack of expertise amongst our seniors. I was to add 'Aircraft Recognition' to my list of unlearnable subjects, which already contained French. For some reason we imported a couple of, non-school staff, young Pilot Officers. They didn't seem to contribute much, spending most of the time posing in their uniforms, with big hats, of which they were obviously very proud. We did have to study for exams - 'Proficiency', 'Advanced Proficiency' etc which had their due rewards. All this was worth enduring for those 'rewards'.

My first was a flight. Remember, this was a Council House lad who had only been in a car once! I can remember that flight so clearly - in an Anson passenger aircraft out of the grass airfield at Roborough on the outskirts of Plymouth. The noise was horrendous, the smell, for the queasy, equally so. I was completely disorientated and recall looking out of the window and seeing the ground as if it were a wall. But it was all sheer magic and I returned home 10 feet tall - my Father had never been in an aeroplane! All this reinforced the Biggles influence of earlier years and my enthusiasm for all ATC

Our school squadron at a summer camp. Mr King, chemistry teacher and CO is centre. The lounging individual, front row, 9th left, is the author!

activities knew no bounds. The natural result of this was that I passed the exams and steadily rose through the cadet ranks and the perks started to come along.

One for everyone was the annual camp where we went to an RAF station. Much of our activity was an extension of our after-school type - lots of drill, lots of chaos, lots of shouting. But there were moments of joy: a visit to the hangars to stand close to real aeroplanes; then to Air Traffic Control with all its atmosphere - and, perhaps, to utterly crown it all, a flight.

There was, for me, an excruciatingly embarrassing start to each of these camps - the FFI inspection - FFI? Freedom From Infection. We were in a military world with not many concession to our youth. We were not going to be excused a tradition of those years which was associated with new groups of airmen arriving at a station. They would be checked *en masse* for 'freedom from infection'. We sheepish young lads were not to be exempt this routine and would be ordered to strip to our underpants and then taken into a hall, to stand in a ring and await the arrival of the Medical Officer. He would walk around the circle, stopping in front of each person who would be required to drop his underpants and raise his arms in the air. On receiving a grunt of 'approval', there would be an 'about turn' for completion of the inspection and the MO moving on to the next. You can imagine the height of my embarrassment. There was one compensation; I was able to determine that I was pretty average, size-wise - and if I was deformed then it was an affliction shared with many others!

So, an aspect of cadet life was that it brought you into an adult world. Another instance, which probably shaped a deficiency that was to stay with me for the rest of my days, was shooting. We were instructed in and fired what seemed to be enormous .303 rifles. They made an awful noise - and they hurt - the recoil was like a kick from a horse. Then there were the RAF instructors - a rough lot who saw to it that there wasn't the slightest hint of indiscipline in the firing range environment. Left in my memory bank is the advice of one NCO on how to lie on the ground for prone firing:

'Imagine it's yer girl friend between your legs!'

This was somewhat unhelpful for someone in my ill-informed state. Mind you, my brother and I had received the one and only piece of sex education from Father, prior to me attending my first camp. I could tell it was about sex, as judged by his unease as he addressed us; this also contributed to his covering of the main topic being less than clear, submerged, as it was, in euphemisms. I think he was trying to warn us off masturbation.

My total flying time was increasing slowly, as proudly recorded in my 'Record Book'. But now it was to be added to, not with hours and minutes, but seconds - but important ones. I was sent on a gliding course on an old disused airfield on the Moors to the north of Plymouth. I made my way there daily - on that ladies' bike. I can recall that many of the trips were in vain - and some very wet.

The gliders we 'flew' were very primitive - and they must have been very strong as our 'instruction' matched the basic nature of their construction. There were no dual control machines - we were simply told what to do and then had a go. Mind you, the 'doing' was very simple. The start was being towed along the ground, on the glider's single central wheel, by winch and cable, and having to keep the wings level. When we were proficient at that we were told to pull the stick back a bit and hop into the air.

'Hold the stick there and you'll land back.'

These 'hops' increased in height until we were ready to jettison the towing cable and needed some serious advice on how to land. Firstly, it was drilled into us that the nose of the glider must be pointing down when we pulled the cable jettisoning knob.

'Then hold the stick there and don't pull it back until you think you are going to hit the ground!'

The photograph from my glider pilot's licence. Would you trust this boy with your daughter?!

I found, in later life, that there were more sophisticated ways of conveying the principles of landing an aircraft. The target for our 'Gliding Licence' was to successfully complete one of these, straight line, flights lasting 30 seconds! Shades of Wilbur and Orville Wright?

In this 'macho' setting there were other things to learn. Many of our fellow cadet students were a lot older than us 'school lot' and were ready to pass on their worldly knowledge. One ginger-haired, pimply-faced individual, with the faintest wisp of a moustache, which he kept sweeping out of the way with a finger, imparted some information on handling a girl's breasts.

'Don't bother with the right one - it's only the left that does any good.'

What's with this 'good'?

So now I was the proud possessor of a gliding licence complete with small round blue badge with a single white gull wing. There were more Air Training Corps 'goodies' in store for me when I moved on into the VIth Form.

St Thomas's Church, Keyham was 'High' church. A lot of wooden mouldings and red, silver and gold paint was used to convey that image.

Chapter 5
The Church

There has been indication that the major influences in my early life, in common with most youngsters, were the home and school (and the ATC). But there was one other for me and that was our local church - St Thomas's.

Mother was the initial influence - Father was definitely 'anti' and it was a wonder that my mother was able to retain her beliefs in the face of such opposition. But go to church we did, regularly - and that is all it initially needs to get children committed. John and I became wrapped up in the ritual - and part of it. We became servers, perhaps known by some as altar boys. St Thomas's was 'High'

Church of England and was not short of its ceremonial and colour, which stood out in the bleak environment of the district of Keyham, Plymouth. Ceremonial meant that there were a number of 'server' roles, with a hierarchy. The lowest starting point was the small boy who held the 'boat' containing the incense. Promotion and physical growth meant moving on to becoming an acolyte and carrying a candle - then the cross-bearing crucifer. But the job everyone wanted was thurifer. He operated the censer; within this holed silver pot on chains was burnt the incense on glowing charcoal. There were so many things to appeal about all this: firstly there was the pyromania aspect. The compressed charcoal tablets had to be heated to glowing red on an electric grill. To keep it in this state in the thurifer, and to distribute the smoke of the incense, required draught. This led to a second appeal - the theatrical. A line was drawn to actually swinging the thurifer over and around one's head but almost anything else was within limits - also attempts to expand those boundaries could be explored in front of an audience. This was a third appeal of all this 'serving', in general; there was an audience for all one's activity - they were called the congregation. If, amongst them, was a young lady that you were out to impress, then that heightened the theatrical nature of one's duties. There came to be such a situation for myself.

But what of religious commitment - belief. Well, we believed in Father Wood. He was incredibly sincere and totally submerged in  his creed. His only desire was to see us equally committed. He had the good sense to realise that, for younger people, church services with associated sermons, were not, on their own, going to do this, so he organised lots of activities - youth club, annual camp, dances, film shows, a pantomime - and these became the social centre of our lives and a considerable influence. An illustration of the draw that such a situation could create is a strange one. For me, it was a film projector which I helped to look after and operate; it was a total fascination for a 12 year-old. When a turntable was added and we could play records for our dances then 'my cup runneth over'.

Another pre-occupation was table tennis. But threading the film into the projector and playing a back hand smash were to be eclipsed by the realisation that a certain Valerie - the one who had been top of Pethy's class and an occupant of the prestigious back row - was quite a nice looking girl. I had plenty of observational experience to draw on to make that decision. I was 'looking about'. The loins were definitely astir.

But let us stay with recognised Church activities and consider the 'Annual Camp'. This too was an influence on later life although the only thing in common with the Church camp and my subsequent nomadic activities was the open air. We, the Servers and Choir, supervised by the Vicar and a couple of men helpers would load the tents, pots and pans etc on to a covered lorry. We climbed on top of all the kit, with our own belongings, and off we set, for a fortnight, to Hope Cove, 20 or so miles out of Plymouth. Camp would be struck in a friendly farmer's field. It was old military bell tents plus an equally ancient ex-Army marquee. The latter would be for the cooking and eating - but an important corner was set aside to contain the portable altar! With canvas screens to hide an earth latrine area, the whole impression was of a refugee camp. But it was heaven - first time away from home - with the lads - and caring adults. Each year it was a paradise away from the Council House estate. I still remember all the words of *'Green Grow the Rushes-oh!'* from the campfire sing-songs. I seem to remember that stew featured fairly heavily on the menu - and one of the men could make doughnuts very successfully. All this was done on a collection of those perilous devices known as Primus stoves. Pour some methylated spirits into a channel below the burner to start off the vaporising of the paraffin in the brass tank that formed the base. Start pumping to build up the pressure in the tank; when this seems sufficient then apply a match - and keep pumping; the result was unpredictable. Either the desired blue intense flame appeared at the burner - or the whole device would become enveloped in a ball of yellow, oily fire! The men helpers returned home at the end of the camp minus their eyebrows.

Cricket was the sport - not football, it wasn't the season. I spent an awful lot of time fielding, interspersed with very short spells in front of the stumps, where I waved the bat, unsuccessfully, in the direction of the ball. The wicket was, more or less, permanently occupied by Graham Stone who obviously had 'an eye for the ball'; it was impossible to get him out. More successful than bowling was an appeal to his better nature to 'declare'.

So, each year was marked by this event - and each year I progressed towards sexual awareness and Valerie and I were becoming very friendly in what was a wonderfully innocent way - but driven by the forces that ensure that the young mature to continue the species. Strangely our 'union' was accelerated by a person who later tried to cool it - Father Wood suggested that Val joined us on the camp lorry. On the cliff top of Hope Cove, we had the biggest 'snogging' session to date. It was the sea air!

So, in parallel with home and school life there was church life - the latter provided a considerable escape from home, where things could get a bit oppressive for Father - having two adolescents around.

It must have been in either the 4th Form or the 5th that it was decided, by the school authorities, that some enlightenment was required for those that had reached that development stage and it did seem as if my ever increasing sexual curiosity was to be satisfied - after school every Thursday in the Spring term we were to take ourselves to Devonport High School for Girls - not for 'practicals', you understand, but for a bit of theory. We were to be instructed in the mysteries of *'Human Sexual Reproduction'*. The title did not seem to totally match the knowledge I was seeking, but it would be a start. I was to be disappointed. We were to begin, literally, with 'The Birds and The Bees'. The weekly progress through the animal kingdom was painfully slow and there wasn't much detail of the actual 'act'. Mind you, we were pretty well informed on this aspect with the behaviour of dogs in the local park! Slowly, week by week, we ground our way towards humans, but we judged that this was going to be pretty tame stuff; if we weren't to be given the detail of, say, two horses copulating, what hope was there for girl and boy. We weren't to be surprised. I remember a lot of activity by tadpole devices swimming towards a watery sphere but we were not to be illuminated on the precursor to this event. I did learn a few words to look up in the dictionary but that was not a fruitful source.

So it might be that Val and I would have to do a bit of DIY instruction!

It has been said that the 11+ was an educational milestone; passing it was the ticket to the Grammar School - and the Grammar School curriculum was geared to the taking, aged around 16, of School Certificate exams at the end of the 5th Form. Two weeks were set aside for these tests carried out in extremely formal and controlled circumstances. Columns of desks were set out in the assembly hall. Exam papers were distributed, face down. At the prescribed moment the 'Go' signal was given; equally precise was the 'Stop'. For those with 'testitus' it must have been agony. You may have gathered that I wasn't one of the most confident of youths but, for some strange reason, I could cope with the tension of the exam system. This, coupled with concentrating my revision on past papers, resulted in me being able to make a fair crack at all the question papers - except French, of course. Val was taking her School Cert at the same time. Up until now we had only been able to meet at the various church and youth club occasions but we used the ruse of me helping with her Latin rote learning to get together in the Top Park. We allowed some time for progressing our relationship.

With the examinations complete, there followed a long summer - the results were not announced until well into August. I had done modestly well, obtaining distinctions and credits. There was a strange thing called 'Matriculation', which one only obtained with adequate results in a range of defined subjects. One of them had to be a foreign language; it goes without saying that I failed French and so failed to 'Matriculate'. I never did determine what was the value of this qualification. I have never been allowed to forget that Valerie 'matriculated'!

My results were sufficient to allow me to enter the VIth Form - status that had been constantly before us for all our years in those lesser grades. I can't remember any positive family discussion about me doing this; it seemed to be assumed - which did put me amongst a select band. There was a lot of assumption, in those days, that offspring should complete an adequate education and then start earning some money, asap, to contribute to the family income. There had to be some purpose to this extra stage of education and it became clear to me that the parental ambition was for me to enter the Civil Service. This reflects the attitude of those that suffered the days of 'The Depression'. If one was an 'established' civil servant, then the job was safe. There was certainly a well trodden path from Sutton High School VIth Form into the executive grade of the Civil Service.

My School Certificate results indicated that I should follow a 'science' path and it was agreed that I should study, in the VIth Form, Pure Mathematics, Applied Mathematics and Physics. There was a gradual realisation with Mathematics, which was to be confirmed in later life, that unless one has the 'gift' then progress in the subject means increasingly getting out of one's depth. I hung on through sheer mechanical effort but the real understanding was not there. VIth Form Physics also started to display much more complexity than had been anticipated from work at the lower grades. A new branch was electricity. Dr Congdon was our rather intense teacher. On Day 1 we were advised that:

'... electricity is very much like water, the wires are pipes; switches, taps ...'

On Day 2 it was,

'... well electricity isn't really like water ...'

This did some considerable damage and a total confidence with volts, watts and amps was going to be lacking through my life; something of a handicap when it came about that, in the course of time, I was to fly the RAF's first 'all electric' aeroplane.

Entry into the VIth Form did not mean a sudden leap forward in maturity ... there was still a lot of schoolboy 'mucking about'. Dear old Dr Congdon took his share. One day the task was to demonstrate to us the Wheatstone Bridge. Mr Wheatstone had given his name to this device which had nothing to do with water bridges but something in the electrical field, the details of which are lost in the mists of time. I do remember that it required wiring up in a fairly complex circuit incorporating a battery. We were instructed in the theory of this and then were tasked with setting up the experiment. The wire used for the circuit was the copper type covered in white thread. In groups of six we set to; in my group there was a wag who decided that a life of conforming was a bit dull. His contribution to lightening this was to substitute a piece of white string for one of the wires in the circuit.

'Please Sir, our thing doesn't seem to be working!'

Poor Dr Congdon ... finding the cause after half an hour of diagnosis, he had a puzzled expression on his face. The point was completely lost on him that the whole thing had been a deliberate act!

My extra-curricular activities continued apace and I was to be the recipient of another Air Training Corps 'perk' which was to push me ever closer to considering a career in the Royal Air Force. I was chosen to spend a month with a RAF bomber squadron, on exercise, in the Suez Canal Zone. By now I was a Cadet Flight Sergeant, but only the tender age of 16fi, when I was plunged into this man's world. I had to report to an airfield in Rutland for a flight, in a Hastings transport aircraft, to the RAF's Egyptian base of Shallufa, by the Suez Canal. The aircraft carried the ground crew for the Lincoln bomber aircraft which departed the base ahead of us. We stopped the night in a place called Castel Benito in North Africa. I was totally bewildered - and lonely. With the age gap, none of my fellow passengers made any attempt at conversation - or assistance - and that was to be the pattern for the month. Strangely, I didn't consider this odd at the time; I was a very small fish in their big pond.

We arrived at Shallufa in the heat and the sand. It was not a very prepossessing place; but I revelled in it. I was near aeroplanes, I could go in them - I was taken on trips in them. The Lincolns seemed massive, particularly when I was allocated the rear gunner's position for a trip; this was probably a devious plot to keep me out of the way! A flight in a Mosquito was fantastic. I had a lot of time on my hands in between these joys and was allowed free rein with a device known as a Link Trainer. It was a very crude predecessor of the flight simulators of today. It looked like a jokey wooden aeroplane mounted on bellows on a plinth. You sat in and there were the basic controls and flight instruments of a full size aircraft. It was intended for pilots to practise flying on instruments. I 'played' with this for hours and it probably stood me in very good stead; with the constant practice, control movements became instinctive - as did reading the instruments.

My very own picture of the Suez Canal! There was the considerable gesture by Father of lending me his camera for the Egyptian trip. This was one of those fold-up bellows jobs and was a quite a responsibility!

There was a lot of bewilderment; I had a bed in amongst 20 men. Perhaps it was as well I was so naive. If I had understood a half of what was being said, I am sure that my sex education would have advanced beyond the 'tadpoles' and the 'watery sphere'. There was puzzlement amongst the local Egyptian staff, clothed in their white galabeahs. There I was, clearly still very wet behind the ears, but I had sergeant's stripes on my arm. A bewildering few days was spent on flying visits to Malta and Cyprus. I really didn't know which way was up - but I probably did 'grow up' considerably in that month. It seemed strange to be back in 53 North Down Crescent after such an experience.

And it was back to Pure Maths, Applied Maths and Physics and the target of 'A' Level exams. Yes, we were in transition time; School Certificate had become 'Ordinary Levels' ie 'O' Levels, and Higher School Certificate, 'Advanced Levels'. A strange thing about the latter's introduction was that results were not graded, other than 'Pass' or 'Fail'. Subsequently A, B etc featured. Homework became more of pressure. It might be thought that, with my progression into advanced mathematics and physics, I would be leaving the homework supervision tyranny of my father behind. But, not so.

Father had completed four years of Dockyard School. What can be the significance of this? Well it certainly meant something within the world of His Majesty's Dockyard. All Dockyard apprentices attended the school for their first year. At the end of this there were exams and the results determined whether you went on to the second year. Half did, half didn't; the latter pursued a greater degree of practical training. This process was repeated at the end of the second and third years. This meant that the 15 or so 'Fourth Years' were the academic cream. With the exams at the end of their year, they competed for positions in the order of merit. Father came commendably well up this list. Achievement of this standard was the ticket, for most, to great things. The very senior management of HM Dockyards (there was Portsmouth, Chatham and Rosyth as well as Devonport) and other Admiralty establishments came from the ranks of past 'Fourth Years'. Many, on completion of their apprenticeship, went on to post-graduate studies at University. There was an opening

The élite - the Fourth Year of the Dockyard School. Henry is in the middle row - 3rd from the left.

into the élite ranks of the Royal Corps of Naval Constructors where 25 year-olds were granted the equivalent rank of RN Captain. One ex-Fourth Year who travelled this path ended up as the technical director of the Clydeside shipbuilders, John Brown & Co, designing and building the *QE2*.

But Father was having none of this. I have mused on this situation, with the benefit of my now senior years, and there is no doubt that he had an attitude problem. He seemed to reason that he had proved that he was pretty bright and now it was up to the hierarchy to pick up on this and use his talents - without any further effort on his part - effort, that is, in any promotion race; he certainly put effort into his assigned tasks, which reinforced his feeling that 'they' should pick him out. The successful amongst his compatriots volunteered for posts that involved moving to another establishment. Father was not prepared to move away from Plymouth. If he wasn't good enough to be promoted where he was then they could whistle. So he soldiered on, in relative obscurity, in the Drawing Office. He was obviously a highly skilled draughtsman. When a new Drawing Office was built many years later, one of his drawings, some 12 feet wide, of a ship's hull, was displayed, framed, on the wall of the entrance hall. He evidently brooked no nonsense from his subordinates - or his superiors. There is no doubt that he carried the label 'Bolshie'. Little of this reached our tender ears. We were aware that Father refused to do overtime. He saw this as a device for the slackers.

'If they put their backs into the job during normal working hours then there would be no need for overtime.'

So, we have the sad tale of a man who never really achieved his potential. He was promoted to quite a senior position during the War (Overseer) but was dropped back to his original status at the end of hostilities. Thus we had a father who had dug his heels in - and his bottom into 53 North Down Crescent, which he wasn't going to leave for any fancy promotion - or to improve the family's way of life. It became clear, even to our young senses that, with the years, the estate area was deteriorating. But Father was to hang on in his Council House until he was in his 50s and then, as has been mentioned, only to buy the humblest of houses.

All this recollection was sparked off by the topic of my VIth Form homework. Here I was, moving into the realms of higher mathematics - but I never exhausted the knowledge of my father, retained for a considerable number of years now. There was the inevitable arrogance of youth as he would peer over my shoulder, realising that I was having a problem.

'You couldn't possibly help me with this latest gigantic leap I have now made in the mathematical kingdom,' I would think.

But out would come his paper and pencil - and I'd be shown a 'similar' problem.

And so it continued, as I progressed through the VIth Form - fortunately for me, it wasn't all work and no play. I had obviously not inherited that almost obsessional desire to achieve academic success which was clearly possessed by Father at my age.

51

Valletta Harbour, Malta

Photographs by that bewildered young traveller.

Street scene, Nicosia, Cyprus ...

... and Valletta, Malta.

Chapter 6
Flying Scholarship

One 'play' ingredient was the cinema. In those pre-TV days it was a magic place for Valerie and I. Part of the attraction was the film. When I catch glimpses, these days, of those films of the time, I am astonished at their awfulness: the awkwardness of the scripts, the falseness of the scenery and settings - but, most of all, the dreadful manner of speaking which was a common ingredient; no matter what the role, it seemed that the characters had graduated from the Academy for the Sons and Daughters of Genteel Folk.

But popular it all was and there was always a queue to get in. This would shuffle along as people inside vacated their seats; yes, they would do this part way through a film because that had been the point where they had come in! This was the amazing norm; screening was continuous so you picked up the story from when your progress to the head of the queue had gained you a seat. You saw the film to the end and then, with a supporting one in between, tacked the beginning of the main feature on to the bit you had already seen - quite extraordinary! Quite extraordinary that the Great British Public put up with it - but that was the way of things in those late 1940s days.

I haven't made much of the low standard of living that was endured after we had WON the War. Whilst we were at war, deprivation was an accepted part of the scene; people had to do their bit on the Home Front. But there was no relief from this with victory. Food and clothes rationing continued - and the amounts were incredibly meagre.

Being sent shopping was a painful experience for me but off I was forced to go, with Ration Books in hand and strict instructions as to which 'cut' of meat, say, was to be obtained. Choice would have been a fine thing. I would find myself in a butcher's shop full of housewives, each trying to negotiate the primest of cuts. It was, no doubt, a relief to the butcher when it was the turn of a lowly being, like me, to be served. Home I would go with my miserable purchase to be berated by Mother. Clearly there was a maternal lesson to be learnt here - but off I would be sent the next week, just the same.

Perhaps it was a feature of the rationing and family finance circumstance but we never seem to have a weekly shop. Every day something would be required from the local Co-op - and off I'd be sent. I can remember my mothers 'Dividend Number' to this day - the way it was said assists the memory - nineteen fourteen two - 19142! This, with the amount of the purchase, was solemnly recorded on small coupons with carbon beneath. The perforated coupon was detached and handed to you. These had to be saved to claim your 'Divi' - a percentage pay out, twice a year. Later, or perhaps it ran parallel with this scheme, we used to be given stamp-like pieces of paper to the value of the purchase. You were also supplied, as required, with one foot square pieces of brown paper which were coated with dried glue. This had to be moistened to take the 'stamps'.

Milk was delivered, by horse and cart, direct from a Cornish farm. Even for my young years, I could not help but notice that the 'milk lady', the farmer's daughter, was a 'robust' young woman. Mother would always boil up this milk and then it was placed in an enamel bowl and allowed to cool. I can still taste the rich cream, quarter of an inch thick, that was scooped off the top.

This was the pattern of our lives, meagre portions of poor quality food with tasty highlights to attack the sensitive palates of a child. It might seem strange to include potato cake in this. Potato cake was made of - well - potatoes, mashed and placed in a flat round tin with a few, very few, sultanas. This was then grilled - a great treat.

One of the deprivations of war was bananas. They were described to us and held in great regard by those who remembered the post-war years. One day my mother decided that she would make us some artificial bananas; no doubt she had picked this up from tips, in abundance, for making do. The ingredients for artificial bananas was banana essence (artificial itself?) and parsnips. Soak the latter in the former. The result? Truly ghastly! It was many, many years before I could eat parsnips as a vegetable - and I'm not that keen on bananas!

Away from food, things were no better with other commodities. There had to be a considerable saving of 'coupons' if a substantial piece of apparel was required. Then there was ghastly 'Utility Furniture'; the adjective said it all. Not that furniture was much of a priority in our house. We had Grandfather's old stuff - suitably repaired or not.

I can remember that a *chaise longue* (don't be misled by this elegant title) and the dining chairs had been re-covered in some brown, inhospitable material that had obviously had some function on board one of His Majesty's ships. Judging by its colour and texture, it must have been something to do with the boiler room.

And then there was the brown paint in the kitchen - chocolate brown on everything - doors, cupboards, shelves, window sills. The tins of the paint bore no description - only the 'broad arrow'. I swear that it must have been the type of paint they apply to poles to stop people climbing them ie it never dries.

To say that the brown paint remained wet to the touch would be an exaggeration - it might be that it was a bit thick coming direct from the tin and some turps had been added. But this did not prevent it being constantly tacky. Pans stuck to shelves; forgetfully lean against the door and clothes' threads would be stuck to the surface as you pulled yourself away, finger and palm prints abounded. There was a rubberised raincoat that had been hung behind a door and there it remained - permanently adhered.

What ghastliness; but it was ignored. Obviously the painting had been a major undertaking and undoing such effort could not be contemplated. And that was the sad state that my mother had to endure. With reflection, I don't think my father ever bought a piece of wood, a pack of screws, a decent amount of paint etc for any job in the house. It was bodge all the way - except for that tea dispenser.

I have read that the success of a crazy, late 1940s' fashion rested on the fact that it signalled the end of austerity. The 'New Look', which had no regard for the amount of material involved in the long full skirts, hit the market. An aspect of church life was that one literally wore one's 'Sunday Best'. This did mean that it was a bit of a fashion parade for the ladies. I can vividly recall the first 'New Look' that walked down the aisle. At the other end of the scale is the fact that one had to be sure that shoes were kept in good repair; the hole in the sole, which would escape unnoticed in day-to-day activities, would be revealed to all as you knelt to take Communion.

Year One of the VIth Form was completed. Val and I were now firm 'friends' and spent all our spare time in each others' company. This meant some late nights coming home - late as I dare, that is, without incurring parental wrath.

It was at that time that I think there was yet another influence on my future attitudes. This one concerns dogs for which I have had a lifelong dislike. The roots of this lay with a fairly innocent creature ... our spaniel. As is the way with our canine friends, 'Ruff' joined the family as a likeable, playful puppy. As the years passed, he developed into a bad tempered, smelly lump.

It was my 'late nights' which really endeared him to me. He slept under the kitchen table. My challenge was to open the back door, switch on the light and get a finger pointing at him before he could utter one bark and alert the whole household to the time of my return. I became quite adept at this and I muse that having to practise this hand/eye coordination in the dark may have helped when it came to my night flying training!

The luxury of education beyond School Certificate was not to be Valerie's lot. There were clear signs that she had considerable potential as a teacher - particularly of young children. But there was no question of continuing on at school in order to go to Teachers' Training College. Her family were very rooted in the traditions of the working class - so it was out to work at the age of 16 and start bringing some money into the family.

Valerie's father had been a Royal Marine; after his service he became a steward at the Royal Navy College at Manadon. There was a little spin-off for Val and myself. The college staff and relations were invited to the annual students' 'concert'. This we attended with some wide-eyed wonder. It was held in the imposing main college building, a part of the RN Devonport barracks - HMS Drake. The content of the revue was something of an eye opener too - very risqué. Remember that we were living in age where, in films, couples (married ones, of course) could not be shown in bed together. Single beds were *de rigueur*; if a pre-sleep kiss and cuddle had to feature then the male participant had to keep one foot on the floor - rather similar to the rule of the billiard table! A thought is that, nowadays, that kiss and cuddle plus 'etc' is just as likely to take place on a billiard table.

'Secretary' was to be Valerie's lot. At the age of 16 she started clerical duties in the Town Clerk's Office. Like so many offices of that time, this municipal one was not contained in the sort of premises that one would anticipate; a mini-stately home in Central Park was its location. The original office was a victim of the Blitz.

There were all sorts of situations like this: shops in converted terraced housing, some curved, ex-military Nissen huts erected to make a shopping centre, Woolworths was just some of the stalls in the pannier market, school rooms in church halls and so on. Life was tough for such a young lady in an established adult world but Val was not one to be put down and she persevered. An escape was to become better qualified and she attended night school to qualify as a shorthand typist. With another eye to the future, she took cookery lessons.

With shorthand speed certificate in hand, she applied for other jobs and was snapped up by an architect's office. This was a much happier environment - and an interesting one. The firm was quite eminent and these were the thrusting days of post-war architecture - perhaps viewed with scepticism now.

Plymouth was certainly in the forefront of the rebuilding surge. It was with some wonder that we youngsters watched the demolition of what was left of the City Centre, after the attentions of the Luftwaffe, and a completely fresh layout for the new buildings take shape. After the austerity that had been suffered, the new shops were something to be wondered.

I remember another post-war 'wonder' and that was *plastic*. It is difficult to imagine now a world without plastic but it will be recalled that there was such a time. There had been the odd 'plastic' type of material - Bakelite comes to mind. But now there was this new wonder material - shiny, brightly coloured and taking many forms. John and I seized on small sheets of the material, an eighth of an inch or so in thickness, and set out to make a jewel box for Mother or some such treasure. Sadly the appearance of the material was not matched by its workability. We would be sawing out a part for one of the sides and - ping! There would be a crack right across the piece. When we did achieve five uncracked bits of a similar size, there then came the difficulty of adhesion. The proof of the attraction of this new material is that we persisted with these forlorn exercises.

Plastic came in strings looking like fine electric cable but with no central wire. This could be bought in Woolworths and was then woven into a brooch or the like to adorn the female of your choice. To shop at Woolworths one had to endure a recognised feature of this establishment in those years. The counters were arranged in a hollow rectangle with the assistant in the centre. The term 'assistant' is used incongruously as it did seem that the girls received special training in ignoring customers in spite of being surrounded by them, only a couple of feet away. Outstretched hands would hold the desired purchase and the payment but all this seemed to be invisible to these girls. It was quite an accomplishment.

So, a working girl had a schoolboy boy friend. In the second year of the VIth form there was a dramatic development for this young man and it came courtesy of the ATC. The Air Ministry had decided that it would sponsor selected cadets to obtain a Private Pilots' Licence. Known as a 'Flying Scholarship', it was a considerable perk - and I came out, top of the pile, for one of the first.

There obviously was a selection process - I went to an RAF station near Bath for interview - and there was a medical. The location of this was something of a trauma for a 16 and a bit Plymouth lad - the venue was London. The precise location was the RAF's Central Medical Establishment (CME) close by the Post Office Tower - except that wasn't built in 1949! I can relate the tower to the position of CME's building, familiar to all sorts of aviators, because I had reason to attend it, for various reasons, over my years, the last being some nearly 30 years after my first. I know now that on this first visit, I was given a full aircrew medical - fill in this form, go and pee in this bottle, height (substantial), weight (not a lot).

'Read the bottom line.'

'I am going to whisper some words ... tell me what you hear.'

'Run up the stairs to the next floor and back down again - then I'll test your pulse and blood pressure.'

The final stage was the examination by a doctor. He did all the usual things with spatula down throat, 'Say aaah.', rubber hammer on knees to test that 'the jerk' was present. I have mused, having been subjected to that test for reflexes many subsequent years, that it would be easy to cheat. That cannot be said about the moment when the point on the end of the handle of the hammer was drawn across the bottom of one's feet! My toes curl at the thought. I was still very self-conscious with regard to the genital area so it was a somewhat embarrassingly painful episode when the doctor cupped my testicles in his hand and asked for the customary cough.

I didn't pass the medical! Not because of the cough! I could not cross my eyes. A pencil was held a couple of feet in front of my face and the instruction was to stay focussed on it as it was brought closer and say when it went blurred. The hidden reason behind the test was to demonstrate eye muscle flexibility. I obviously did not possess sufficient eyeball mobility.

The incredible thing is that this insignificant ATC cadet was not just sent on his way; I was given a card on which there were some circles and instructions on eye exercises, using it. I returned to CME six weeks later and passed. I often think how odd instances of fate can add together to determine one's future. This CME incident is a prime example. If I had been sent home, 'Aircrew Medical failed', then it is unlikely that I would have made any progress along the aviation highway.

A library photograph of a Tiger Moth, with less sky and grass, could have been used here - but this was taken at the actual time!

Plymouth had only a small grass airfield, on the edge of the Moors, that was just used for club flying. It was here I was to be taught to fly. Things were pretty primitive, although they were normal for those years. The aircraft used was a yellow Tiger Moth, a two-seats-in-tandem training aircraft where, rather oddly, the instructor sat in the front. It was a biplane with open cockpits - real white silk scarf in the slipstream stuff; but at the age of 17 I was not sufficiently self-possessed to match that image.

Communication between instructor and pupil was a rather odd affair. In films involving old ships you will see the orders from the bridge to the engine room being conveyed by voice pipe - simply a tube with a mouthpiece cum earpiece at each end. The 'transmitter' shouts his order down the mouthpiece to be received at the other end by the earpiece being placed to the - well - ear. The Tiger Moth was a little more sophisticated in that there were two mouthpieces - one in each cockpit. These were connected by tubes which led into ear pieces in the flying helmets of each occupant. Imagine this system in use with the background noise of the engine and the slipstream. One might get an approximate idea of what was being said.

I progressed through the essential initial exercises - I recall spinning being particularly bewildering - and moved on to practising take-offs and landings. There were good days and bad but I obviously hit on a run of good ones for my instructor to say those magic words.

'Fancy having a go at your first solo?'

'No, I'm too scared,' said my heart. But I managed to suppress this and blurt out an enthusiastic:

'Yes please!'

It is said that every pilot remembers their first solo; I am no exception. It was not an ideal day; the wind was blowing in a non-prevailing direction so we hadn't used that particular stretch of grass in the build-up. It was a bit short but my instructor gave a reassurance.

'We'll close the road at the end so it will be OK to run over it onto the next bit of grass.'

In later years I took my turn as an instructor so I know the feeling when one takes the gamble - and that is what it is, essentially - of sending Bloggs off on his own. The instruction is to take-off, complete a circuit and land - relief all round!

I must have caused my Tiger Moth mentor some anxiety for, on my first approach to land, I felt I was too high - running across that road didn't seem a good idea to me. Around again I went and you will guess that on my second approach I was too low. I think, at this stage Mr Instructor probably went into the club house for a large Scotch! My third approach was spot on.

We cadets - there were two of us training - were regarded with some aloofness by the Flying Club. Clearly we were a very useful source of income but we definitely did not fit into the club scene. So we behaved with due deference to this. The club steward very rapidly assessed our status and we were persuaded to keep the clubhouse coal bucket filled up and complete other chores which lightened his load. But none of this detracted from the magic of learning to fly. You might think that such an achievement for one of a relatively young age would somehow improve that person's confidence and self image. Not for me - returning home, I would be brought back down to earth. A loaf of bread would be required from the Co-op ... nineteen fourteen two.

In fact, it was being despatched on such an errand that established my determination to leave home.

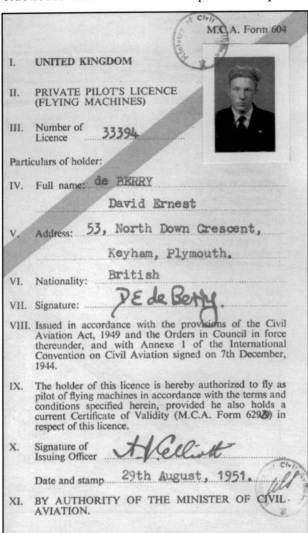

I should have looked a little happier about obtaining such a document at an early age!

Chapter 7

'He's leaving home - bye-bye'

With reflection, it is some amazement to me now that I achieved the necessary standard for a Private Pilot's Licence, given the primitive conditions for instruction and my complete bewilderment with the whole thing. Success was not due to the 'say so' of one's instructor; there was a final flying test with an independent examiner and a solo three-legged cross country flight had to be flown, landing at an airfield *en route*. All this was accomplished within just 30 hours of flying.

With Flying Scholarship complete and Private Pilot's Licence in the pocket of this 17 year-old, it was time to concentrate on those A-levels. I remember applying my 'past papers' technique. There was the risk of some new dynamic examiner coming along and demolishing my preparation method but, luckily, it appeared that the examination compilers were a pretty conservative lot and 'my' questions came up. Because of the curious way A-levels were introduced with just 'pass' or 'fail' grades, we were not sure how well we had really done - I was quite satisfied to let the level of my three 'passes' remain a mystery - just in case they were a bit marginal!

At home, my future career had obviously been a topic of discussion. I have mentioned that Father's determination was that I should enter the Civil Service. I was equally determined, as much as I could be in my cowed state induced by those years of paternal oppression, that I should join the Royal Air Force. As I had demonstrated with my ATC activities, and in particular the flying, that I might have some potential as one of the 'Boys in Blue', it was reluctantly agreed that I should have a go at being accepted for the Royal Air Force College, Cranwell.

Father had obviously done some research and had found out that this was the place for the *Crème de la Crème* and from it graduated future Air Marshals - so he allowed this fruit of his child rearing to be subjected to the selection process for this élitist establishment. It perhaps would have helped if some effort had been made, over the foregoing years, to build up that offspring's confidence and worldly wiseness.

The selection process was lengthy - a week in all. Firstly it had to be proved that we future leaders were capable and fit enough to fly an aeroplane so, for the first few days we underwent the normal tests of potential aircrew. The medical ones were rigorous - no 'ifs or buts' - one leg quarter of an inch shorter than the other, or whatever, or not able to cross one's eyes, 'Out!'

Then there were the aptitude tests; firstly, paper ones which bore a similarity to those Mensa type things - number sequences:

1 1 2 3 5 8 13 ... 'What is the next number in this series?'

Five blocks of patterns:

'Which one of the following four would be the sixth one?'

And so it went on, page upon page, all to be completed within a time limit. That done, it was time to move on to the coordination aptitude tests.

'Move this control to hold that light lined up with that line.'

One test was to keep a pointer on a wavy line on a rolling cylinder. I have mused on how the assessors must have had to change their tests with the advent of the 'computer kid' raised on games needing the ultimate in the required coordination - and there is also the thought that might such a breed be better prepared to fly and fight with sophisticated high speed aircraft anyway?

This stage over, it was time to assess our leadership potential and we moved from RAF Hornchurch to some country house location. Things became a bit military here. We were allocated to teams

- blue, red etc, dressed in khaki overalls with an appropriate coloured top bearing a distinguishing number. That was to be our identity for the duration of the tests. These can be imagined.

'Using these poles and pieces of rope get those drums over this imaginary river - Red Eight you are the leader.'

Red Eight would attempt to influence the activities of his fellows; some of his fellows would attempt to demonstrate their own assertiveness and ingenuity. Red Eight might not be looking too good. Half an hour of struggling with the poles etc over, it would be time to move to another imaginary obstacle for Red Six to take the helm - and so it went on. Less physically demanding, but intellectually so, would be discussion groups.

'You are in a boat with an eminent brain surgeon, a terminally ill woman and your baby niece. The boat begins to sink and you can only save one of them. Which one would you choose?'

It can be imagined that whichever candidate you put forward, this could be challenged by the interrogators. After a few hours of this where your:

'Well I would save the brain surgeon as he has the potential to save more lives ...' being countered by:

'But what will you tell your sister about her baby?', one's inclination was to declare:

'Well, actually, I'll go along with whichever one you say.'

Which, of course, would not do for a future Air Marshal. Whilst I did not utter any such words, perhaps my demeanour suggested them. For whatever reason, a few weeks later a letter arrived advising that I had been unsuccessful in my application. I think that Father probably breathed a sigh of relief - Civil Service executive officer was back on. I was a disappointed young man.

But lo, a few days later another OHMS letter arrived: His Majesty would be very pleased for me to join the Royal Air Force as a pilot on a short service commission (eight years). I was over the moon - Father was unmoved.

'Forget it - just eight years - the Civil Service is for life!'

It was about this time that there was some sort of punch-up about going to fetch that loaf of bread from the Co-op - I was now approaching 18 years old!

'I'm off!'

Sensibly I didn't do anything dramatic like walking out the door but just wrote a letter accepting the offer. The atmosphere in the house was distinctly cool.

There then followed a strange period. In the July, I left Sutton High School for Boys, with no feeling of sadness, and it seemed then that the working class principle of offspring bringing in money to the household was applied and I found myself, with no conscious effort on my part that I can recall, in a government office as a temporary clerk. This was another bewildering time. Forms were thrust in front of me with the briefest instruction from indifferent staff. I seem to recall that it was all to do with the social benefit scene of those days so there were probably some poor Plymouth souls whose deprivation was increased by my incompetence.

I did discover my major role and that was to man the office whilst all the permanent staff bogged off to lunch. The nightmare of this was the switchboard; again I was given cursory directions but I never did master the thing - and this is someone on the threshold of entering the Royal Air Force to train as a pilot!

The call came - report to RAF Cardington on 10th October 1951 - transport would be provided from Bedford railway station - which is where this story began. The motley crew that assembled was gradually sorted into some minor semblance of order with the segregation of potential air and ground crew, technical and clerical ground crew - and the issue of uniform and other accoutrements. Some of this was puzzling: what was this strangely shaped piece of brass - a button stick? I was soon to find out its purpose. Equally puzzling were the pieces of webbing - what use could this possibly be to a future pilot? Again I was soon to find out - find out that there was a testing and tiresome hurdle to be crossed before getting anywhere near an aeroplane. It was called 'Initial Training'. But even the surmounting of this barrier was to be delayed. This was the time of some considerable expansion in the Services. After the trauma of WWII and the rush to demobilisation, it was time to build the Forces of the future; a force established in peacetime to efficiently maintain that peace. Some edge was put on this by the Korean War and the realisation of the threat of Communism. Undoubtedly the offer to me of a commission was part of that expansion. Obviously the system was under some strain to cope with this rapid growth and we were told that the start of our training would be delayed and that we were being sent to an Aircrew Holding Unit at RAF Driffield, Yorkshire. 'Useful' ways would be found to pass the time.

Sending potential pilots to Driffield was rather like showing show jump horses the obstacles that they are going to have to tackle - with demonstrations of the odd one crashing into the poles - and some of them breaking their necks! Driffield was an Advanced Flying School (AFS) to which trainee pilots came, having completed their basic training. The latter was on simple piston-engined aircraft. The purpose of the AFS was to train these pilots on the more advanced jet aircraft that they would be flying on their eventual squadrons. The aircraft were the twin jet-engined Meteor - fast, complicated and fairly critical to operate in its day - it did hold the World air speed record in its time. The speed, complexity and difficulties were obviously too much for some of the trainees for the accident rate was horrendous.

All of this should not be put down to the aircraft; some of it was due to the gung-ho attitude to flying in general and training in particular that was a legacy of the wartime years. An example was the approach to practice asymmetric flying - a necessary exercise to train for the occasion when an engine fails on a two or four engined aircraft. Over the years the rules about this changed to reduce the training risk to the point where actually shutting an engine down deliberately was confined to only the most experienced instructor pilots - and even for them, some stringent rules applied.

Back in the Driffield days, Pilot Officer Bloggs, with a mere ten hours or so on the aircraft type was told, on his solo flights, to shut an engine down before making his final landing. Add to this the fact that the Meteor, with one engine shut down, had the unfortunate propensity to turn on its back and dive into the ground, if one forgot to put the air brakes in and lowered the undercarriage, and you had the recipe for a military funeral. The churchyard at Driffield will bear witness to this; indeed, we 'rookies' had to form the escort party for one of these burials.

We were kept well informed, by the ill-intentioned, of the latest flying disaster. One particular murky day two students had died, their aircraft flying into the cliffs of Flamborough Head. With an aircraft flown by a leading instructor, the two students were practising formation flying. Flying low level in from the sea, in poor visibility, in a 'V' formation, the instructor suddenly saw the cliffs and pulled up; the students had no such opportunity. No doubt there were drastic recriminations about this but, overall, the general attitude was that such things were an inevitable part of flying, particularly flying training. All this was to change markedly over the years.

Our days were spent cleaning and polishing - our barrack block and ourselves. Time hung heavy - but Christmas was approaching and we were to be sent home. Orders for departure day were to 'fall in' outside the barrack block at 8am dressed in our best blues and greatcoats and that webbing which we had learnt to blanco and brass polish. Kit bags completed our pseudo- military appearance. Duly assembled at eight we anticipated the transport arriving to discover that we were MARCHING to the railway station! My journey from Yorkshire to Devon by train was horrendous. The look on my Mother's face, as I stood on the doorstep of 53 North Down Crescent, said it all about my appearance after such a journey. But recovery was rapid particularly with the anticipation of being reunited with Valerie.

We had left Driffield with the prospect of returning after the Christmas break but a letter came extending the leave, with a (meagre) pay cheque enclosed, until 2 January 1952 when it was, 'Report to No.1 Initial Training School, RAF Cranwell.' Yes, I was going to Cranwell but to humbler parts of that station far from the sacred halls of the College.

Picture Lincolnshire in January in a wooden hut with two small solid fuel stoves in the centre of that cavernous space. We had to be restrained from stealing coal! It was going to be a long hard three months. The clear intention was to harden us up and possibly eliminate any weaklings. An awful lot of time was spent on the parade square under the jurisdiction of hard-nosed corporal drill instructors who treated us like shit whilst addressing us as 'Mister Bloggs'. I was re-acquainted with the dreaded .303 rifle of my ATC cadet days. They hadn't become any lighter and we were expected to move them pretty smartly with lots of noise of hands against wood, slaps on the webbing strap and butts to the ground etc.

We all tried hard in order not to draw attention to ourselves. Fortunately there will always be one or two in such a squad who cannot tell their left from their right with any guaranteed success rate or keep in marching step, moving arms, legs, rifles in unison with everyone else. A silent prayer of thanksgiving is deserved for the distraction that they created.

The regime was a strange one; above the aforementioned corporals there was a couple of sergeants who, by comparison, were fairly humane - undoubtedly age had matured their outlook. The next up the hierarchy were some young pilot officers of the Education Branch. They were only slightly drier behind the ears than ourselves - National Service men. They had obviously only recently endured a routine similar to ours and so were well equipped to inflict a similar treatment. On one early morning parade we were being inspected by one of these individuals. He stops in front of me, giving time for my reflection that he was not much older than me.

'Did you shave this morning, Cadet?'

'Yes Sir,' I lied - I was still at the stage where, with my fair hair and skin, standing in a strong wind was probably enough to keep me clean shaven.

'Well next time stand closer to the razor!'

This was obviously a pearl he had picked up from his own recruit training. At the top of the tree was a rather sad looking, older Flight Lieutenant with war medal ribbons. Undoubtedly he was mourning the loss of his flying, exchanged for the miserable job of looking after us lot.

I do not recall too much academic work - with all the square bashing there was little time. We were future officers so one of the subjects was 'Customs of the Service'. From these lessons and associated text book we learnt of some of the archaic traditions. We needed to obtain visiting cards of a specified size and style; with a rank less than Flight Lieutenant they carried the mere appellation of 'Mr'. On arrival at a new station we were to leave two cards on the silver tray in the Officers' Mess foyer addressed to the Station Commander and the President of the Mess Committee.

Another part of our grooming was the matter of dress. Initially we were not permitted to wear civilian clothes but for the last half of the course they were permitted - and a hat was *de rigueur*. It had to be the right sort of hat and I had a trilby of which Humphrey Bogart would have been proud. Picture such an object sitting on my still boyish head! Then there was the matter of our uniforms for our

One thing to get used to with Service life is having a label ... number, rank, name. This example survives on the cover of the diary we were obliged to keep:

'A diary is to be kept by all pilots and navigators throughout their training.

The objects of keeping the diary are to train all cadets in:

        (a) The power of observation.
        (b) The power of expression.
        (c) The habit of orderliness.'

Reading the contents, my object seems to have been to present our overseers with what they wanted to read and, hopefully, make a good impression. The result is rather 'sugary'!

future officer rank. We were to receive an allowance to pay for this and there was a group of tailors on hand to ensure that we spent it all. In fact we really did not have any control over this at all. We were measured and a week or so later had a first fitting. On the second fitting, a member of the staff was present and it was his 'say so' whether this was up to standard. This was repeated on a final inspection. These uniforms were tailored for young, slim, fit eighteen year olds - standing to attention. It is no wonder that occasions in later service calling for the wearing of 'Best Blue', produced a lot of bulging buttons and held in stomachs. A sad uniform postscript is that ours came complete with a black arm band. King George VI had died and officers were to wear these armbands for six months.

I do remember that, in the classroom, we started learning the Morse Code - or trying to learn in my case. I have already spelt out my dyslexic way with French and aircraft recognition - I was now to add Mr Morse's fiendish dots and dashes to the list. The thing in common with these subjects? No logic! I was OK learning E I S H - one dot, two dots etc - and T M O - one dash, two etc; opposites - A and N etc. But what the hell was J? If I could have remembered them, there was no way I could recall them at the speed at which they were transmitted, either by light or buzzer. We were supposed to achieve a speed of four words per minute.

Somehow I managed to escape being tested and slipped through the net. In later life the only occasion I was required to read Morse was to identify radio beacons. They constantly repeated their code letters. So, with the help of an *aide-mémoire*, it was possible to get by. Mind you, in order to sustain some credibility, I had to hide my 'crib' from my fellow crew members.

The overwhelming memory of that three months training was cleaning. Obviously we cleaned ourselves; we cleaned our kit - buttons, boots, webbing; we cleaned the hut - every nook and cranny. The floors were buffed to a mirror finish and then we moved about by sliding our feet on thick pieces of felt. I learnt a useful fact for a future pilot - a good finishing shine can be given to windows using old newspapers! We didn't actually have to paint the coal white - but it came close to that. Each week there was a kit inspection. For this,

all our service possessions had to be laid out on our beds in a precise, prescribed manner. At the head of the bed was our bedding rigidly and squarely folded. If the intention with all this was to break our spirit then it came perilously close to being realised.

And so the miserable three months dragged on in the miserable Lincolnshire winter weather. One bit of sunshine was a weekly phone call from Val. I had to go to one of the few public telephone boxes and wait for her to ring - she was now established in the architect's office and used to do this telephoning 'after hours' with the office to herself.

But Red Letter day was approaching. I remember one agony I had to endure was our 'end of course' party in a local pub. I was no drinker and it was an ordeal. How I compensated for that in later years!

I think this party was the final highlighting of what a mixed bunch we were. Rather like school, there were 'boys' who were men; also there were a number who were much older - when you are 18, a 24 year-old can seem like someone of another generation. Then there were the 'youngsters' like myself. The older element were in their element with the party. The wildest thing I had attended was a 'Social' in our Church Hall, so I felt distinctly uncomfortable in 'The Red Lion'. That over, it was the passing-out parade which, naturally enough, we had rehearsed a thousand times over.

With that, it was all over - could we believe it? We had passed and would shortly be commissioned into the dizzy rank of Acting Pilot Officer on Probation - an extremely low form of life - and start our flying training.

Chapter 8

'Off we go into the Wide Blue Yonder'

With hardly any delay, I found myself at No.1 Flying Training School, Moreton-in-Marsh for my basic flying course: nine months leading to the award of the coveted RAF pilot's wings. Moreton, set in rural Gloucestershire, was an idyllic place after Cranwell. It was May.

Alongside other choices, Moreton-in-Marsh would have been classed as a 'standard' Flying Training School (FTS) of which there were four or so. There were a number of schools which were equipped with Oxfords, a small, but twin-engined aircraft. Students selected for these may have demonstrated, during the selection procedure, a suitability for larger aircraft. Other 'non-standard' FTSs included some run 'under contract'. They were civilian-manned on civil airfields with a variety of aircraft. Some of my compatriots at Cranwell went to schools in Canada. All this demonstrates the burgeoning nature of pilot recruitment and training in the early 1950s.

Moreton-in-Marsh was an old wartime station. This meant that we did not escape the wooden huts. But this time it was a room to yourself - and you didn't have to clean it. We were in a strange limbo - tokenly, with the rank of Acting Pilot Officer, we were officers and enjoyed associated privileges. This included membership of the Officers' Mess and a batman to do that cleaning. Each morning he would appear with a metal jug of hot water. The washing facility was direct from a safari tent - a metal bowl supported by a folding wooden tripod. But it was all heaven after the miseries of Lincolnshire.

I say tokenly we were officers; we were regarded with very low esteem by the 'real' officers. Ours was a probationary status depending upon success on the course. I have in my log book one of those certificates that, from time to time, one was obliged to complete. This typewritten one reads:

```
I ............... certify that I fully understand the
petrol, oil, ignition, brake and hydraulic system,
action in event of fire and method of abandoning
Harvard aircraft.

Instructor's signature ..........................
Student's signature     ..........................
```

After the 'I', I inserted '*Plt. Off. D E de Berry*'. This has been amended, in the same ink as my *real* Pilot Officer instructor's signature, to '*A/Plt. Off. D E de Berry*'. Had I found a Freudian replacement for my father?

It is curious that the idea of commissioned students was introduced; it went alongside the new policy that all pilots and navigators would be commissioned. For a time, this produced a lot of anomalies in the Royal Air Force in general; some experienced senior pilots on a squadron being Sergeants and Flight Sergeants and 'sprog' new arrivals, Pilot or Flying Officers. Some ex-wartime officers rejoined the RAF prior to the commissioning policy and became NCOs. I knew a Flight Sergeant who held, from his wartime service, the Distinguished Flying Cross - an 'officer' award.

But ours was not to reason why - Acting Pilot Officers we were. One initial magic of the Flying Training School was the frenetic airborne activity - and the realisation that, shortly, one would be part of it. Two aircraft featured - the Prentice and the Harvard. The latter had a particularly penetrating propeller noise contributing largely to the overhead circus. The pattern for our training was that

74

we would spend the first three months on the Prentice and the last six on the more advanced Harvard.

The Prentice was a strange beast; a product of the Percival Aircraft Company, its origins were clearly in a rather sedate small passenger aircraft. That was the Proctor. The cumbersomeness was something of a self inflicted injury; the RAF made it a requirement that its first post-war training aircraft should be capable of carrying three people. This is a considerable penalty on performance as there is the extra weight and the necessary size and shape of the canopy. Why three? A Flying Training School would generally have a satellite airfield; an FTS airfield could be incredibly busy, interfering with instruction. So there would be a nearby 'relief landing ground', often a disused, apart from the runways, wartime airfield, which would take the pressure off the main base. Some committee, somewhere, decided that an instructor should be able to take his aircraft and two of his four students to this airfield for the morning/afternoon. It might be seen that this 'two student facility' was not really a compelling reason to influence the performance of the aircraft but it was insisted upon. From Moreton-in-Marsh we had a relief landing

ground - Edge Hill. I only recall the three of us, instructor plus two students, going there once.

So, the Prentice was heavy, slow and not very agile. A distinguishing feature was that it had turned-up wing tips. It was alleged that this had to be done as it was found that the aircraft was more stable upside-down than the right way up! Turn it on its back and it would display a shortcoming attributed to sheep. There was a compensation for the Prentice's sluggishness and that was, for straightforward flying, I have in mind take-off, circuit and landing, it had the quality of being easy to fly. Combine this with a patient, kindly instructor and the result is a first solo after six hours of instruction.

My amenable instructor was a Canadian, 'over here' on an exchange posting - a British instructor would have gone to an FTS in Canada. Flight Lieutenant McClean gave me a good start. Perhaps the lumbering nature of the aircraft combined with his gentle manner are the causes of me remembering very little of this stage of training. This was not going to be the case with the next six months on the Harvard.

The Harvard was an American training aircraft, produced in their thousands for the instruction of wartime US military pilots. They were on loan to the RAF as part of the post-war assistance of the USA to the UK. Driving a two-bladed propeller (the tips of which went supersonic, producing all that noise on the ground previously referred to) was a big radial engine, sitting up in front obscuring the view, on the ground, of the student and instructor, riding in tandem.

'When you're taxying this aircraft, Bloggs, you'll have to weave the nose to see ahead - and make sure that you weave it enough so that I can see as well!'

The complete antithesis of the Prentice, the Harvard was powerful, fast, slim bodied and very manoeuvrable. With its origins in the small fighter world of the immediate pre-war years, it was quite a handful to fly - and I had an instructor who was at the opposite end of the amenability spectrum to the Canadian. Pilot Officer L was younger, fiery, impatient. With the benefit of experience I am able to say that he was not a good instructor. One day I was tested by an outside examiner and I had never been taught half the things he

'... the Harvard was powerful, fast, slim bodied ...'

asked me to do. 'Well, I would say that, wouldn't I?' Whilst the eternal staff/student wall kept the truth from me, I did have the feeling that, as a result of my test, Pilot Officer L was in the dwang.

A feature of the slim-bodied Harvard was a 'slim' undercarriage track to match; the distance between the two main wheels was small and this led to an undesirable landing characteristic. If a Harvard was not kept fairly positively straight after touchdown then the 'swing' would start to tighten up to the point that it became uncontrollable and the aircraft would complete an ever decreasing circle until it disappeared up its own asshole - no, forget that - until, possibly, the undercarriage collapsed. It was known as a 'ground loop' and was to be avoided at all costs! It certainly was discouraged by the hierarchy. There was a FTS in Rhodesia, in the immediate post-war years, which was equipped with Harvards and it had a unique tradition for keeping students on their toes. There was a spare Harvard wheel and the supporting leg - not an insubstantial piece of equipment. If a student did a ground loop then he had to push this wheel everywhere he went - to lectures, to the flight lines, to meals. The relief from this only came when another student 'ground looped'; then the wheel was handed over.

If I jump forward a considerable number of years, I can tell of another association with Harvards. I was serving at The Aeroplane and Armament Experimental Establishment, Boscombe Down and, somewhat amazingly, we had three Harvards; they were incredibly ancient but loving care compensated for this. They were not there for decorative purposes; part of the trials work was associated with parachutes and the Harvard was ideal as the 'chase aircraft'. A photographer with a video camera flew in the rear seat. The Harvard would position alongside the despatching aircraft, typically a Hercules, and the exit of the load, cargo or human, would be filmed. The Harvard, with its manoeuvrability could then follow the parachute in its descent, allowing the filming to continue. What amused me was that considerable precautions were taken with the operation of these three aircraft: only selected pilots flew them and these were, in the main, test pilots; three point touchdowns were not allowed, the aircraft had to be 'wheeled' on to the ground, main wheels first; to guard against 'ground loops', only exceptionally was operation off and on to a runway permitted, grass was the 'norm'. All this caution was taken with the aircraft that we 18 year-olds, with virtually zero experience, were expected to fly to its limits. If we had done a 'wheelie' landing instead of a three-pointer then it would definitely have been a rap over the knuckles.

There is an extremely sad postscript to those Boscombe Down days. One day, a very well established test pilot took a younger, but experienced staff pilot for a Harvard trip. Part of the purpose of the flight was that the staff pilot was a potential candidate for the test pilots' course and some tips would be passed on to aid his selection. The aircraft took off and all contacts with Air Traffic Control were normal. It is known that the aircraft did a practice spin and recovered; it is believed that it then immediately entered into a practice forced landing. It did seem that when overshooting, at low level, from this that the engine did not respond. It crashed and both the occupants were killed. The subsequent investigation did not reveal any apparent mechanical fault. One of the routines with the Harvard was not to let the engine cool down too much, which it was inclined to do if left at idling power for too long. Our training routine was to give the engine a 30 second burst of high power at intervals during the forced landing practice - the 30 seconds and amount of power could be judiciously adjusted if one was getting a bit low to make the chosen field! Could it have been that the Boscombe Down Harvard did the spin (power off) and the forced landing (power again off) with insufficient engine warming? That will never be known. But what was underlined was that the aircraft was one that needed to be taken seriously - and we young 'sprogs' flew it!

I have done some foolish things in my life; high on the list is low flying in The Vale of Evesham. It was our low flying area and we were sent there, solo, to low fly - but not as low as I went. On one occasion, with the adrenalin still pumping, it was time to return to base. From my last low level pass, I turned in the direction of Moreton-in-Marsh. Now, the name 'The Vale of Evesham' indicates that, when you leave, there are some hills to climb. Up I went. About two thirds the way, I realised that the rate at which the ground was rising was exceeding the rate at which I was climbing - the throttle was hard forward. The brow of the hill was just ahead and it did look as if I might just make it. In an effort to increase the rate of climb, the cheeks of my ass were squeezed hard together. With this contribution, the Harvard did make it over the top - just! A very subdued student landed back at RAF Moreton-in-Marsh.

There has been a comment on the attitude to flying accidents. We had one. Part of the night flying phase of the course was a solo cross country. Whilst flying this, one of our compatriots crashed and was killed - why he crashed we knew not; but little was made of it. A couple of his friends from the course attended the funeral; the rest of us just carried on as if it had never happened. With hindsight, it is an uncanny reflection on the attitudes to flight safety in those days.

It was whilst I was a student at Moreton-in-Marsh that I

witnessed a notorious flying accident. A number of us had been given tickets for the 1952 Farnborough Air Show and off we set in an RAF coach. It was at this show that a prototype swept-wing naval fighter, the DH110, flown by John Derry, broke up in mid-air, right in front of the crowd.

From where I was standing, I saw the pieces of the airframe hit the runway. But the awful sight was above; there the two engines went over our heads. Initially they were in the same position, relative to each other, as they had been in the fuselage but as they proceeded, they gradually parted. They were close enough for us to be able to identify components; in fact, I recall vividly that they looked exactly like the engines that we had just seen on stands in the static display area - pipes, nuts and bolts, pumps - the whole engine twisting slowly about the fore and aft axis. Then there was the sickening sound of a double crunch and the realisation that the engines had plunged into the crowds that packed the small hill behind us. John Derry and his observer died, as did 28 spectators ... 60 more were injured.

Our basic flying course progressed - landing the aircraft in various configurations, flying the circuit in different ways, practice engine failure after take-off, aerobatics, steep turns, spinning, stalling, practice forced landings, flying complicated patterns on instruments, making an approach to the airfield in simulated low cloud and poor visibility, cross country flights of increasing difficulty, night flying, formation flying - there was an enormous amount to cover and in which to become competent.

Half the day was spent on this flying, the other half in the Ground School where we were taught aerodynamics, meteorology, technical matters, navigation theory, flight instrument principles and several other minor topics - including a padre's hour! Our parade ground instruction continued in a subdued way more suited to our pseudo-officer status.

Some time was put aside for a terrifying 24 hours - an escape and evasion exercise. We were transported, in covered lorries, for small groups to be dropped off in various parts of Gloucestershire and neighbouring counties. This was just as night was falling. The

Student pilots ... the author, John Armstrong and Bob Deas.

object was to get back to the airfield but the build-up to this exercise was sufficient for us to believe that every shadow contained 'the enemy'. It was during this caper that I collected a scar across my forehead that has stayed with me through life. If the angle of it is examined it will be seen that it corresponds to that of the supporting wire of a telegraph pole, into which I ran. I developed a lifetime respect for electric fences that night. Walking into one in the pitch black can be a bit of a nasty surprise - and a painful one. The ordinary man, who is not obliged to engage in such bizarre activities, will possibly be unaware that the average height of an electric fence coincides with the distance above the ground of his goolies!

All the learning was not confined to aeronautical matters - there was an awful lot about life for this council house boy to master. Luckily I had joined the Royal Air Force during that rapid recruiting phase when the net was, perhaps, being cast wider than usual. So, I found that a lot of my contemporaries had, seemingly, similar backgrounds to myself. There were one or two who felt somewhat superior but ability to fly is a great social leveller; we had our own class structure - those who were doing well on the course were definitely the upper strata.

I have often mused on the RAF's pilot recruiting policy in the years subsequent to my start; the emphasis gradually shifted to recruiting graduates - or, if the candidate was younger, those that might be considered of that calibre. Yet, we fought and won the war with, virtually 'lads off the streets'. These were the gutsy sort required. The peacetime junior pilots gradually became older, perhaps already with domestic commitments, possibly more interested in the prospect of obtaining a mortgage than a social life with fellow aviators.

Perhaps there is something psychologically sub-conscious about my view. Am I really trying to defend the fact that we appeared to spend an enormous amount of our leisure time getting pissed?! My particular friend on the course was John Armstrong. We seemed to have a lot in common - except that he had a car! This was quite an exceptional state in those days. Admittedly his jalopy was of the Austin Seven genre - but it was a car. He took me to his family home one weekend and we seemed to spend most of it getting there and getting back. I have said that, in certain respects, we did enjoy officer status. This applied to most Mess facilities and those still had a traditional air to them. One of these was that you could ring a bell in the ante-room and a steward would appear to take your drink order. It was still our early days and perhaps John and I were not too confident about the bar situation; for whatever reason, we rang the bell.

'Two pints of Worthington, please Steward.'

These duly arrived and were, duly, consumed. The bell was rung again. My subsequent capacity for beer clouds my memory of how many times we did this but I will put it at four. This would have been more than enough to have caused Yours Truly and J Armstrong to be in the condition commonly associated with newts. Am I ashamed to say that this opened the door to a lifetime of enjoying the pleasures of drink? No!! But I don't feel very proud of the fact that around that time I took up smoking; I would blame this on peer pressure - everyone smoked. The habit stayed with me for ten years.

With all this 'far from home', in all senses, activity, had I escaped the 'tyranny' of my father? I wrote home as often as my conscience troubled me. My first letter from M-in-M proudly pointed out that I should now be 'addressed' as Pilot Officer D Berry (us probationers dropped the 'Acting' for 'outside' purposes), my service number was not required (that was an 'airman' thing) and the address was Officer's Mess, RAF Moreton-in-Marsh, Glos. Father, who hardly ever corresponded, on a personal level, with anyone, added a PS to Mother's reply pointing out that I had the apostrophe in Officer's in the wrong place!

Staying with the home connection, I did get some vibes that now I was 'earning' I should be repaying part of my 'debt'. Even if I thought this to be justified, doing anything about it would have been impossible - without giving up drinking and smoking! Seriously, we were incredibly lowly paid. I did attempt to salve my conscience on Mother's birthday that FTS year and went to Oxford and bought an electric toaster; a somewhat, in those days, new, up-market electrical gadget. What I forgot was that, for some curious reason, the voltage in our part of Plymouth was 200 volts - not the

Our 'Passing-Out' photograph on a wet January day. A Harvard is the backdrop. Judging by the hat angle, the author (back row, 2nd from the right) might have been at the Worthington 'E'!

normal 230. Father took charge of solving this problem and, undoubtedly with one of his elaborate letters - he was prolific in the complaining/putting the World to rights etc area - asked the manufacturers for a replacement. They sent a 200 volt toaster but didn't ask for the original one back. It will be revealed later why this story is of significance.

Having covered: flying - in detail; drinking - in passing; smoking - dismissively ... what of sex? Well this was, through force of circumstance rather than lack of desire, a bit low key. This might explain an unfortunate period of my young life. It was Officers' Mess Summer Ball time - a traditionally grand occasion where considerable effort is put into every aspect - the lavish decoration of the Mess, the best in music, the most elaborate buffet that could be produced, ladies dressed in their finery, 'free' booze. But what, on this intensely social occasion, were we young blades to do? It seemed to be all part of the seamless effort that went into such an event that an invitation was issued to the nurses in residence in the Oxford hospital and a coach load of them appeared, putting an obligation upon us to entertain them for the evening.

In the course of that evening, I became totally smitten with a dark haired young lady whose name has disappeared in those mists of time which seem to constantly roll across this text. There did appear to be considerable mutual feeling. I have mentioned that I have done silly things but this beats low flying stupidness; on the strength of this one night of boozy 'magic', I wrote to Valerie saying that our understanding had to end as I had now found 'Miss Right'. There is an ethical wrong about this but there is also a practical one - don't give up what you have until you have secured something to take its place! A cynic would remind me that, 'A bird in the hand is worth two in the bush.' I'd always thought that the bird referred to was the feathered variety ... perhaps not. 'Dark haired nurse' and I never met again for, basically, logistical reasons - me at M-in-M, no transport, she in Oxford. There was also the problem of a subsequent detected lack of enthusiasm on the female side. Obviously, a good night out was one thing but ... This was sadness because it made me realise that I really loved my childhood sweetheart ... and now I had lost her.

But life moves on ... the end of basic training was marked with many tests - Ground School, final navigation, instrument flying - and finally, finally, the final handling test. A light-hearted end to the course was an aerobatic competition. A 'knock-out' was first held where the likeliest students flew with one instructor to demonstrate their aerobatic skills and that instructor selected the six best to fly, solo, in the final competition. It was landing back from this selection sortie that, for the first time, I nearly ground looped! The instructor was kind enough not to allow this to influence his choice and I was selected to fly in the 'final' - and I won! This summed up for me the lucky escape I'd had - 14 months before, I was 'going up to the Co-op' for a loaf of bread ... nineteen fourteen two!

86

Chapter 9
'Fast Jets'

FTS was our *basic* flying training. It will come as no surprise that this was followed by *advanced* flying training; equally unsurprising is the fact that this was completed at an *Advanced* Flying Training School (AFTS). To match the number of FTSs, there were a similar considerable number of AFTSs. Most of these were equipped with Meteors or Vampires - jet aircraft with fighter origins; the former twin-engined, the latter with just one engine. There were other AFTSs tailored, aircraft-wise, to the needs of students who would go to squadrons flying transport, bomber or maritime aircraft.

I was sent to a strange AFTS at Tarrant Rushton, Dorset, the home of Flight Refuelling Ltd, a firm that pioneered and persisted with the idea, for very many years, that there was a place in aviation for the ability to refuel one aircraft from another. That persistence was eventually to be realised; I have often wondered if Flight Refuelling Ltd profited sufficiently from this. The company had secured a contract to service the AFTS's Meteor aircraft and provide airfield facilities at their home base.

The instructors were RAF. We were not accommodated at Tarrant Rushton but at an old military camp of some sort which went by the unassuming name of Grimsditch. Here we swapped our wooden huts for Nissen ones - not an upward step. Each morning and evening we were transported, by coach, to and from the airfield.

The Gloster Meteor aircraft already had a history. It was developed just in time to see some wartime service. Its claim to fame then was that they were used in an attempt to thwart the 'doodlebug' attacks on SE England. These V1 and V2 rockets were proving a real menace, creating widespread death, injury and damage, with an associated lowering of civilian morale - and this just as we thought that the war was more or less sewn up. The attacks were particularly difficult to counter. One method used was to pursue the missiles with the Meteor and attempt to shoot them down. Some pilots tried and succeeded in tipping them, off course, with their wingtips.

This is a later version of the Meteor, the Mark 8, with its all perspex canopy, more sophisticated tail shape and larger engine nacelles containing more powerful engines. There were also improvements with the flying controls.

This indicates that the Meteor was a sturdy aircraft; added to this, it had the potential for development. This ensured that it was well represented in the Royal Air Force fleet for many years. One development was to produce a two seat trainer, the Mark 7, and this would be our introduction to jet flying. When we had covered the necessary exercises and proved our competence, we would be sent solo in the Mk7 with the back seat empty. Our subsequent solo flights would be in a single seat version.

Tarrant Rushton was unique in still being equipped with those wartime aircraft, the Mark 3. Other AFTSs had Mk4s. The Mk3 did look somewhat ancient: a short stubby engine just the length of the chord of the wing and with a wire grill over air intake. This was only a feature of early jet engines to prevent the ingest of stones etc. This is an eternal problem with a jet but, obviously, the wire grill was not a solution.

Starting the course meant establishing relationships with a new set of instructors. To match the increase in performance of our training aircraft, the average age of the instructing team was lower - or would have been if one of them had not looked about 50 years old. Flight Lieutenant D was my instructor. No doubt my assessment of his age was distorted by my youth - but he was bald, pipe smoking and very set in his ways. There was an inclination to glance down at his feet to check whether he was wearing his carpet slippers! I did get the feeling that he was not entirely happy in the back of a Meteor Mk7 with, up front, some young pup with moisture behind his listening devices and perhaps lacking in some grey matter between them.

But we duly proceeded with the required exercises. Many of these were carried out in the new environment now available to us, that being 25,000 feet and above. This added new stresses: having to breathe oxygen, experiencing rapid pressure changes and enduring high 'g' forces. Effects of compressibility associated with getting towards the speed of sound had to be demonstrated, controlling high rates of descent, generally coping with much higher speeds and making allowances for the delayed reaction time of a jet engine - all these major differences from the Harvard had to be mastered in an incredibly short space of time.

Then, to complicate the normal problem of getting accustomed to landing a different type of aircraft - and one with a nose wheel instead of a tail one - there was the matter of having two engines - which doesn't make that much difference if they are both working but coping with one failed was something completely new.

This had to be heavily practised. It has already been stated that the Meteor was not the best behaved aircraft when on one engine.

There was, undoubtedly, a more gung-ho attitude to this stage of training compared with the basic one.

'You're big boys now - destined to become fighter pilots - get on with it!'

So, with just 1 hour and 50 minutes hours dual instruction spread over three sorties, I found myself alone in this, for its day, mighty machine. All went well - it's amazing how fear can concentrate the mind. With first solo accomplished, there followed two months of steady progress through exercise areas similar to basic training ie general handling, instrument flying, navigation, night flying and formation flying.

A moment is taken to reflect on one of these training topics - instrument flying. The ability to fly an aircraft, safely and smoothly, in cloud and/or poor visibility is an absolute essential for safe operation and, therefore, has to be practised, during training, to an almost exhausting degree. Such a regime does not cease then and stays with a pilot throughout his career.

The obvious way to gain experience, to practise and to be tested flying in cloud and/or poor visibility is to actually fly in cloud and/or poor visibility. But, although we may have a low opinion of UK weather, it would be impossible to carry out sufficient instrument flying practice in 'actual' conditions; so these have to be 'simulated'. This is done in a variety of ways. Why is the topic raised here?

Well, at this stage of our training, we had experienced two methods of simulating flying in cloud; the first, in the Prentice, was highly effective but horribly isolating for the student. The aircraft was fitted with concealed amber screens which could be pulled up, from their stowage, to cover the normal glass. The student then donned blue goggles. Blue and amber obscure all light so there was no way you could see out - the instructor, wearing no goggles, was able to, thus maintaining a safe lookout for other aircraft.

Through the blue the student could see the flight instruments - very clearly; the luminosity of the figures and needles seemed to be heightened. It might be that the student would complain that the goggles were misting up, more than likely from the sweat of his brow. This eventuality was covered by having a tube leading from inside the goggles to a hole in the side of the aircraft. With the end stuck out in the airstream there would a flow of air through the goggles. It is surprising that, to my knowledge, the Prentice was the only aircraft to be fitted with this highly effective, but horrendous for the student, system. I, for one, was very pleased not to meet it again.

It might be considered that this blue/amber system, with its hideaway screens, was quite a sophisticated scheme. Alongside it, every other method might seem to have emanated from someone closely related to Mr Heath Robinson. A common idea was called a visor but it was more like a hood - imagine a baseball cap with a huge curved aluminium peak.

With this, one stayed more in contact with one's environment but this could be to the point of 'cheating' - taking a fleeting glimpse of the horizon. Another idea was screens - solid ones - in front and to the side of the student. This idea was not entirely satisfactory from a safety aspect as it tended to obscure the view of the instructor. The final solution did not depend on any equipment; quite simply, the student, or pilot under test, was trusted to keep his head down and not to look outside the aircraft.

This was the norm for practice and tests on squadrons. It led to a familiar quote. But first it should be understood that the success of instrument flying depends on a good scan; it is fatal to concentrate one's attention on a single instrument. There are six instruments on a basic instrument flying panel: air speed indicator, artificial horizon, altimeter, turn and slip indicator, compass and vertical speed indicator (ie rate of climb or descent). Eyes should be moving constantly from one to the other with some priority for particular ones, depending on the manoeuvre - this is good scanning. The quote?

'One glimpse outside is worth a thousand scans!'

Social life continued much as before, essentially revolving around the Mess. John Armstrong and I had been split up - I never met him again. A new compatriot was HC; if I revealed it, there would be many who would groan on hearing his name and would recall some outrageous story. I can follow this pattern: H was one of those few car owners - a Ford 8. One day we went into Salisbury. Driving towards the centre, at a crossroads, an idiot motorcyclist drove straight into the side of us. H leapt out of the car and, seeing that the rider was OK, proceeded to berate him for his stupidity. A policeman appeared on the scene and quickly assessed the situation. He then turns to me.

'Would you come with me, Sir.'

He walks me back some 25 yards up the road on which we had approached the crossroads. Stopping and turning, he says:

'Would you please read what is says on that post.'

'Halt at Major Road Ahead,' I croak!

This was the story of H's life. In later years, he was attending to the engine of his car in his garage, leaning over the radiator. Somehow he accidentally turned over the starter motor and the car was in gear. Two broken legs were the result!

I was never touched by the motorcycle phase - as much a lack of desire as lack of finance. One of my fellow Grimsditchians had a bike and he lived in Plymouth. One weekend, seeking to half his petrol bill, he offered me a lift. This was my one and only ride on a motorbike and it left me with no inclination to repeat the experience. I remember that when the numbness of the cold wore off, I became aware that my body seemed to be still vibrating in sympathy with the now distant engine.

It must have been this weekend that, to my relief, fences were mended with Valerie. I say this weekend because there was a subsequent one where she sent me the money for the train fare down to Plymouth - greater love hath no man! Apart from an indication of strength of feeling, it also points to my impecunious situation.

With the end of the course approaching, it was once again testing time. As one of the people who survived this training process, I was lucky not to feel like so many of my compatriots. For them it seemed like a continual attempt to suspend them from training. They would narrowly scrape over some hurdle only to see another one ahead. Eventually they would go down; the suspension rate was very high. So, a percentage of us successfully completed this advanced training stage to move on to the next.

In subsequent years, trainee pilots endured dreadful delays between the training phases. This was not my experience - in fact, perhaps a bit of a breather might have been welcome. But no! Destined now to become a fighter pilot, the next port of call was the Operational Conversion Unit (OCU) for Meteor fighter aircraft.

This was located at Stradishall in Suffolk - a God-forsaken, remote place. It came as no surprise for me to learn, in later years, that it had become a prison. This closely relates it to the way I felt during my two months 'banged up' there. If advanced training compared with basic seemed to possess machismo, then the atmosphere at the OCU was a bigger step still.

The 'Battle of Britain' spirit was not dead! In double quick time (45 minutes) we were checked out in the familiar Meteor Mk7 and then thrust into the air in the very much more sophisticated and powerful than the Mk3 Meteor, the Mk8. For one thing, we had an ejector seat for the first time. On this first Mk8 trip we were told to do a 'sector recce', this being gung-ho language for 'have a look around the local area'. I duly did this and landed back at Stradishall. I was summoned to the Flight Commander's office.

'Your sector recce - on it you called Air Traffic twice for a bearing!'

This was a facility available whereby, with a short radio transmission, Air Traffic Control could pass you your bearing from themselves. It seemed a good idea to me to use this aid as a reassurance that my map reading was not up the spout. The message I was given was along these lines.

'Big boys don't use such mamby-pamby things - you're in Fighter Command now!'

This was the atmosphere that prevailed from the Wing Commander Flying down. That be-medalled gentleman was definitely from the Spitfire and Hurricane stable. He had the misfortune to suffer from a stutter - but this did not hold him back from delivering long tirades to us students. One of his *bêtes noires* was us sitting in the crewroom.

'G -g-g-get out-outside and w-w-w-watch the air-aircraft - y-you m-m-might p-p-pick up s-s-some t-t-t-tips.'

Woe betide any student who fell asleep in the Mess ante-room after lunch; this was another of his pet hates.

Flying an aircraft fitted with an ejector meant being introduced to a curious training device which would have looked more at home in a fairground. The ejector seat trainer was towed from one establishment to another to give pilots periodic training. On arrival, the horizontal gantry would be raised to the near vertical and at its base would be the ejector seat. Into this Bloggs would be strapped; body braced, with a handle at the back of the top of his head, he would pull a blind over his face; for an ejection for real, this would do something to preserve, from the slipstream, his handsome fighter pilot features for the subsequent impression of the females in his life.

The blind was linked to the cartridge firing mechanism and Bloggs would be fired up the rails of the gantry. If he wasn't sitting correctly he might not end up with essential equipment functioning, to accompany his good looks. There was also the agonising thought that you hoped, when it was your turn, an over-strength cartridge had not been loaded. Space flight was still a number of years away.

Seriously, the Martin-Baker ejector seat was a life saver and a truly remarkable, all British, product. It is amazing to muse on the development days when a single seat Meteor aircraft was modified with space for another occupant behind the pilot. Into this was fitted a prototype ejector seat - and into this was strapped a gentleman by the name of Lynch. And yes ... the aircraft would fly along and Mr Lynch would pull the handle! At a meeting of pilots who owed their lives to the Martin-Baker ejector seat, I'm sure he wouldn't go short of a drink!

A large amount of the Meteor OCU course, for us would-be day fighter pilots, was spent learning to fly 'in battle'. This was a loose formation for four aircraft designed to prevent an attack from behind by an unseen enemy. If you hold out your right hand, palm down, and imagine an aircraft on each finger nail and the leader is your second finger - with the distance separating them being some 800 yards or so - then you have a basic idea of a Right Hand Battle Formation. This was conducted at around 30,000 feet where the aircraft's reaction to power changes was extremely slow.

With this handicap, one struggled to get into position - too far back, put on full power, initially no effect but up one slowly crept, but then that slowly became fast as the aircraft's inertia was overcome. Before you knew where you were you had overshot the correct position, back on the power, perhaps a touch of air brake - you can guess the outcome ... you are back where you started.

All this happened whilst your instructor leader was flying in a straight line. But now he wants to turn, which is not unreasonable otherwise we would end up possibly crossing the Iron Curtain. Turning in this spread out formation requires some juggling otherwise the guy on the outside of the turn would drop hopelessly behind - and the one on the inside would find himself leading. So, during the turn, the outside man would cross to the inside position, the inside to the out - all without hitting each other; we are now in Left Hand Battle Formation. It really was a tortuous and frustrating pastime.

The instructors were relative youngsters who had completed their first three or four years on a fighter squadron, no doubt not very pleased to find themselves surrounded by blockheads who seemed possessed with the anticipation capacity of a brick. The debriefings were very acrimonious. Student morale at Stradishall was low - if this was Fighter Command they could stuff it!

The formation described above seemed almost to take place in slow motion compared with the last hectic five minutes of each flight where we joined up in close formation for the approach to Stradishall - the run-in and break. The four aircraft were flown in echelon starboard - the right hand portion of an upside-down 'V'. Over the runway, on the command, 'Break, break', each aircraft would turn sharply left to fly the circuit in stream. It was this activity we were urged to, 'W-w-w-watch!'.

The end of training is in sight. Throughout it, we had been required to take our turn at the station duty of Orderly Officer. During one's spell it was a bit difficult to write, salute and carry out various other hand actions, as fingers were permanently crossed that nothing untoward happened. One day I examined the new list of duties and found my name down twice. On the 6th, say, Plt Off Berry was listed; then on the 12th, Plt Off de Berry. This was something that was to plague my Service life. You may have been puzzled already to see, on a couple of reproduced documents, that my full name is David Ernest de Berry.

You will recall the de Rippe story; Grandfather was Percy de Rippe Berry; Father, Henry Ernest de Rippe Berry - de Rippe was a first name, the family surname was Berry. When it came time for me to be named, Father decides, for what reason I know not, that the Rippe bit should be dropped. Thus, the endless confusion over whether my surname is Berry or de Berry. I have firmly called myself David Berry for a number of years now - but the de Berry still comes back to haunt me, now and again.

My memories of Stradishall are rather like its location - sparse. One highlight was one of those Summer Balls and I persuaded Val to come. This was quite something for someone who had really never been away from home before. The place to stay seemed to be Cambridge - all at considerable expense mainly footed by her good self. It was great that she was at the Ball but the week in the hotel in Cambridge was really a disaster. I depended on HC for lifts; we socialised with him and his wife of what was going to be a crumbling marriage. What were we two innocents doing, tangled up in all this?

It was with some relief that I completed the course and the list of postings was published. The choices seemed much of muchness as many of them were just names: Horsham St Faith, Wattisham, Waterbeach, Leuchars and more. Against my name was:

No.65(F) Squadron, RAF Duxford near Cambridge

This seemed as good as all the rest. It turned out to be a pleasant assignment.

Chapter 10
Fighter Pilot

During training there was an enclave to which you could retreat - the company of fellow students. Here feelings could be vented about, say, particularly idiotic instructors and the whole training system reorganised; confidences could be exchanged, with those you trusted, of your latest flying difficulty - or, indeed, achievement. But now, accompanying the big moment of being on your first squadron, was the fact that you were 'on your own' - well, certainly for a while until you became established. There were fellow pilots of your own vintage - well not quite. They had been on the squadron a couple of months or more and were anxious to maintain that seniority - you were a 'new boy'. Above them, age and experience-wise there was a curious mix. I find it odd to reflect what an odd ball lot they were. I will bow to convention and start at the top.

The 'Boss' was a Squadron Leader - these were the days when RAF ranks did still bear some resemblance to status. His nickname related to the colour of his hair - and the colour of his hair related to his temperament. He wore his hat in a rakish style and he led his squadron in a rakish way - but it was still shades of Battle of Britain days and that was the way to do things. I have to admit that, in those early days, I lived in complete awe of those in positions above me. Perhaps it is for this reason that I remember a particular incident involving this boss which demonstrated that he was only

You pick out 'The Boss', the 'Senior Flight Lieutenants', the 'Flight Sergeants and Sergeants', the 'Junior RAF Pilots' amongst which were the 'gregarious, the shy, the over confident and the under, the tall, the short, the good fliers and the poor ones ... There was a university graduate and an ex-Modern Secondary one' ... the Author!

human. Nothing to do with flying; he was the father of a young boy who was perhaps endowed with some of his father's 'devil may care' spirit. The son's outlet was to unscrew the petrol cap of the family car and, carefully, start filling the tank with sand!

I also remember that he took me on a formation trip - just the two of us. We spent most of it in cloud with him twisting and turning and me trying to simulate the qualities of a certain substance and a blanket - I stayed 'stuck'. Although nothing was said, I did feel that this was some sort of 'baptism of fire' - and test of competence.

Next down in the hierarchy were the flight commanders - senior Flight Lieutenants. One was an incredible personality, a real Cockney who, pre-war had been an high speed ice skating ace and held some sort of record for the number of barrels jumped. He took such bravado into the war and earned himself a DSO. It is strange that he was regarded as just part of the scene and yet, when he died many more years later, he had a substantial obituary in '*The Times*' - not an inconsequential testament to one's standing.

The distinguishing feature of the other flight commander was that he was a small time racing driver. There was obviously 'money' and he owned a splendid classic two-seater. There were other 'elderly' Flight Lieutenants - one was a member of the car family that built the Jowitt Javelin car.

The next squadron members by age and experience were Flight Sergeants and Sergeants. One was, shall I say, worldly-wise and the story went that he once owned all the one-armed bandits in Blackpool - but something had 'gone wrong'.

Moving to the younger members, there was a group of three that stood out; they were ex-Cranwell graduates. A thing that distinguished them, apart from their superior air, was their Best Blue uniforms. It seemed to be part of the post-war bucking-up of the Royal Air Force image that the traditional uniform was discarded; this was the very familiar one with large pockets at lower fronts of the jacket. These were scrapped - just the plain material in their position - and the wings were in wired gold. It looked like something out of a stage musical. The unfortunate three obviously were passing through the uniform equipping stage when this uniform policy was in force. They

were unfortunate, as it seemed to last for an incredibly short time; the old style was re-established.

Finally, there was the humble majority, the post-war bulge of people of my vintage. We did make up the bulk of the squadron and therefore had to be reckoned with; this must have been very hard for some of the old timers. Within our ranks, in spite of the fact that we could carry a common label of 'Junior RAF Pilots', we had the mixture that can be anticipated with any group. There were the gregarious, the shy, the over confident and the under, the tall, the short, the good fliers and the poor ones ... There was a university graduate and an ex-Modern Secondary schoolboy; a Royal Australian Air Force Flight Lieutenant who, in subsequent years, rose to a high rank in the RAAF; there were several who had nothing about them at all. I should have fitted into that bracket but I seemed to get on OK. I was able to identify what was required, and being someone always anxious to please, came up with the goods.

Senior ranks were populated by men with distinguished war records; there was the share of 'characters'. Our Commander-in-

Chief was Air Chief Marshal The Earl of Bandon. The much told story about him concerned a time when he was rising through the ranks. It was in Cairo that he'd had an over-indulgent lunchtime. Sitting on the steps leading up to the Officers' Club, in blazer and flannels but tie askew, he was looking distinctly the worse for wear; he was accosted by a gentleman, also in mufti.

'What a disgraceful sight you are ... letting the side down ...'

' Oh, go and ...', the Earl suggested some unhealthy activity to the complainant.

He takes exception, 'Do you know who you are talking too? I'm Major, The Right Honourable Bloggs.'

'Well I'm Wing Commander The Earl of Bandon ... so that's got you on two counts ... now go and ...'

A well known surname was Atcherley; there were two of them - twins. They both achieved senior rank and one of them was also, in turn, a C-in-C ; he went by the rather disrespectful sobriquet of 'Batchy' ... not without reason. The stories about him were legion. In spite of his senior rank he still flew as often as possible. One day he used a Vampire jet to visit one of his stations. Unfortunately he neglected to lower his undercarriage before landing which resulted in lots of sparks but, luckily, no fire. The fire engines rush to the scene and one firemen leaps on to the fuselage and starts attempting to break through the canopy; 'Batchy' winds back the hood. The airman shouts.

'Let's get you out of there quick, mate, the C-in-C's due in here any minute!'

'I am the C-in-C - now just go away for a minute whilst I collect my thoughts!'

A sad postscript to the Atcherley story is that Batchy's twin brother went missing on a solo flight from Cyprus. 'Batchy' flew, day after day, in a Meteor, searching for him ... in vain.

No.65(F) Squadron - we were a 'Day Fighter Squadron' with our Meteor Mk8s. I have often reflected, with the experience of other flying jobs, that a fighter pilot's is a strange one; life is one big practice for something that never happens - well rarely. How long did a post-war pilot, who stayed in the fighter world, have to wait for some real action? Until the Gulf War? Subsequently there have been jobs of the Bosnia/Serbia sort. Both commendable but, with many other flying roles, there is the satisfaction of actually doing a job, even though it is peacetime - I have in mind being a flying instructor or a transport aircraft pilot. It will turn out that I would say that ... wouldn't I?

I went through a 'check out' phase on the squadron - very relaxed and informal compared with the training days. There followed a number of solo trips to get used to the local area and the airfield.

One feature of the Duxford Air Traffic Control was that a point some 30 miles out from the extended centre line of the main runway was identified by the code name of 'Luxembourg'. This was useful for the radar

A fairly low level 'run in and break'. The cameraman rather over anticipated the speed of the Meteor!

station controlling aircraft on, say, an interception exercise. At the conclusion, the radar controller could position the formation at 'Luxembourg' and then hand over control to Duxford ATC who would immediately put the aircraft into a descent for a 'run in and break' or for an instrument approach.

A solo aircraft, like mine on those initial sorties, could call the radar station and ask for a course to steer for 'Luxembourg'. The OK phrase was:

'Request pigeons for Luxembourg.'

The 'pigeons' word emanated from the homing instincts of that feathered species. The time came for me to return to base and I duly called.

'Yucky Radar this is Jubilee Mike Bravo, do you read?'

'Mike Bravo from Yucky Radar loud and clear - go ahead.'

'Yucky Radar, Mike Bravo, request pigeons for Amsterdam.'

I *was* under a bit of stress! There is a pause and Yucky Radar comes back.

'Mike Bravo your pigeons for Amsterdam are steer zero seven zero, seventeen hundred miles!' - or some such message. Silly bugger - he knew what I really meant.

So, our life was practice, practice, practice ... of that dreaded battle formation - but one did get better; close formation, mock interceptions - and exercises, being either the defender or the enemy. There were those personal proficiency skills to keep honed: instrument flying, navigation, asymmetric work. With all this, punctuated with bad weather, leave, sickness, life was full enough.

What about the 'real thing'. Well, we were required to take our turn, along with the other fighter wings, at what was called Exercise 'Fabulous', a not, altogether, appropriate code name for the possible outcome. To not put too fine a point on it, I now reflect that we are talking about launching World War III. The gravity of what we were doing was somehow lost in the routine.

'The Duty Wing this week is Duxford.'

Four aircraft from our 65 Squadron and our compatriots at Duxford, 64 Squadron, would 'arm up' ie put live bullets 'up the spout'. We were then on day-time stand-by to intercept any suspicious incoming aircraft.

Perhaps it was my still continuing naivety but I cannot, honestly, recall anyone telling me precisely what to do, given that I, personally, was faced with the aircraft that was going to drop an H-Bomb on the centre of London. Perhaps it was assumed that us lesser mortals were always going to be led by more experienced beings.

However, the one time that I remember being 'scrambled' in anger, I found myself as Number One. The thought might have crossed my mind that I should have applied more effort to my aircraft recognition - Bearcat - Dingbat!? In the event, it really was a Soviet aircraft but it was flying as part of the Cold War game that was constantly being played - fly with intent towards the UK but turn away before there was any infringement of territorial rights. I let it go - well that's what Yucky Radar told me to do - and had a few beers that night, satisfied in the knowledge that I had not precipitated World War III!

An enormous amount of time was absorbed by particular

events. One that comes to mind was a visit to RAF Duxford by the Emperor of Ethiopia, Haile Selassie, 'Lion of Judah, Elect of God, King of Kings of Ethiopia'; he had numerous other titles which seemed a lot to bear for a man of such small stature.

The plan was that the whole of the Duxford Wing's (64 and 65 Squadron) aircraft would be lined up along the long aircraft apron, the pilots and ground crew standing in front, for inspection by the eminence. We stood there, at attention, with weeks of work on the aircraft - and our own personal appearance. The Emperor went by on

his 'inspection'. I have that picture of a small man wearing a uniform style hat - flat top, peak - but it seemed huge, as did the sword which he trailed along beside him. And not a glance, to left or right, at our pristine turnout.

Ah well! Time to do the flying bit. Thirty two aircraft started up - at a command they all moved forward 20 feet and, with a further prompt, turned through 90°. Now in line, we taxied to the runway, to line up and take off, in pairs, at 30 second intervals. To reduce the effect of wake turbulence after leaving the runway, the first pair would stay low, the second pull up and so on,. Describing all this in words, cannot convey the pilot and machinery anguish that was involved. 'Please let it not be me who has a wet start,' would be a silent prayer offered up by each pilot. (A wet start is a failure to start a jet engine due to initial over-fuelling because of a mechanical fault or, more likely, mishandling, down to pilot anxiousness.) The machinery? Jet engines being operated in the wake of other jet engines, rapid power changes, heavy use of wheel brakes - all to keep your aircraft in line. I wonder if Mr Selassie was that impressed.

We would have been airborne to fly two 16 aircraft formations in line astern. Each 16 would be made up of four sets of four aircraft flying a diamond shape - one aircraft leading, one on each of his wings and one in line astern. Each four would, in turn, form a larger diamond formation - a diamond four of diamond fours. My hands are going crazy trying to describe this!

I am amazed, these years later that we, and the other fighter wings, survived all this without incident. This Haile Selassie display was not a 'one off'. We used to fly the formation quite often: on the occasion of HM The Queen's official birthday, for instance, and each time Her Majesty returned from a, frequent in those days, overseas visit. These would be over Buckingham Palace.

Another of my reflections is that, as a very junior pilot, aged just 21, I was given a tremendous responsibility in these formations. I led the diamond four on the port side. This meant that I was concentrating on the leader, keeping the correct position with smooth, small power changes; if I started using rapid, large throttle movements then the three formating on me would have required even quicker and bigger ones - possibly beyond the capabilities of the engine. Similarly my flying control movements had to be, well, controlled. It would be rather like driving a car, in a motorway situation, with slow reaction to the steering wheel and a very stiff accelerator pedal and poor brakes. Most importantly I had to maintain the correct distance out from the leader to ensure that my starboard wing man didn't collide with the leader's port wing man - my hands are going again. There was enormous trust in my flying ability; that starboard wing man was looking at me and had to hope that I kept that correct distance.

Once more my mind slips back to that Co-op loaf of bread - nineteen fourteen two!

Manoeuvring such an enormous formation required careful planning, especially when, for those London flypasts, it wasn't just the Duxford Wing but all the Meteor wings - Waterbeach, Wattisham, Horsham St. Faith etc, flying in a stream. Careful timing was needed of each Wing's take-off so that they could fly a route and slot into their place in the, one wing behind the other configuration, at one minute intervals, over the Palace. A critical aspect for Duxford was that it was close to Waterbeach so very little time elapsed before that first rendezvous. So, the day that our wing leader got it wrong and took off a minute early caused a little difficulty!

We were due to drop in behind Waterbeach but now we would be level with them. Thirty two aircraft did a 60° left turn for one minute, followed by a 60° right for another minute and then another a 60° left. With the minute lost we were behind Waterbeach but us lot, in formation, felt as if we had done a day's work already. Remembering that particular Wing Commander Flying, I know he would not have had the good grace to feel any embarrassment about this.

One of our other excitements was air-to-air firing. That is what we were about; all this practice battle formation, interceptions, exercises were only the means of rehearsing getting within shooting range of an enemy aircraft. But then comes the crunch: can we shoot that aircraft down?

Obviously we could not test this by having a go at real aircraft so our skills were evaluated against a banner. This was what its name implies. One of our compatriots would tow behind his aircraft a rectangular piece of nylon-type material, some 20 feet long by 6 feet high. It was kept taut with a tubular bar at the front which had a heavy weight at the bottom to make the whole thing fly vertically. The duty 'Joe' would line his aircraft up on the runway. Alongside him, but pointing the wrong way, he would see, lying on the edge of the runway, the banner. The cable for it would run back from the banner and then be turned through 180° to be attached to the underside of his aircraft. This would mean that, when he released the brakes, with full power applied, the aircraft would have a bit of a chance of accelerating before the load of the banner was taken up. For such a seemingly dodgy exercise, it did work - most times.

That drama over, the tug aircraft would make its way, slowly, otherwise the banner would come off, to the East Coast firing range. The firing party of the day, two or three aircraft, would take off, at a suitable time, to rendezvous with the tug over the range. It might be appreciated that none of this was easy to arrange and, what hasn't been mentioned is the ground crew side.

Apart from all the day-to-day stuff of getting the aircraft ready for flight, for firing sorties the guns had to be prepared and loaded with ammunition; the points of each round would be painted a different colour for each aircraft. Prior to the firing day, the guns would have been 'harmonised' (lined up) with the gun sight. Film would be loaded into the gun sight for subsequent analysis of the firing. All this technical and flying effort weighed heavily on the mind as one prepared to have a maximum of three or four 'goes' at the banner, in just 10 second bursts each time.

A great deal of coaching went on before the actual sorties, which didn't really relate to shooting down real aeroplanes - it would have been a strange enemy that, obligingly, flew along, at low speed in a straight line, whilst you executed the following manoeuvre. There was an ideal position to take up before the attack on the banner; this would be a 1000 yards or so abeam the tug aircraft, slightly ahead and 1000 feet higher. When set, and within the boundaries of the firing range, it was time to go in with a diving turn towards the banner. When at 90° to it, the turn would be reversed and, hopefully, the banner could be brought into the aiming ring of diamonds of the gun sight. The big moment had come - decide when everything was just right and squeeze the firing trigger on the control column. Do it too soon and you would be out of range - leave it too late and you stood a good chance of shooting down the tug aircraft - not an activity to be encouraged.

Refinements were advocated by the experienced who advised that the dot in the centre of the gun sight should be allowed to drift from the upper front corner of the banner to the bottom rear as one

Waiting for the banner ... once again ... spot the Author!

pulled the trigger - fat chance! I applied the same technique as I did with darts in those home years: don't over concentrate, relax and 'fire' - intuitively. Whether this policy worked with a banner would be tested on return.

Guns empty, the firers would return to base; slowly bringing up the rear would be the tug, hopefully nursing the valuable banner back to base. Flying low and slowly up the runway, it was his turn to squeeze the firing trigger but, in the case of the tug, this was wired up to the attachment hook underneath the aircraft and released the banner.

Collected by the Squadron Land Rover, it would be brought back to the front of the crew room and laid out on the ground. The whole squadron would gather for the solemn ceremony of counting the holes - and, more importantly for the individuals in the firing party, identifying the colour of those holes. Remember, each aircraft had different coloured paint on its shells. There would be disappointment and surprise. It really did seem like pot luck. The day you thought you had it licked, hardly a hole your colour; another day - bingo!! But what had you done that day? The film from the gun sight would reveal all; the day you missed, you thought that you were holding the banner firmly in your sight; the film showed a banner briefly flashing across the screen. Try harder next time.

There were the odd sensations. Occasionally the film would reveal a picture of the tug aircraft. As this could have only have happened when the guns were firing then there would be a few beers owing. A particular friend of mine, noted for a rather bulldog attitude, developed a new theory and decided that the last part of the attack should be at a sharper angle, then one could hold one's fire until at a very close range with no danger to the tug. I said there was a substantial metal bar and weight at the front of the banner - he came home with it firmly embedded in the leading edge of his wing.

Once a year we attended an Armament Practice Camp - a month devoted to firing and located in Northumberland where there were bigger range facilities. Happily, the 'Camp' was a, name only, legacy and we were safely tucked away at nights in the comfort of the Officers' Mess at RAF Acklington. There would be the odd foray to sample the Northumberland social scene. It seemed a good idea, one Saturday evening, to visit a local dance. There were several stories to be told later. One of my compatriots reported the remark of his dancing partner.

'Cor, I ain't 'alf sweatin'!'

The 'Camp' enabled us to try our hands at firing at higher altitudes - the firings 'at home' were limited to 2000 feet by the size of the ranges off the East Coast. There was an element of competition at these Armament Practice Camps as an annual trophy was awarded to the squadron producing the highest scores.

Our boss decided that we should prepare ourselves for operating at these higher altitudes and, for some weeks beforehand, a banner was towed to the great height and we did simulated attacks on it - squeezing the trigger merely operating the gun sight camera. The results would be analysed and advice given.

Towing the banner for live firing exercises was something of a thankless task but perhaps the thought of all those bullets flying behind you made the time pass quickly. But the really tiresome job was towing for those high level sorties. One of my compatriots was so engaged. As he droned along over East Anglia, he saw ahead an enormous cumulonimbus cloud developing. He thought that it would look good on his gun sight film - so he squeezed the trigger. Go back some lines to remind yourself that, with a tug aircraft, the trigger releases the banner! This is quite a substantial piece of kit to be hurtling earthwards and it can be assumed that there wasn't an East Anglian located at the impact point as we heard nothing of the incident.

A strange feature of our lives was that none of us - and you are talking about 25 blokes - seemed to have nothing better to do than hang about in each other's company. This would be natural when flying was in progress but we would get days of bad weather and we all would sit about in the crewroom - or not sit, as the case may be; the problem was that there were not 25 chairs! This would result in endless attempts by the chairless to get the chairbound on their feet so that a seat could be won. Coming in the door and calling to Bloggs, 'You're wanted on the phone,' didn't work after a very short time. Many ingenious schemes were contrived. Life became a bit complicated, 'Bill, the Boss wants to see you.' No joy, Bill was not going to be had - but the Boss really did want to see him!

It was probably during one of these 'brain in neutral' occasions that we dreamt up 'The Letter'. The coffee bar was, and still is, a great feature of crewrooms. Endless cups of coffee, tea, cocoa, Bovril, whatever, are consumed. Indeed, in those far off days, the powers-that-be decided that we needed the 'energy' from these beverages and the squadron received an allowance to support the coffee bar. On one of our bad weather days, someone discovered, on opening a new tin of cocoa, that there was a bug of some sort inside. All 25 minds set about composing a letter of complaint. The start of the finished result went something like this:

`Dear Sirs,`

`On opening a tin of your maggots, recently, we were disappointed to find that it mostly contained cocoa ...`

We didn't receive any reply!

Our desire to stick together extended into our leisure time, which I, rather shamefacedly, have to report was mainly spent in the Mess bar. Not the whole time, you understand ... we spent some of it in various local hostelries. I don't think there was any hidden psychological reason for this; we just enjoyed each other's company and it was one big laugh. Things rarely got out of hand - there was some mischief! This might be sparked off by the raw materials available - bricks and eggs come to mind.

The bricks were to hand because some Mess building work was in progress. Late one night we built a temporary wall across a corridor sealing off the rooms containing the WAAF officers - it seemed quite a jape at the time but I don't think the humour of it stands the test of time.

A cleverer idea was 'The Eggs'. An 'old' Flight Lieutenant - probably about 35 - who lived in the Mess, used to disappear at weekends to some country retreat. He would return on Monday with his stock of fresh eggs for which he had established a demand from the families on the station. All this marketing seemed to be somewhat stressful for he was always first in the Bar at six o'clock, opening time. By nine o'clock he would be in a highly collapsed condition and would stagger off to bed. We young blades drank on and, on this particular evening, hatched a fiendish plot.

A team went to the Flight Lieutenant's door; assured by the snores from within, they entered and spied the stock of eggs. These were then carefully spread out all over the floor. This done, a master touch was to remove the bulb from his bedside lamp. The door was quietly closed. Then followed some urgent knocking on said door with calling of name and the general indication that there was an urgent reason for him to get out of bed and come to the door. You can picture the rest - it was a dirty trick but did have the merit of being a clever one!

Dogs were a feature; several of my fellows considered that a canine companion created the right image - or perhaps they just liked dogs! Labradors and Alsatians were popular; one of these dogs was a particularly long-legged breed - a boxer of some sort. JD was a

Beau, the adopted dog, is bottom centre. The tribly of Cranwell days has, clearly, been abandoned by the author - as has consciousness!

good friend but he did have some outlandish ways. One of these was that his dog was a particularly small, scruffy specimen which he had adopted on a Northumberland beach during one of our 'Camps'. It flew back to Duxford on his lap! One day, the owner of the above mentioned boxer was due to go flying and he charged his compatriots to look after his dog; this required particular attention as the bitch was 'on heat'. If it had been known that he was to return to the crewroom prematurely - his aircraft was unserviceable - then the project of assisting JD's 'Beau' overcome his height disadvantage would not have been in progress.

I said that we, as 'Junior Pilots' were a strange mix. One of my compatriots was a worldly-wise Londoner - something very removed from my roots. Perhaps it was the realisation that my horizons needed broadening that he decides to take me to London and show me a thing or two. Amongst the activities was a visit to the Windmill Theatre. This was very *risqué* for its day ... nude women, but standing perfectly still, as required by the law of the land at that time. So, really it was the front cover of *'Health and Efficiency'* revisited, this time in 3D.

An astonishing feature on the drinking scene of those years was 'Merrydown Cider'; I think it must have been about 15% ABV! A baby would be born and the new father would give birth to a barrel of Merrydown to celebrate. Its effect was lethal - three halves and I was anybody's - along with my companions. On our cultural visits to Cambridge, one of our 'ports of call' was a pub by the bridge where the students jump into the Cam on May Ball night. Perhaps they are on the 'Merrydown', which was sold at the pub, 'On Draught'.

On our sojourns around the local area we must have considered ourselves as, somewhat, debonair - or something similar. This
was dampened, one summer evening, when standing around an open
Cambridge pub window. Someone made, probably not too quietly, a
remark about some passing Teddy Boys. An arm reached through the
window and grasped a soda syphon. We had a good soaking. Teddy
Boys, 1: Fighter Pilots, Nil.

Inevitably, for those years, another accident story creeps in.
Duxford lay to the south of Cambridge; to the north was Waterbeach,
equipped, like ourselves, with Meteors. On a particularly foul day, all
our aircraft had recovered to base and we were engaged in crewroom
pastimes.

Word came from Air Traffic Control that there was a problem
at Waterbeach. With four aircraft still airborne, the decision had been
made, because of a swing in the wind direction, to change the
'Runway in Use'. This usually could be done quite speedily, the
major task being the moving of the large trailer containing the
Ground Control Approach (GCA) radar. But there had been some
hitch with this and the aircraft had to hold off whilst the radar was
being set up.

The weather worsened. It was decided that trying to land the
four aircraft at Waterbeach be abandoned and they should divert to
Duxford. Now, their fuel was running perilously low; the visibility
and cloud base at Duxford were as one ... very poor.

The four aircraft started their approaches, one behind the
other at three minute intervals. We went and stood outside our crewroom. In the distance, the first aircraft could be just heard as it made
its approach; then there was the roar as full power was applied ... the
pilot had not been able to see the runway and was overshooting.
Moments later that engine roar suddenly died; seconds later there
was the unmistakable crunch of an aircraft hitting the ground.

This was repeated three more times, the only variation being
that, on two of the occasions, the 'crunch' was preceded by the
explosion of an ejector seat being fired at a low level. The outcome
was that the four pilots were seriously injured. As the ambulances
drove past, our gloom matched that of the weather. It needed a few

beers to get over that one.

A facility that we were allowed, which I found difficult to believe in later, more stringent times, was the loan of an aircraft for the weekend! On a number of occasions I took a Meteor to Exeter Airport and then caught the train to Plymouth!

As we were a 'Day Fighter Squadron', night flying was not a major feature. But it was decreed that we should have a session, once a month, to 'keep our hands in'. It was strange how the briefing for this could have been taken straight from one of those wartime films - pilots lounging in chairs, the wall display, stick pointing to features, notes on a lectern, the met man adding his bit, cigarette smoke hanging in the air, the final word from the Wing Commander Flying, ending with, 'Good Luck, chaps.'

The edge of the runway was crudely marked with 'goose necks'. They were like metal watering cans with a wick in the spout and paraffin in the container. It was not unknown for a number of these to be extinguished by a not too well controlled landing.

We did not want to push our luck by carrying out too many landings during our one hour sortie so we used to go off and have a bit of a look at some of the local lights. Even in those days of lesser aviation, there must have been rules about flying over London. If there were, we were oblivious of them. Circling overhead the capital, we tried to pick out landmarks. With all that successfully over for another month there would be the need for a few more of those beers!

Was it all squadron and Mess life? Sounds like a bit of a monastic existence.

Chapter 11
'Do you, David, take ...'

During the first year on the squadron, matters back at Plymouth once again took a bit of a dive; Valerie and I were 'estranged' for while. I cannot remember the precise reason why but, undoubtedly, it was my fault. One thing for sure, I was regretting the state of affairs and was doing my level best to restore 'relations'. I am not sure how I managed it but Val was persuaded to attend the RAF Duxford Officers' Mess Summer Ball - the, already reported, traditionally grand occasion. She stayed with our young RAF doctor and his family, which was very successful, young children featuring - a *forte* of Val's. I have been a bit hazy about some of the detail but one thing I remember well is that I accompanied her to Paddington Station for the journey home and it was at that romantic spot that she agreed that we should marry.

But it was not a straightforward matter for a 21/22 year old RAF officer to enter into matrimony - it was not encouraged. A major barrier was financial; full marriage allowance was not paid until the age of 25 and one did not qualify for other privileges and payments associated with the married state eg a married quarter or an allowance payable on posting together with the expenses of the removal van. To underline all this, the 'under age' officer required the permission to marry from his Station Commander. Group Captain Jamie Rankin was an ex-Battle of Britain ace and I don't

This really is us on Paddington Station. An American tourist wanted a picture of a genuine English farewell. He sent us the photo later!

That very important Summer Ball when the the question was 'popped' and answered.

116

That holiday at Bournemouth.

suppose he was that much bothered about the fate of this love-struck Flying Officer; but he went through the motions, offering advice in a kind, fatherly way and ending with permission and good wishes.

Obviously there was considerable enthusiasm about Val and I being together and we arranged an autumn week in Bournemouth. Rather daringly we stayed in a reasonably smart hotel - but in single rooms!! How times have changed. It was quite a memorable time and was a happy confirmation that we had made the right decision.

Back home, at St Thomas's Church, Keyham, Devonport, Plymouth, this was going to be a wedding of some local note. The Sunday School teacher, Girl Guide Brownie leader and occasional solo soprano singer at other people's weddings, was to marry one of the chief servers (altar boys) who had left home to fight for Queen and Country. Happily for me, that commitment excused me from all the preparatory detail.

The wedding itself was a curious occasion when viewed from the distance of time. We were so young. I was still extremely self-conscious and couldn't wait for the day to be over! For the initial part, Father had his influence. Pre-wedding, I was at home - not the old council house but the new abode; at the age of 50+ the bold decision had been made to buy a house. But it was a humble affair - a terraced late Victorian one amongst acre upon acre of similar abodes - each with only a mean backyard.

On the wedding day, Mother, Father, brother John (my Best Man) and myself awaited the wedding car to take John and I to the church. Father was 'champing at the bit' - he was now a driver with his own car, an Austin A30,·which was quite a natty little car in its day. He was set to drive Mum and himself to the church when the Groom and Best Man were on our way. The minutes ticked by; Father's agitation increased.

'It's no good, something's gone wrong ... get in the back.'

Jumping forward to post-ceremony, the first few moments alone with my new bride, in the wedding car driving to the reception, were occupied with the driver giving me a 'bollocking' for being impatient and not waiting to be picked up.

'I was there in good time - and you'd gone!'

Picture the ceremony. Valerie and I had grown up together under the umbrella of the church so there was a lot of intensity on the part of the priest - our Father Wood. It was very family on V's side - with May and Henry's history of coming to Plymouth, the Berry's were a bit short of relations. I think the only contribution I made to the day, apart from being there, was to suggest that we hired a Plymouth Corporation red double decker bus to take the guests from the church to the reception - which, for its day, was quite a kinky idea.

The wedding reception was a standard affair, including my duty few words, which I managed to get through. What was remarkable, compared with weddings of later years, was that we were changed into our going away kit and on the train to Exeter by late afternoon - in fact we were in Exeter in time to go to an evening concert by Eddie Calvert, 'The Man with the Golden Trumpet'. It was as good a way as any to, temporarily, take one's mind off later activity!

The reason for Exeter was that we were to fly to Jersey the next day for our honeymoon proper - good hotel at St Brelades Bay; all rather grand for an impecunious, under-25 couple. A moment I will always remember was the one when we were being ushered into the dining room for our first meal.

'It's Mr and Mrs Berry?' queries the head waiter.

Val blushed to the point where, as I followed her, I could see the red back through her rather diaphanous white blouse. The days passed in the blissful way of honeymoons - I assume this, with just the experience of one. On one of the days, we happened to be sitting on the rocks above the beach of St Brelades Bay when I heard, in the distance, a familiar sound - it was Rolls Royce Derwent jet engines. Searching the sky, I saw three Meteors, in formation, approaching - and they flew smack overhead. It was my mates from the squadron! How many newly-marrieds have had such a salute? It is certainly something that would not have happened in the more disciplined later years.

With the euphoria of that fortnight over, it was time to return to the real world. I had managed to find some suitably priced accommodation close to Duxford. It had to be ' suitably priced' and 'close' for we had no money and no transport. It was the upper half of a house - why don't I say the second floor? Well, it was more like the roof space made into rooms; access was an outside iron stairway. It had no running water; there was a tap at the bottom of the stairs. We had the use of a toilet in a lean-to of the downstairs accommodation. I really do not know how we managed - it must have been 'true love' that carried us through.

I recall that Valerie set the pattern for later life and did her best to prepare good meals with the most limited facilities. Those night school cookery classes and the associated notes were utilised. Part of one those evening lessons was dedicated to the really OK method of making coffee. Rather strangely (to me) it involved the use of mustard. All the, saucepan simmering, processes complete, the final part of 'The Method' was to strain off the brew. Val stood at the sink staring at this strainer full of coffee dregs, completely puzzled for a moment as to what had gone wrong. The coffee was down the drain!

She found a job at a company which was, strangely, locally placed; a well known product now, 'Araldite' was in its early days and the manufacturer, Aero Research Ltd, was based in Duxford village. I returned to the Squadron, now somewhat isolated from my boozy mates by my recently acquired marital situation.

It is strange that I remember so little of those days - it must have been happiness! Apart from no water, we had no radio, limited social contact - certainly 'no money' was beginning to bite. This condition was going to stay with us for many a year.

I was approaching the end of my second year on the squadron and thought that I had another six months to go before posting. This was the days of the firmly rooted policy of pilots being moved every 2½ years on the principle that 'It will be good for you'. We were all regarded as future Air Marshals and the broader the experience of those of lofty rank, the better. The fact was ignored that it meant that we climbed one ladder in the 2½ years, and became pretty competent in that role, only to be kicked to the bottom of another ladder to start the ascent all over again. With not quite two years under my belt, the posting came as something of a surprise ... not just the timing but the job. I perhaps should say potential job as there was a selection process involved.

I was commanded to attend the Central Flying School (CFS) at RAF Little Rissington, in the Cotswolds, for interview. CFS was the training establishment for flying instructors. You may be as surprised as I was that someone who had only finished his own training barely two years before should be considered capable of teaching someone else to fly. But, it was 'new policy'; younger blood was required in the training machine; selection of someone of my limited experience was, possibly, over zealous application of this principle. Attitudes towards becoming a QFI (Qualified Flying Instructor) changed over the years. In the 1950s it was, undoubtedly, a prestigious qualification to obtain. In later years, spending time instructing came to be regarded as a bit of pain and an interruption to one's real flying career.

So, it was with some enthusiasm, and trepidation, that I presented myself at CFS for the selection process. The final part of this was an interview with the Commandant, an Air Commodore. I have already said how senior rank tended to over-awe me and I was only referring to Squadron Leaders and Wing Commanders; the sight of the broad blue band on the sleeve of 'The Commandant' was, indeed, somewhat daunting. But, as I very much discovered in later years, it is generally the case that the more senior an officer, the more pleasant and amiable is his attitude towards subordinates. 'It's the bastards on their way up, using you as a stepping stone, you have to watch out for!' This was a kindly Air Commodore and the interview pleasantly progressed ... but he saved the bitter pill to the end.

'I think you are well suited to the CFS course - but I would like you to live in the Mess whilst you are completing it.'

He was obviously of the opinion that I could not cope with the complications of 'The Principles of Flight', learning to deliver the 'patter' that went with airborne exercises and all the like content of the course, and the demands of a new bride! With the benefit of hindsight, I might agree that he had a point ... but it was very hard to take at the time. Val kept her chin up! Picture this young lady, away from home for the first time, being on her own in a strange area, from Sunday afternoons to Friday evenings - in the grotty accommodation that was our lot.

With a good send-off, two of us left the squadron to start the course. John M. was older than me although with the same flying experience ... he had attended University before joining the RAF. We shared a room in the Mess and got on well, in spite of him being a bit of a 'clever clogs'. This turned out to my advantage as I am sure it made me work harder at the academic stuff, of which there was an awful lot. Old hands would tell you that the CFS course, 'will do you good!' But I have to admit that this is true. During one's own pilot training there is so much to take in and the constant anxiety of being 'suspended from training'.

Completing the CFS course allowed you to have a second go at all the basic flying principles and in so much greater depth. After all you were required to understand those principles etc in sufficient detail to pass them on to your trainee. I will always remember a classic example of this and that was during one of the exacting flying exercises we had to carry out. Each took you through the flying syllabus of an *ab initio* student. The first one would be 'Effect of Controls'. Your CFS instructor would demonstrate this, acting out the part of a flying school instructor with his student. It would be your turn, on the next flight to 'teach' him. If you didn't get it quite right eg if there were two ways of interpreting what you had just said, then you could be sure that this 'dim' student would follow the alternative instruction to the 't'.

So, what was this classic example of having the chance of re-examining basic principles and understanding them so much better the second time around? Well, the instance occurred in this very first lesson. I was obviously told it during my training and applied it, intuitively, subsequently, but one's skill was greatly enhanced by having been brought back to basics, once more.

The simple concept that was a new enlightenment - and fellow pilots might scream at its basic nature - was that, 'the elevators control airspeed and the throttle rate of climb or descent'. It is not entirely that clear cut as there is some inter-action and it is this that blurs the perception of the experienced pilot. Nevertheless, it is something to always keep in the back of one's mind, no matter the aircraft type and the manoeuvre being flown. I will jump forward a considerable number of years for an example: a flapless approach and landing in a four, turbo-prop, engined Britannia aircraft!

The first half of the course was completed at RAF South Cerney, near Cirencester, on the then current basic trainer, the Percival Provost with its Leonides piston engine. This was a big improvement on the ghastly sluggish Prentice, of my student days. The Provost was a lively aircraft but a Harvard could have held its own against it. One major difference between the two was that the Provost was side-by-side seating compared with the Harvard's tandem. Side-by-side was considered a good thing as you, the instructor, could look at the student, as required, when instructing him. It also meant that he could be sick all over you! I had a good instructor; he, in his turn, representing the quest for more youthfulness in the training arena. His agreeableness was demonstrated when one had to fly with another instructor; there was one who clearly showed signs of mental instability. The whole of a flight with him would be overlaid with him playing the stupid student; taxying for take-off:

'Oh, Sir, look at all those people stopped in their cars looking at us - can I give them a wave?'

One evening it was the misfortune of three of us to have to do our night flying with this guy. We were sat in this room for his briefing, during which the signs of a deranged mind increased. We squirmed in our seats, wondering what to do. But the word had obviously spread for the door opened and he was called away. We never saw him again. I think that this was an extreme example of the post-war syndrome for the 'old hands'. It must have been very difficult for some of them, after the traumas that they had faced, to accept this new Air Force and its fresh-faced new members.

I was very happy with this Provost stage of the course and seemed to be doing OK; in equal measure, I was not overjoyed with the subsequent half. The first half would qualify us to teach the basic stage of pilot training. The second was aimed at those destined for the advanced stage. We all did the lot as our destinies were not decided until the end of the course.

This advanced stage was carried out, at RAF Little Rissington, on the de Havilland Vampire. This, in its day, had been an excellent single seat, single engine fighter/ground attack aircraft taking the post-war stage alongside the Meteor. But CFS was equipped with the T11, the trainer version of the aircraft. The single seat Vampire Mk5 was a small aircraft but into its only slightly increased, modest dimensions had been squeezed two seats, side-by-side, and ejector seats at that.

This meant that it was a bit of a tight fit for someone 6ft 2ins tall. Add to this the fact that my co-student (we flew together a lot to practise our 'patter' on each other) was very keen on high 'g' force and I spent a lot of those flights unconscious and you might get the impression that I didn't enjoy this product of the de Havilland Aircraft Company very much.

Actually the acceleration forces on my body were good training for the weekends. I am not, of course, referring to delightful intimate activity but the car rides from South Cerney/Little Rissington and return. John M. was the proud owner of one of the early Morris Minors. This model broke new ground in road holding and John demonstrated this to the full ... indeed, he often went very close to proving that even the Morris Minor's remarkable adhesion to tarmacadam could be overcome.

To describe the journeys as hair-raising would be an understatement - but I was very grateful for those trips to weekend bliss.

To add to the problems of Valerie's lonesome weekday state, her father died. Any lesser person would have then stayed at home with her mother. But there was the job - and me. So when things had settled, after the funeral, she was back at Duxford.

The very bright light at the end of the tunnel was the conclusion of the course and, assuming I successfully passed, a posting to a Flying Training School with life together restored and, hopefully, some improved accommodation. What was to be our new locale?

Before moving to that, a PS to this wedding chapter. I return to the topic of that 230 volt toaster that I bought, by mistake, which Father had replaced with a 200 volt one - and the company failed to recover the original. What was our wedding present from the Berry parents? You've guessed!

CENTRAL FLYING SCHOOL

This is to Certify *that*

FG. OFF. D.E. DeBerry.

has successfully graduated from the
Central Flying School

as a Qualified Flying Instructor

DATE: **11TH. OCT. 1955.**

AIR. CDRE.
COMMANDANT

Chapter 12
Qualified Flying Instructor

I passed! I had joined the ranks of the pilots who could describe themselves as QFIs. It was an odd thing: one completed this particular six month course and the qualification stayed with you for life and could influence your career, even outside the establishments devoted to *ab initio* pilot training. Obviously there was that ladder to now climb in this instructing world; graduation was with a humble B2 category. Ahead were the hurdles of B1 and A2 to cross. A few 'clever clogs' might achieve the exceptional A1 grade.

Not unnaturally, I had stated a preference for basic training, the Provost. There was no hesitation in consigning me to that pool so, obviously, my dislike of the Vampire showed. Now was pot-luck time; there were five or so Flying Training Schools from which to choose. I think that I was lucky to be selected for No.2 FTS, RAF Hullavington in 'Darkest Wiltshire'. This began, what was to be, a very long association with that county.

So now Valerie and I knew what was to be our new area but what about somewhere to live? Remember that this was a penniless, car-less couple, so picking affordable places and viewing them was not an easy business and there was the matter of being within a close range of Hullavington. Some postal negotiation was started and it did seem that there was a suitable place to the north of Chippenham, which was lucky. Equally lucky was the fact that one of my fellow

 students, also posted to Hullavington, was able to offer me a lift to view. This was a bit ironic for him as he was also seeking to rent and was a bit green when he saw the place that I had 'landed'. Steinbrook Bungalow, Kington Langley was converted stabling which belonged to Steinbrook House, a fairly grand Victorian abode. The title 'bungalow' conjures up an uncomplimentary picture; the conversion had been done quite tastefully and we felt incredibly lucky. What is more, it was only three miles from Hullavington - cycling distance - if I had a bike!

Now came the matter of moving. Our possessions were modest but having to use the train and not having sufficient suitcases did present a challenge. We must have had around 12 separate pieces of luggage - including a couple of brown paper carrier bags. The route was Whittlesford to London, Kings Cross then London, Paddington to Chippenham. Somehow we were standing on the Whittlesford Station platform with all our kit - in the rain. I had, long ago, discarded that ghastly trilby hat from those Cranwell days but the rain forced me, for head protection, to resort to an old RAF beret minus cap badge.

So, there is the picture; surrounded by our miscellany of packages, in the rain, we must have resembled something from a refugee camp! Then, who should appear to say farewell to us but the Station Commander. The beret was quickly whisked off my head into a pocket. I find it difficult to relate to this farewell. Why he (not Jamie Rankin, but his successor) should choose to say goodbye to us I will never know - and how he knew we were catching that train, again I am mystified ... but it was a pleasant gesture.

The next piece of drama was the bit across London; we needed a taxi and I can remember a porter moaning about the number of pieces of luggage that we had - courtesy was not a key word of those railway days. Chippenham to the bungalow was another taxi; this put a considerable strain on the Berry finances. What seemed an endless journey was over and as we unpacked in our new abode, we felt very pleased with ourselves. We were going to have to remember that pleasure when it came time to pay the rent bill - or be unable to pay it, as was the case a number of times. The monthly amount was really outside our means.

I am in residence at Kington Langley but my first day of work was looming and that was at Hullavington. A walk into Chippenham was called for. I must have had at least £1 in my pocket for that was the down payment on a bike at Halfords to be followed by 12 monthly payments of £1. At least I could cycle back home. Monday brought 'Day 1' at Hullavington.

This was rather like that start on the Meteor squadron. After the camaraderie of one's fellow CFS students, there was the feeling of being somewhat isolated. But, on my allocated Flight, I was with a kindly lot, albeit that I was the youngest by a long chalk. My youthfulness must have been the cause of some wonder; this novelty was to be diluted as time progressed and the policy of having a younger instructing force took hold.

A feature of a RAF pilot's life is that you have never actually ever 'passed'. In spite of the fact that I had just completed the CFS course to the satisfaction of that staff, I was 'checked out' by the supervisory body of the FTS. This completed I was ready to start instructing my first students.

I think I matured considerably in those first few weeks. Having to act out a superior role, in spite of inner feelings of inadequacy, is an ageing process. There was also the considerable responsibility of having the success or failure of a student resting on one's shoulders - subject, of course, to their own ability.

With pilot training there is that ultimate early test and I have referred to my own experience - the first solo. Sensibly, I was not exposed to this immediately; the Flight that I had joined was part way through handling a course and I joined in with the latter stages of instructing - formation flying, instrument flying practice etc. The very first student I flew with is only noted in my log book as 'Watts'. I wonder what he made of this 'boy' with whom he was flying?

A couple of months passed in this way and then it was time to start a new course. Perhaps, rather appropriately, the length of the basic stage of pilot training corresponded to that of the human gestation period. An instructor was allocated three students and he took them through each stage. It might be seen that this was quite a testing relationship. Page after page of my log book registers 'Kiernan', 'Rivers', 'Moore'. Apart from indicating the treadmill aspect of this, it also shows that I sent them on their 'first solos'. Much is made - I have done it - of the student's experience of this occasion. Now I was to appreciate the somewhat nail biting situation for the instructor! It is a testing time ... send a student off too soon and disaster is invited ... leave it too late and confidence can be destroyed. But all was well and the course progressed and my first students graduated.

Having mentioned 'gestation period', it is appropriate to record that some of that had been going on at Steinbrook Bungalow. There, a conversation along these lines had taken place - one to be repeated a number of times.

Val: 'I think I'm pregnant.'

Me: 'You can't be!!'

You can guess who was right. Never mind the joy of prospective parenthood; for us it was a bloody disaster. Financially we were struggling and the only reason we were keeping our heads above water - well, perhaps it would be more accurate to say not totally plummeting to the bottom - was that Valerie was working. She had a secretarial job in the not too salubrious surroundings of the Westinghouse factory in Chippenham. I can picture her now, visibly 'bigger', standing at the road by the bungalow, in the rain, waiting for the lift to work. I particularly remember the shoes she was wearing ... the only pair possessed. What were we to do?

Her Majesty, for all her youthfulness, came to our rescue. Coinciding with the day that Val had to stop work, the Services had the biggest pay rise for years - perhaps in history. This is, of course, all relative. We were receiving a pittance until then - grossly under-paid. Now we were to get a reasonably fair reward; from 'pittance' to 'reasonably fair reward' was quite a steep climb. All this meant that now our nostrils occasionally brushed the fresh air above the sea of our debt. Were we gloomy about all this? Not at all. As with most young people, we found money for the things we wanted to do and, eventually, for those we had to do. Perhaps falling within both brackets is 'the small black dress'.

This item of clothing was required for a 'cocktail party'. In the hands of Group Captain A, the Station Commander at Hullavington, the old Service traditions were safe. One of these was the six o'clock to eight cocktail party and we received an invitation. So, there would be some scratching around for the rent; the correct attire was required.

Further proof that we could find money for the things we wanted is that we sorted enough out for the down payment on a TV set. Black and white, of course, and it was an enormous box for the size of the screen, but a source of real wonder and we were completely hooked by it. We watched everything. It was in those early TV days that Richard Dimbleby played his April 1st joke of 'The Spaghetti Tree'. As he walked about, amongst these trees draped with spaghetti, explaining the complexities of its harvesting, we took it all in.

'Well, I didn't realise that spaghetti grew on trees!'

But this was more a reflection of the way of most people's lives rather than our particular naïvety. Diets were still very traditional - pasta was definitely something only 'them foreigners' ate.

The pregnancy progressed ... we really were too young for all this, but '... *for, whatsoever a man soweth, that shall he also reap ...*' Val's mother's pre-marriage words came to haunt us; her response to Valerie saying that we would wait a couple of years before having children was, 'Well, some people think they are very clever!'

One night there was panic as 'things down below' - the euphemism habit dies hard - started to go drastically wrong. On my bike, I flew the mile up the road to the phone box and in a remarkably

131

short time we were in an ambulance on our way to a hospital in Bath. The prognosis was not good; the GP told me that the baby would not survive. But she was not taking into account Valerie's fighting spirit. A corner was turned and all *was* well but rest was called for; there followed an agonising fortnight of a pre-natal ward. I visited each evening ... bike ride to Chippenham Station, train to Bath, walk to the hospital. As I stood waiting at the ward entrance, with the fathers or potential fathers, it was my dread that one of them would tell me I was in the wrong place - this was the Maternity Wing. I, surely, being so young, wanted another part of the hospital.

On one of the visits, things started to 'happen'. These were the bad - nay, good - old days where the delivery room was no place for fathers. I scooted off home. Simon was born in the night and mother and child were doing well.

So, now we had parenthood to add to our lives. There were times when I really did feel that all this had happened too soon - but we were happy. It is incredible how we coped compared with the parents of later years. With Simon only a few months old the question of a summer holiday arose - it was to become our tradition that we would take such a holiday - regardless. One of my elder flying instructor compatriots offered us the use of his caravan. We took this up; we all travelled to Bournemouth with DS towing and he then left us there for the week.

It was our return, by train, which illustrates our spirit. With all our baggage and baby in pram, we walked to the Bournemouth railway station. The train took us to one of the Bath stations; our train to Chippenham was from the other one. So, Simon was carried and the luggage put in the pram and we walked across Bath. The exercise was repeated for the three mile journey from Chippenham to home!

DS is worth a few words. Larger then life, very excitable, he was a bit of a character. He had seen the tail end of the War and on demobilisation had become a bit of a Bristol entrepreneur in a market suffering from post-war shortages. Ice cream was one of his projects. At one stage, he had so much, allegedly, black market milk powder stored in his roof space that the bedroom ceilings showed signs of collapsing. It was rumoured that he rejoined the RAF in order to escape a closing web of investigation. He obviously came back with a little nest egg for, in what was almost a car-less community, D had a series of new ones. In those early post-war years, quality was not a key word in the car manufacturing business; a factor in considering this was that DS was a strong man. So, when he tightens up a painted fuel cap with the palm of his hand he finds himself with a disc of paint in that hand. One day, his attention from the road ahead was momentarily diverted; when he looks back ahead, a collision is imminent. DS applies the brakes with such force that the pedal breaks off and the back of his seat collapses!

Hullavington saw an interesting development in pilot training during my time there. It has been said that we were equipped with the piston-engined Hunting Percival Provost. It was a good trainer, sporty enough to keep a student on his toes but not going to the extremes, in that department, of having handling vices. To my mind, a quality that it possessed was that a student was required to be able fly an aircraft sufficiently well to do a three point landing ... touching down, simultaneously, on the two main wheels and single tail one. This was, very much, a three dimensional exercise. The *ab initio* needed to master this at an early stage in order to be sent on his first solo. This meant that some lack of coordination and ability were revealed at that early stage and the student's training would cease.

It is my contention that as the training aircraft that replaced the Piston Provost did not have this 'three pointer' requirement, consequently, coordination in three dimensions was not tested fully at this early time and a lack of real ability was only revealed at a later point. I believe that many of these latter day students went through training right up to the operational stage and it was only when they came to another demanding three dimensional exercise - air combat and firing - that the weakness was revealed. But I digress and get ahead of myself.

Our Air Ministry masters decided that, as an increasing percentage of operational aircraft were jet-propelled, then so should be the basic trainer. Perhaps rather astonishingly, instead of starting with a new design, the manufacturers of the piston-engined Provost put a jet engine into that airframe and fitted a nose wheel in place of the tail one and declared that this could be the new trainer. Equally astonishing is the fact that this was reasonably successful, if lacking in some aesthetic quality. This particularly applied to the first models which retained the original, necessarily long for propeller clearance, main undercarriage legs of the Piston Provost. This made it look rather gawky - something similar to me in those short trousers!

Not unreasonably, the new aircraft was called the Jet Provost and sufficient were initially built to equip one of our Flights at Hullavington to test the efficacy of the aircraft using real instructors and students. This was obviously deemed a success, with the Jet Provost becoming the RAF's basic trainer for many years. Interestingly, when age dictated that it was time for them to be replaced, the aircraft chosen, the Tucano, was propeller driven - but only because a turbo-prop is more economical than a pure jet - but it was fitted with a nose wheel. So, my opinion on 'three-pointers' declared above was ignored ... such is the price of obscurity!

A feature of a Royal Air Force officer's life is 'Secondary Duties'. Obviously the primary one is to pilot, navigate or whatever; but there are a mishmash of jobs, on a Station, that have to be covered - Officer i/c Sergeants' Mess springs to mind. In this, there is, again, an element of, 'It'll do you good.' Mercifully, at Hullavington, with my slender maturity, I escaped any onerous tasks. The minor role that came my way was No.2 in the Station's Guard of Honour; tallness was to see this sort of task come my way, over the years. With my home-to-work transport means ie bicycle, I had to make some fairly detailed arrangements in order to appear, on parade, in Best Blue with sword to hand. I was to be further involved with a Guard of Honour ... the story will follow.

I progressed with my instructional task. My log book lists names and only to a few of these can I link faces and memories. With my first real students on 116 Course there are Kiernan, Rivers, Kiernan, Rivers *ad infinitum,* with the interjection, now and again, of another instructor's student. There was a strange interlude in the middle of Kiernan, Rivers, Kiernan, Rivers in that I returned to Duxford for 'Reinforcement Training'. It would seem that there was some realisation of the possible usefulness of the skills that I had gained during my two years as a day fighter pilot. It was short lived ... it was the only time I was so summoned.

Kiernan, Rivers, Kiernan, Rivers - I seemed to accept responsibility also for Sibbring and Copeland as the course progressed - continued for the duty nine months and they successfully graduated - I should be more conscious of those very first students - I *can* picture them, vaguely.

I have already made the observation that, as an RAF pilot, you have never ever totally 'passed'. Each of us, no matter the role, had to maintain an instrument rating - an assessment of competence to fly in cloud/poor visibility. The frequency of this test (six or twelve months) depended on one's ability and experience. Within each pilot's role (fighter, bomber etc) there would be a testing hierarchy. With reflection, I think there was some accidental cunning in this. A structure, which drove one to increase one's stature by proving that one's skills had improved, must have some spin-off for general raising of standards.

I passed out of CFS as a B2 category instructor - the only *real* thing to be was an A2; in between was the 'inconvenience' of B1. Qualification for the latter was 'local' and really depended on 'good behaviour'. After a duty six months, I duly qualified. But the step to A2 required a return visit to CFS, which meant that the test was independent. For this, one was coached by the home-based team responsible for maintaining the unit's instructional standard. The number of A2 instructors was considered very much a measure of their success ... in turn I received their attention after just a year's experience and was duly despatched to CFS. I passed! Still slightly damp behind the ears, 23 year-old Flying Officer Berry was an A2 instructor - and I was a father. Was this all too much for those young shoulders to bear? I had to do my best.

My best was required with the start of our next course of students. Two of my students had good old Anglo-Saxon names, Brunt and Horsfall ... the third was Sinjackly ... he hailed from Iraq. An illustration of how international relationships can change over the years is the fact that back in 1956 there was an agreement to train students from that country. We had the first batch and it has to be said that they were outstanding young men. Undoubtedly, being the first, they were the *crème de la crème*. All sorts of local 'legend' built up about them - their connections in Iraqi high places, wealth, success with women! Sinjackly was a keen, intensely polite young man - but ours was to be a stormy relationship. The start was as with any student - a progression through the early flying lessons *viz* Effect of Controls, Straight and Level, Turning, Climbing and Descending.

I did my instructor patter bit and Sinjackly appeared to be taking it in. Certainly he was plentiful with his, 'Yes, Sir,', 'I understand,', 'Thankyou very much, Sir.' I think it was on about the third or fourth lesson that I asked him to take his feet off the rudder pedals so that I could demonstrate a point ... 'Yes, Sir,', 'I understand,', 'Thankyou very much, Sir.' His feet stayed planted on the pedals. I concluded that I really needed to start all over again! But we got there and Sinjackly, along with my Anglo-Saxons, successfully went on his first solo. There started the long road to graduation and as time progressed it was clear to me that Sinjackly was not doing that well.

In the instructing business of those days we, perhaps, anticipated later legislation in the employment market. Warnings of shortcomings had to be advised and time for improvement allowed before suspension from training. It was known as being put 'under review'. It would not be a happy student day but Sinjackly's reaction was a bit excessive ... he threatened to commit suicide. We managed to calm him down and explain that all he had to do was try a bit harder rather than fall on his sword. It worked and things improved. There was the odd lapse.

One day there was a call to the Flight from Air Traffic Control. My presence was required in the tower - Sinjackly was on a solo flight and had become lost. ATC were having difficulty getting him to obey instructions that would get him back to base. These were the days of air driven gyro flight instruments. Amongst these was the 'direction indicator' and the pilot had to set it to agree with the magnetic compass for the information it was giving to be meaningful. Also, gyro instruments topple when doing aerobatics. Sinjackly had done his aeros, no doubt with more brute force than finesse, and now set course for base - without resetting his direction indicator (DI).

136

Nothing fitted his map and panic set in. Air Traffic assistance was requested but their guidance was meaningless when applied to an incorrectly set DI. When I arrived at ATC Sinjackly was saying that all he could see was water. Bearings told us that he must be somewhere over the Bristol Channel ... or out in the Atlantic, south of Ireland!

'Hullavington, this eese tree zuro - I see land!'

Sinjackly made for it and Allah was smiling on him; there was an airfield close to the coast. He landed at Rhoose, near Barry Island, South Wales. As he turned off the runway, the engine stopped - he was out of fuel!

The night flying phase brought another bit of excitement from another of the Iraqi students. He landed and swung off the runway, charging through those paraffin flares that lit the runway edge. At a halt, his aircraft was approached by a Land Rover containing his instructor. Jack Colston climbed up to the opening cockpit hood.

'What the **** are you doing??!!' Jack was the gentlest of men, in spite of his size - but he was an ex-Royal Marine and, now and again, it showed!

'Well, Sir - the aircraft - she swung off zee runway!'

'Well, why the **** didn't you keep it straight?!'

'Sir - if Allah say aircraft swing off runway - then aircraft swing off runway!!'

The Iraqis departed - 129 Course started - Whelan, Hawes, Harris - all this was becoming quite routine. At this time, I made a rare appearance in a review of accidents - I led quite a charmed life in that area. As I was carrying out some aerobatics the left rudder pedal broke off - shades of DS and his brake pedal? 129 graduated.

RAF life is a rich field for rumours - most not realised - a few come true. It had been in the Hullavington air for some time that our days there were numbered. It would seem that there was going to be some rationalisation of the Flying Training Schools. It is always amusing to look back on such plans, with the benefit of hindsight, and see that they were not the ultimate solution and there would be further change. In our case, it was mooted that the FTS at Syerston, which specialised in RN pilot training, was to move and we, No.2 Flying Training School, would take its place. Rumour became substance and

137

in November 1957 we moved. Never mind the service organisation required; what of the domestic upheaval. The Berrys were well settled in Steinbrook Bungalow.

1957 was the year of Suez which had ramifications for many sections of the Royal Air Force but little effect on a Flying Training School. But there was one personal impact. Petrol was short and one of the economies was to cancel driving tests. Rather astonishingly, as this might be seen as unfair on some people, it was decided that learners could drive unaccompanied. Our landlords, Mr and Mrs Eric Gardner, had been very kind to us during our tenancy. This now extended to teaching me to drive. It is a measure of the 'different-to-now days' in which we lived that I was a qualified pilot with some four years experience, teaching other people to fly and I could not drive a car! Eric Gardner took me out a couple of times in his market garden business van and then sent me solo. The van was loaned for family excursion and if there were any deliveries or errands then I was given the opportunity to carry them out.

But now there was another aspect to driving; we were going to have to move and the only real way would be to hire a van. But driving tests had now been reinstated. I booked one and a driving lesson in Bath a few hours before. All our moving plans now rested on success as we were set to hire a Dormobile the next day. I passed - and we duly set off for Nottinghamshire. I had been given the opportunity to visit the Syerston, near Newark, area beforehand and had secured an upstairs flat in the village of Lowdham. It was a far cry from Steinbrook; not only was there the upstairs flat aspect but below, the rather eccentric French landlady bred Scottie dogs. The house was next to the railway station. But we had to be pleased; furnished accommodation was in short supply, especially with a whole unit moving into the area. When we had moved to Wiltshire two years previously, it turned out that Val was 'in the family way'. This was going to prove a bit of a pattern. Settled into Lowdham, the conversation once again took place.

'I think I'm pregnant!'
'You can't be!!'
Guess who was right, once more!

Chapter 13
More Instructing

In a remarkably short time the FTS was settled into Syerston. It being November, we soon had cause to ponder on the wisdom of the move; situated on the banks of the River Trent in pre-smokeless zone days, the weather factor was poor. Once a 'clamp' became established, it could last for weeks.

The treadmill restarted with 132b Course - number one student, 'A', was standard Anglo-Saxon - but number two - Soemantri? Indonesian! An incredibly polite and self-contained young man who did well. 'A' was a bit of a struggle but he graduated. A considerable number of years later, like 40 or so, I was in a social situation with a retired Air Commodore. After a long and pleasant lunch, the Air Commodore suddenly has a question.

'Were you ever a QFI?'

'Yes,' I reply, 'My first job was at Hullavington and then Syerston.'

The Air Commodore smiles, 'I was one of your students! Well - you weren't actually my instructor but I was on the same Flight and we flew a few times - but I'll go and get somebody who was your student!'

He disappears and returns a while later with 'A' - another retired Air Commodore! But I did not contribute directly to his rise through the ranks - he was suspended from pilot training at the jet stage and transferred to the navigator role. But he said he was grateful for my attentions of the past. Well, he would say that, wouldn't he?

Lowdham was some seven miles from Syerston so a bike would not really do. But I was now a driver, so to the secondhand car  dealers I went. The Wolseley I saw seemed OK; it was one of those models that used to be police cars. I was given some chat that it wasn't immediately available as it was being looked at by some highly qualified motor mechanic who was desperate to have it. This worked - I couldn't wait to buy. £125 - on hire purchase. It did do us amazingly well for more than a couple of years; especially considering that I didn't have a single piece of routine servicing done - again those were different car days.

We set off in it, with the back converted into a cot, for a visit to Plymouth, calling on the Gardners on the way. It took forever and night fell. I was feeling totally knackered. With just 15 miles to go, we had a puncture. I was a bit pushed to know where the spare wheel was stored ... it was flat. This saved the exposure that I didn't have a jack! I'd had it; all I wanted to do was sleep. The baby was quiet and Valerie and I slumped in the front seats. I was just dropping off when a police car pulls up behind us. Out I get and explain our predicament and willingness, indeed desire, to see the night through and sort things out in the morning. The policemen obviously had a long night shift in front of them and were ready for a chat.

'RAF pilot, then ... I've always wanted to fly ...'

I've always wanted to go to sleep when dog tired.

In the morning I walked to the, mercifully nearby, village which, again mercifully, had a garage. I returned to the car with a borrowed jack - and milk plus cornflakes. Wheel off, wheeled back to the garage, puncture repaired, wheel back to car, wheel on, jack back to garage. All fairly straightforward really!

On one of my trips home from Syerston a fault was revealed; in the rear view mirror I could see I was leaving behind a dense cloud of smoke. In fact I learnt that some of it was steam. One of my mechanically knowledgable compatriots diagnoses, 'You've got a split cylinder head gasket.' With the minimum of tools - a mole grip wrench featured large - I removed the head and fitted a replacement gasket. This was quite an achievement for someone with the mechanical ability of an orang-utan. Immediate result: no smoke. Subsequent result: the gasket would fail at intervals of around 1000 miles! 'You've got a distorted cylinder head - it needs skimming,' advises the automobile professor. I settled for changing the gasket each time - I became quite good at it!

After flying, one day, I reluctantly (!) became caught up in the celebration of a birth of a son to my compatriot, Jack Colston. Later, I arrived home to tell Val:

'When I got out of the car there was a funny hissing noise!'

This was a rather stupid way of announcing I had a puncture.

'But I think the baby is starting!'

The French landlady was recruited to take Val to Newark whilst I looked after two year-old Simon. This must have been arduous for I fell asleep ... French lady has to wake me with the news.

'You have another baby son!'

Timothy John had joined the clan. I should feel quite shame-faced about this when set alongside, say, Tim's involvement when his sons were born but, to repeat a used theme, these were different days; chauvinism was something of a norm. I did change, over the years!

Syerston, during this time, was the scene of a tragic accident. It was an air display day and, by chance, a Victor bomber was returning to nearby Hucknall. The captain was asked if he would do an impromptu flypast. Whilst executing this, there was some structural failure of the wing; slow motion photography reveals the skin of the wing peeling back. The aircraft crashed on the airfield, killing all the occupants; mercifully, no spectators were victim. We Syerston residents had the grim task of collecting up all the small pieces of wreckage, to be pieced together for the benefit of the accident enquiry.

Soemantri and 'A' gained their wings; next on the scene was a course of Royal Navy officers. Lieutenant Notley and Sub-Lieutenant Phipps definitely had a different approach to flying than their RAF equivalents - and for a good reason. They were RN career officers and flying was just a passing speciality. There was also a hint of the 'Senior Service' being present. It was interesting and challenging to be dealing with maturer students.

There was further 'rationalisation' at this stage and the FTS at Feltwell, in Norfolk, closed and the staff and students joined our unit. Our Flight's share was a couple of instructors and some - wait for it - Iranian students. We were cosmopolitan, if nothing else. Prior to their arrival some senior person took upon himself to address us on the sensitivity of having these Iranians. It would appear that there was some delicacy about the arrangement and we were to be careful in the diplomacy area. My first awareness that they were with us was the raised voice of a Flight Sergeant instructor, who, along with his students, were members of the group transferred to us from Feltwell; he was addressing his Iranian student on his failings whilst completing some pre-flight paperwork. He was using every swear word under the sun - and the moon as well! To acknowledge this spell I have, in my log book the name of Officer Cadet Dodo-Sutarmo. Where are you now?

In September 1958 I entered the ranks of the over-25s and thus, eventually had qualified for the full privileges of the married, the first being the full marriage allowance; in our still parlous financial state, every penny counted. As importantly, we now qualified to be an occupant of a Married Quarter. In those days of having to scruff around in rented accommodation, as we were doing at Lowdham, a house on the Station was a most des. res. But there was a barrier: the number wanting exceeded the number available - so a waiting list was established. This list was weighted in favour of the more senior, the longer married, the more separated - those whose surname did not begin with a 'B' - ignore that! It was tough; we sat in our grotty upstairs flat watching our name creep up the list only to see it kicked down five places by some ancient Flight Lieutenant who had just served 500 years in RAF Station The Back of Beyond. But we eventually made it; No.6 Inholmes Road was ours.

'Marching in' is the curious title for the taking-over procedure of a Married Quarter. One is taken over the house for a check of the contents and a note of any defects. A fact of life was that all this could be rather cursory, if one didn't watch out, compared with the process at the end of the tenancy - 'marching out'. Then great attention was paid to detail with the intention of extracting payment for any repairs.

Removal was numerous car journeys and when complete we were well pleased with our new abode - a detached, red brick house with substantial garden, three bedrooms and a spacious downstairs. It lacked central heating and double glazing but that was how things were. The group of quarters was very close to the Mess and ten minutes walk from work ... all very pleasant.

It was around this time that there started a curious turn of events. For some reason, which I have never really been able to identify, the Station Commander started selecting me for a series of jobs. Group Captain John Blount was a charismatic leader, socially well connected but able to relate to individuals. His surname was pronounced 'Blunt'. At a formal dinner the Group Captain was seated next to a lady, not of his acquaintance. She peers at the name on his place card and turns to him.

'It is pleasant to meet you, Group Captain Blount,' pronouncing the name as spelt.

'It is pleasant to meet you, Mrs Smith ... my surname is pronounced Blunt - and I'm John to you,' is the response.

'Oh, how can that be. If Blount was pronounced Blunt then Count would be ... Oh, I am a silly woman!'

One day, minding my own business on 'B' Flight, I was summoned to the Station Adjutant's office. This gentleman was a senior

Flight Lieutenant of the old school.

'Goin' on a spot of leave on Monday ... bit of shootin' and fishin' ... the Station Commander wants you to take over as adjutant for that time.'

He was unable to conceal his astonishment at delivering this message to, in his eyes, this abject example of a commissioned officer standing before him; we were definitely poles apart in whatever field you care to choose and he could not see how I had been selected as the temporary substitute for his 'Upper Class' service to the CO. But Adjutant I was for that fortnight and all subsequent leave occasions of Flight Lieutenant Superior. This is really the only proof needed that I obviously did the job to the satisfaction of JB. I think all this came as some surprise to my compatriots!

The next event was associated with the Officers' Mess. Traditionally the Mess Secretary - a secondary duty - was someone pretty senior with matching maturity. For some reason it was decided, undoubtedly by the Station Commander, that younger blood was required; it couldn't come any less old than mine - and I found myself in the post. The surprised people this time were the old cronies associated with the Mess organisation who had been very happy with the old way of things.

Can that be it in the extra jobs line? No! There is the story of the Station Guard of Honour. One day I was summoned to the presence of the Station Commander to be told that I was to take charge of the Station's ceremonial flight. It came as no surprise to me that the post was vacant for the tale of my predecessor's performance, the previous day, had spread like wildfire. The Guard of Honour had been formed up, with Flight Lieutenant W in front, to pay respects to the Air Officer Commanding. He arrived by air, the aircraft stopping in the precise place, right on time. The Air Marshal descended the steps. The Guard Commander started putting his men through the traditional routine.

'Guard of Honour, Slope Arms.'

'Guard of Honour, Present Arms.'

His sword went to the salute. Then he made a fateful mistake!

'Guard of Honour, Order Arms.'

144

For those of less mature years, denied the joys of Arms Drill with the .303 Enfield rifle, some explanation is required. A Guard started with their rifles at the 'Order', that is with the butt resting on the ground and held against their right legs. The next command was 'Slope Arms' when the rifle was moved to the left shoulder. The final part of the ceremony was the 'Present Arms' when, with much banging and a little foot juggle, the men 'presented' their rifles before them, a symbolic 'giving'. Having held this position for a few seconds, the process was reversed... 'Slope Arms'... 'Order Arms'. Those were the positions and that was the essential order!

Return now to our doomed Flight Lieutenant. He, in a position of some disadvantage ie facing forward, his back to the men, had given the command 'Order Arms' when the Guard was at the 'Present'! The 'rules', just outlined above, do not allow for this! Consider the plight of his men.

Some remembered a basic tenet, from their training days: if you are given a wrong order then you 'stand fast'. Therefore these, possessed of good memory, stayed at the 'Present'. Others, perhaps of a more pragmatic nature, thought, 'Well, what he really means is Slope Arms,' and duly went to that position. The remainder, possibly with lesser imagination, thought that, as 'Order Arms' had been given, they would go to that position, which they did in a variety of ways! Picture the scene now, as the Guard Commander, oblivious of the chaos he has created, marches smartly forward, gives his sword salute and proudly shouts the traditional invitation.

'No 2 Flying Training School Guard of Honour ready for your inspection, SIR!'

The response from the AOC was a little less conventional.

'When you get that bloody lot sorted out, I'll inspect them!'

This caused the Flight Lieutenant to 'lose his cool', as, with sword in hand, he looks back over his shoulder and mutters, 'Christ!' But he has been told to sort it out, and he returns to face his men. After a pause, during which the contortions on his face revealed the torture in his mind, he issued this unique order.

'When I say Go, those at the Slope stand fast, those at the Present and at the Order go to the Slope.'

'GO!'

A rather nervous successor was appointed the next day. That 'small black dress' was called for, one evening, when we were summoned to attend a Station Commander's cocktail party. We went armed with the knowledge that these occasions were strictly 6 o'clock to eight affairs and, as the hour approached, we made our move to leave. Mrs Blount quietly speaks to us.

'We're asking half a dozen people to stay for some supper - I hope you can join us.'

Again that special treatment! The occasion did have its social agony ingredient - the meal was Spaghetti Bolognaise, somewhat *avante-garde* for those days and new to us. Eating red, sauce-coated, long spaghetti, in a civilised manner, is a matter requiring experience - and we had none! But we survived. The thought did cross my mind that it was rather lucky that we had read the *exposé* of Richard Dimbleby's April Fool, spaghetti prank otherwise I could have blurted out, at the table, 'It's difficult to believe that this spaghetti stuff grows on trees ...' or something even more devastating!

I am sure that the attention of Group Captain John Blount was a powerful influence on my maturity and I will always be grateful to him for that. Later events, therefore, were a great sadness to me. Subsequent to the Syerston post, he retired from the Royal Air Force but was promoted to the honorary rank of Air Commodore; this was part of the process of him being appointed the Commandant of The Queen's Flight. One day he was a passenger in one of the Flight's helicopters which suffered a catastrophic mechanical failure; all occupants were killed, instantly. What a sad end for a fine man.

Mott, McCrimmon and Coghlan shared my attentions to the duties of Adjutant, Mess Secretary and Guard Commander ... it was a busy life. But it wasn't all work; I recall Val and I enjoying the Mess social scene.

I originally joined the Royal Air Force on an eight-year Short Service Commission and that commenced from my commissioning in 1952. So, with 1959 upon us, time was running out. Conveniently, there was a decision to introduce a new 12-year engagement and those of us eight-year people, who had kept our noses clean, were offered those extra four years. I gladly took it ... RAF life was being kind to me and, no doubt, I was, subconsciously, starting to be glad of the comfort of its cushioning from the 'real world'.

The ambition of every short service commission officer should be to obtain a permanent commission which put one in the promotion lane and meant service to the pensionable age of the rank achieved. Each year we were assessed by our seniors, their findings being recorded on a Form 1369 - the Annual Confidential Report. Unlike enlightened (?) subsequent years, this was completed in great secrecy. The only part that the subject of the report saw was the first page where he recorded his flying hours for the year etc.

There was also a section where a preference for a next posting could be stated. I, along with other aspirants after a permanent commission, were advised that our chances would be improved if we showed an interest in widening our experience by completing a tour of duty as a staff officer. With hindsight, I am sure that this was a devious plot of the administrators who had great difficulty filling those posts; short service guys would normally be dragged, kicking and screaming, into such jobs. But, Muggins took the bait and wrote: *Group or Command Air Staff Officer.* I can picture the rubbing together of hands at the 'Postings' Palace'.

'We've got one here, Fred!'

Surprise, surprise ... Flight Lieutenant D E de Berry is posted as Air 3 HQ 25 Group! I'd had a good run as a QFI, four years in all, which exceeded the normal 2fi.

So, the Berry family was on the move again - to RAF Manby, near Louth in Lincolnshire. It was time to survive that 'Marching Out' process, with minimum cost.

On the day before, a Sunday, we were waist deep in cleaning materials, packing boxes, kids etc when who should stop outside the house but Group Captain Blount and his wife. On their way home from church, they had stopped by to say farewell.

Chapter 14
An Air Staff Officer!

A fresh location meant repeating the pattern of finding some furnished accommodation near the new Station, and then waiting for one's name to, hopefully, creep up the Married Quarters' list. The abode I found this time was a bit different. It was quite a large house, white with something of a Mediterranean appearance but not in a, sympathetic to that style, locale.

It was on the Lincolnshire coast near Sutton-on-Sea, only a few yards from the shore but with a sand dune cutting off direct view

of the sea - and, thankfully, some of the unobstructed effect of an East wind. The reason that the rent for such a large residence was within our price bracket was that this was a 'winter let'. The house was someone's summer retreat and they were only too pleased to have it occupied for the winter. It was a great house to live

The staff of HQ 25 Group - what on earth was I doing there?! Squadron Leader Eddie Lawson is front row, extreme right. Stan Greenhow, middle row, 3rd right. Master Navigator Norman Pullen is middle row, extreme right.

in, incredibly well equipped, and it was quite a novelty being so close to the sea, with two small boys, especially as we had a bit of an Indian Summer on arrival.

The old Wolseley kept going for our move and it was now a necessity as Sutton-on-Sea was some ten miles from RAF Manby. But we did not have to move our belongings this time; being over 25, we were entitled to a removal van. So we settled in, Valerie having to get used to another locality and me leaving her to it as I restart work.

Air Staff Officer - sounds rather grand, but it was in the smallest Group HQ that one could imagine and there was no doubt that I was the most junior member of it. Hullavington and Syerston were in 23 Group, the one accountable for all pilot training. No.25 Group was responsible for all the other aircrew training: navigator, flight engineer, signaller. The headquarters was entirely staffed by older, more senior persons than myself. I shared a room with two Squadron Leaders 'who had seen life'. Stan Greenhow had been a Sunderland flying boat captain; Eddie Lawson, my immediate boss, was a very experienced transport aircraft man.

The two of them were examples of 'men of promise', on the career ladder and therefore having to endure this 'good for you - and somebody's has to do the job' period of their lives. Eddie, in particular, was like a bird with clipped wings. His heart was in the air. Transport Command was just being equipped with the four turbo-prop Britannia and it almost amounted to mental cruelty that Eddie could not be there.

Apropos of nothing in particular, he liked to write Sexton Blake type stories:

'*The rain drops sparkled golden in the light of the street lamps and bounced off the roof of his white sports car. He sat hunched in the driver's seat, the collar of the white raincoat turned up, partially hiding his face; the brim of the trilby hat was down over his eyes. He pulled a cigarette from the packet with his lips and, with a flick, lit the gold Zippo lighter. The light from the flame danced on his tired face ...*'

The fact that I became aware of this is an indication that we were not exactly working our socks off. Stan was a countryman at heart and his major occupation was running the Station pig farm. This was a feature of RAF Stations of the 50s/60s, converting the substantial supply of swill from the Messes into pork.

My predecessor had a week to hand the job over to me - an hour would have been more than enough. He was like a dog with two tails: he had a good job to go to and he was getting shot of being Air 3! I settled into a routine - it really was a nothing job. There was some apparent activity; files would placed on the desk but 90% were material being circulated to all members of staff, in turn, eg a Flight Safety magazine. But, at least, it was something to read.

The days were long and I couldn't wait to get home. The winter set in but we were cosy. There was a huge solid fuel boiler which looked as if it could have done ship service - there was a door at bottom front into which you threw shovels full of coal. We rapidly learnt that we could not afford to feed this monster so we depended on the open fires - which was fine.

Before I was married, I would say that my hobby was being a social animal. I did little else. With matrimony, this activity was denied me and I spent an awful lot of time just poking about. It has already been seen that TV was a great filler of time. But I was looking for something and I hit on the idea that, with two sons, I had the excuse to build a model railway. The detail I wanted to achieve was not likely to fire them up; I built a very simple, there and back, layout with a few sidings. But my satisfaction came from making the buildings and scenery etc as realistic as possible. I spent hours at it.

Time will tell that this pastime did not last but what did happen was that it led me into woodwork - I had to build a structure to support the layout. Woodwork did become a hobby of a lifetime. This was a real turning of the corner as, from then on, I have been a great one for always having 'something to do'.

Our financial position must have been improving; this did not mean that we had some money left over at the end of each month - we just took on more commitments. One of these was our first NEW car! It was a humble thing - a Ford Popular. Fords had the policy of stripping bare an outgoing model and marketing it as the 'Popular'.

In our case it was what had been the Anglia minus any 'goodies'. But we were delighted with it. One offshoot was that Val learnt to drive, partly under my instruction.

This had its traumatic moments. We had the airfield on which to practice and, on one occasion, we had been doing some low speed manoeuvring eg reversing, three point turn. I emphasised that, in these situations, speed could be controlled with the clutch. We moved on to normal driving and went down a hill at the back of the airfield. We were using engine braking but going faster and faster ... some foot brake was required; I urged Val to slow down a bit - she depressed the clutch pedal and we shot into the verge!

'But you said to control speed with the clutch!' Is there any answer to that?

We saw the winter through and with the Spring came our arrival at the top of the Married Quarters' list and we moved into No.4 Hunter Avenue, RAF Manby, a house identical to our Syerston one. We were well pleased.

One feature of this MQ was that we had part share of a batman; this archaic system still survived though it was to disappear in a few years. Mr Lawson was our man; he was old, an old soldier, quite unfit, each task was accompanied by a lot of puffing and blowing. He was a traditionalist and was there to serve but one had to allow for idiosyncrasy. One of the items of furniture was a writing bureau and the very first job was cleaning the brass handles. That done, his attention turned to shoes. Fires would be laid, coal fetched - he kept on the go for his allotted time. Valerie remembers him for his ability to hand wring nappies until they were nearly bone dry!

153

Nappies - nappies - what's all this? I have mentioned that a pattern of life seemed to be that with each move there was a pregnancy. This one was no exception - Alison Margaret was born in the October. Perhaps I should have been paying more attention at those Secondary School sex lectures!

I did find one way to occupy idle office time. It was time I took the second set of promotion exams to qualify myself for elevation to the rank of Squadron Leader, come the time that I was considered worthy of such status. This story will reveal that a considerable amount of water was to be passed - sorry - was to pass, under the bridge before that was the case ... but one had to be seen to be trying.

I dutifully started with the syllabus and the relevant books; with time on my hands, I was able to go through this process; but nothing was sticking. The weekend before the exam, I panicked and locked myself in a bedroom - we had plenty from which to choose. I then concentrated on that old school technique of mine - past papers. Obviously the setters of 'A' Level examinations had been drafted into the RAF. It worked - I passed!

In the late 1950s, early 60s, there was a policy towards pilots in particular, perhaps aircrew in general, that if they had the misfortune to have to do a ground tour then they might 'seize up' and forget that moving the control column back brings the aircraft nose up - or whatever. Steps were taken to see this didn't happen. Aircraft were specially provided for the 'ground-borne' to fly. My pilot compatriots in HQ 25 Group went whizzing about in a Meteor 7. I tried it once but found that, in spite of my still tender years, four years of plodding about in a Piston Provost had coloured my attitude towards the jet age.

But there was to be salvation for me and relief from the stifling boredom of the office. The Group had its own, passenger carrying, Avro Anson. If anyone, from the AOC downwards, needed to visit one of our Stations, then the Anson could take them. A pilot and navigator were established to operate this aircraft. Flight Lieutenant BS was older than me but not old enough to be an ex-wartime veteran. He was just one thing old - old for his years. His navigator had the disappearing rank of Master Navigator.

In the immediate post-war period, it had been decided that most aircrew would be non-commissioned. In view of this, a special rank structure was required. Instead of the Corporal, Sergeant, Flight Sergeant, Warrant Officer of the ground trades, equivalent ranks were created of Pilot 4 and 3 (or Navigator, Engineer, Signaller) - Corporal, Pilot 2 - Sergeant, Pilot 1 - Flight Sergeant, - and, top of the pile, the Warrant Officer equivalent, Master Pilot.

To accompany this curious idea was a bizarre rank badge, the common theme of which was, what can only be described as a laurel wreath within which was one, two or three stars or three stars and a crown. The Masters had the traditional Warrant Officer coat-of-arms within their leaves. All this, well nearly all, had died a death by the time I entered the Service in 1951. I am not party to the reason why but, no doubt, a contributory factor was the policy to now commission pilots and navigators. For whatever reason, the ranks of Pilot 4 and 3 were replaced by Corporal Pilot (if ever used), Pilot 2 by Sergeant Pilot and Pilot 1 by Flight Sergeant Pilot. A remnant of all this was that the rank of Master Pilot - and Navigator, Engineer and Signaller - was retained.

All this is to give you a picture of Anson navigator, Master Navigator Norman Pullen. A real gentleman, he must have been close to retirement - bald, a good weight - it would have been more appropriate to have seen him setting out for a game of bowls than walking out to an aeroplane. BS introduced me to the Anson - this was a significant day for me as it was in an Anson that I had my very first flight as a young ATC cadet.

We had just two flights together, which struck me as not enough, before I was sent off solo - well not quite solo; poor old Master Navigator NP was required to accompany me. I can picture him now, as I desperately tried to locate the runway in the haze that prevailed, in a machine with which I felt none too comfortable. The look on his face was that of a long-service man wondering if he would, after all, be collecting that pension. I found the runway and landed - that was quite enough. Many say that becoming a QFI changes you; I'm not too sure of that but it certainly teaches you to respect an aircraft and to realise your own limitations. In this instance I don't think I received enough instruction and I was sent off solo in unsuitable conditions - BS was not a QFI!

But, on more suitable days, I built up my experience and was declared competent to carry passengers. I became No.2 pilot to BS so whenever he was not available, it fell to me to convey the 25 Group staff officers to wherever. Surprisingly, I accrued quite a number of hours in the year. It was a welcome relief from the boring office.

It might appear that standing-in was becoming a major commitment; there was another such post awaiting me. In the traditional way, the Air Officer Commanding (AOC) had an ADC. When he went on leave then I was required to fill in. With my deference to rank, I had a bit of a problem accepting that Squadron Leaders were normal people; so coping with an Air Vice Marshal was a bit of a strain.

Only slightly down the stress curve was the fairly frequent contact with the Senior Air Staff Officer (SASO) - a Group Captain. On the wall of our office was a device reminiscent of an 'Upstairs Downstairs' situation in a grand house; it was a box with a glass front. Behind this there were two holes; a ting on a bell and a red star appearing in Hole One indicated that Eddie was required by the SASO - Hole Two ... mercy! The AOC was demanding. And, if Eddie wasn't there I had to go.

The first Group Captain that we had was, at that time, the youngest of that rank in the Air Force - a fact that heralded he would, one day, be an Air Chief Marshal. Such men, though not all, in their early years of ascent, are pretty ruthless in their personal relations. On the occasions that I answered 'the bell', I would be immediately dismissed; there was clearly nothing that I could contribute to whatever was the matter in hand. His successor was quite a different personality; kindly, interested in his subordinates. He gave clear indications that he was as bored to tears as the rest of us and often his 'bell' was just to have a chat. I remember that one of his topics was QFIs, of which he was highly contemptuous and I had to defend my corner.

I note, from my log book, that one of the people who flew in 'my' Anson was Squadron Leader DS. The whisper in the corridors of Group HQ was that he had been court-martialled on his last flying tour. This was on the four-engined Lincoln bomber.

As often occurs with military flying, one can be in particular locations with no specific task. It would appear that DS, at the helm of his Lincoln, found himself cruising over some part of the ocean when he spied one of those huge US Navy aircraft carriers. A gleam is in his eye - it seemed a good idea to make an approach to the carrier as if he was going to land on it. He circled the ship and descended and positioned himself on a final approach to the landing deck - wheels and flaps were down and power was low for the descent. It is alleged that the Americans started pushing their aircraft over the side to clear a landing path! If this is true then I suppose one court-martial against a quantity of lost aeroplanes seems fair, on balance! The final outcome was not an unusual one for those days - if you make a name for yourself, in whatever way, you'll get noticed - and noticed people stand a chance of being promoted. DS was!

How would you feel if you did a job for a year and then it was decided that it could be dis-established? It happened and all I felt was total relief! The only disgrace was for others; it should have occurred before I was put in that post. But what was to happen to me now? There was that 2fi year tour pattern - and also I was in a ground tour and it is hard to 'trap' fliers into those. So 'early release' was not on the cards.

It so happened that a ground job was falling vacant at Manby. We, HQ 25 Group, were an extremely small unit on the Station; the major concern was the RAF Flying College. This was a prestigious establishment with a long history. Its purpose, in these years, was to give a course to General Duties (ie Flying) Wing Commanders and Group Captains who were destined for even higher things. Also, within the College was a 12 month course for navigators, the Specialist Navigation Course (Spec N for short), a highly academic and demanding year for top drawer navigators. An increasing responsibility of the Royal Air Force then was 'Guided Weapons'. As well as the air-to-air sort, we had our own ICBM, Thor, and the surface-to-air Bloodhound. All this demanded a specialist course and this fell within the bailiwick of the RAF Flying College.

Three, high powered, courses each with a timetable, visiting lecturers, outside visits etc, required an administrative backup. For the next year, I was to be a major part of that - the description of the post was Flight Lieutenant Plans.

I sat in an office where the walls were covered in pieces of card slotted into columns and rows of fabric tape pinned to boards on those walls. The columns represented days of the year and the rows times within those days, with a block for each course.

My task was shared by a Civil Servant; this was the first time that I come upon a member of this species. I have to be careful what I say, for my own brother John had joined the ranks of the Civil Service. In spite of an early setback through ill health, he was to make considerable progress through its hierarchy. But I digress from Mr A. He had been doing his job as the clerk in this Plans Office for years and had seen Flight Lieutenants come and go. But it was not for him to reason why - well, that was his demeanour. He was the original Mr Invisible ... he would, for example, slip from his desk and move some cards on the wall that he knew, from years of experience, needed moving, and then slide back into his chair.

'What did you do then?' I would politely enquire.

He would, equally politely, give me an answer. As the complexities of this emerged, I rapidly realised that it would be as well to let Mr A, slip from his desk and do whatever he had been doing for the many years before I had appeared on the scene.

Sitting back in my armchair of maturity, I can reflect that I have been a good communicator. I can, without unnatural effort, relate to most people. I never related to Mr A. I'm not sure whether I even established whether he was married or single - perhaps I had not fully developed my skills of communication at that stage.

It might seem that, with the expertise of Mr A, I was in another useless office job. But this did not seem so. You might gather that he was not the great master minder so the overall management did come down to me and I found that I was respected for the part I played in the running of the College - which is more than I can say about 25 Group!

An intriguing aspect of this Plans job was my role as film

projectionist! The Air Warfare Course, that high powered one for Wing Commanders and Group Captains, was visited by suitably high powered lecturers. The Commanders-in-Chief of various Commands were pretty standard fare. They would arrive, to be welcomed by the College Commandant; I would be, dutifully, standing off stage, right. The pleasantries over, there would be the nitty-gritty of the lecture and out would come the visitor's slides for the projector.

There is a feature of such slides, when they are flashed on to the screen: the first is that they can be the right way up and the right way round ie the text on them is identifiable as English and not something related to some foreign land; the second choice is for the slide to be the right way up but the text is that mirror image. Then we start with upside down cases: in that state, but the text only readable by those with 180° neck mobility. Finally you are catering for those with complete fexibility of mind and body - upside down and reverse of picture and text.

With my first couple of C-in-Cs, whoever, I made the assumption that some minions on their staffs would have made certain that their masters would not be embarrassed and had ensured that the slides would be correctly arraigned in the holder. I rapidly came of the opinion that there were many minions deliberately mixing up said slides! I learnt to check them.

To perhaps labour this subject, it took me back to those early cinema days when the film broke - the audience would hiss, boo, slow hand clap whilst the poor projectionist, who after all hadn't broken the film himself, attempted to restore 'service'. There would be a frosty silence in the RAF Flying College lecture hall when Yours Truly, on cue, flashed on to the screen a slide - and it was misaligned. I would say to the Air Chief Marshal:

'Excuse me Sir, but this is entirely not my fault and I think that you need to have a word with your staff when you get back to your headquarters.'

Forget that - I didn't ever say it - I'm just fantasising!

An offshoot of all this was that, as a very junior Flight Lieutenant, I was privy to some incredibly high powered information. Apart from the C-in-Cs, the likes of Sir Stanley Hooker, the aeroengine designer supremo - and Dr Barnes Wallis, inventor of, amongst many other things, the Dambusters' bouncing bomb, were typical 'stars'.

The latter, an incredibly memorable man, started his lecture by reminding the audience that the content would be commercially security sensitive. Bewildered by the complexity of what followed, I concluded that his secrets were safe with me.

I now knew, as ground tours went, being Flight Lieutenant Plans in the RAF Flying College was a 'good' job. I attached myself to a number of the visits. A memorable one for me, possibly because of, on reflection, its historical significance, was to a Thor Inter-Continental Ballistic Missile (ICBM) site ... did we really have that facility?

But time was going by - the end of my 2fi years of being 'in the wilderness' was drawing nigh. What was to be my flying tour?

Chapter 15
Rule Britannia!

W hat *would* be that next posting? Strangely, I cannot recall what I put down, in that preference section, on my 1369 (Annual Confidential Report). This possibly reflects my uncertainty at the time of my future - or, indeed, potential. One thing for sure, I did not declare an inclination to fly long range transport aircraft - it was an unknown world to me. The 'Postings' People' move in dark and mysterious ways. One morning, amongst all the other files and pieces of paper arriving on my desk, I found a 'Posting Notice'. It is strange, on reflection, that I wasn't summoned to the presence of someone in the hierarchy to be told the news - perhaps they felt a bit sick about it! Translated, the message was that I was posted to RAF Lyneham to fly, initially as a copilot, the Britannia, the role of which was worldwide transport operations. Eat your heart out, Eddie Lawson!

I was completely gob-smacked by this - it had no real meaning. But it did for many of my contemporaries.

'Cor! You lucky bugger!'

What was it all to mean? We were left in no doubt by some who had been acquainted with the transport world.

'He'll be living out of a suitcase, most of the time, Val - you'll only see him now and again.'

But, it was our lot and we moved towards it.

162

Step No.1 was a flying refresher course. Quite rightly, these had been established for the likes of me who had not flown for a while - an end had been declared to having aircraft set aside for the occasional use of the deskbound. As I was going to fly a multi-engined, propeller driven aircraft it would have been appropriate for me to have completed the Manby-based, twin-engined, Varsity refresher course. But those 'dark and mysterious ways' were at work again and I found myself doing a Meteor course, almost equally conveniently situated at nearby Strubby.

Then was the time to start a familiar routine: find some suitably located furnished accommodation, pack up the married quarter, march out, removal van, arrive at new home, unload. This time it was a cottage, by the name of 'Red Cottage' - in fact, two knocked into one - in the village of Aldbourne, south of Swindon. Family settled, it was time to make acquaintance with Lyneham.

It had a long history and most of the wartime and post-war part was associated with transport operations. It was appropriate, therefore, that the two latest additions to the RAF Transport Command fleet, the Comet and the Britannia, should operate from there. This meant some building work etc to accommodate the requirements of these aircraft, which added to the general higgledy-piggledy nature of the Station's layout. Redevelopment went on continuously prompting the remark:

'Lyneham will be great - when it's finished!'

The decision to buy Britannias had been made in the early 1950s as the post-war defence requirements became clear. Part of the new strategy was to have a smaller Army but one that was mobile. This required a far bigger air transport force and part of the expansion was the purchase of 23 Britannias. This aircraft was developed for the civilian passenger market and it should have been a world beater. A simple thing it possessed was that it looked good - and aircraft that do that are, generally, successful. During the development stages, the specification for it was increased, time and time again, in step with the increasing expectations of civil aviation. The ultimate design could carry 100+ passengers over a distance of 2000+ miles.

It was powered by four Proteus, turbo-prop engines. These

were part of its success - but contributed towards its failure. The success was that these new turbo-props were efficient, thus economical; they were also smooth and quiet. The down side, for the Britannia, was that a major problem with the Proteus was not revealed until the aircraft had reached the stage of being put to test by one of the biggest customers - British Overseas Airways Corporation (BOAC). On these route trials the aircraft experienced serious engine icing problems.

This was due to two factors: the design of the engine where, to cut down overall length, the flow of air through it was reversed and the fact that the BOAC aircraft met climatic conditions which were unknown at that time - the heavy concentration, in the tropics, of water droplets at 20,000 feet, the operating height of the Britannia. It was a disastrous event and, whilst a palliative was developed, the introduction of the aircraft into airline service was set back by two years. In that time, the pure jet, principally in the form of the Boeing 707, was taking centre stage.

The RAF's choice of the Britannia may seem a strange one unless the decision is related to the time. Tailor-made designs for military transports were on the drawing board - but that is all they were. Undoubtedly, the Americans had some suitable aircraft but we were very much in a 'Buy British' post-war phase. So, the Britannia emerged as the choice - it perhaps did this on the grounds of being the least unsuitable rather than the most suitable. Using an aircraft, as a military transport, that was designed to operate out of civilian airports carrying fare paying passengers, did present problems.

But never mind all these lofty thoughts; what did a posting to Britannias mean for me? We, the new course, assembled. This was a lot of people; one thing I was going to have to get used to was that this aircraft needed a minimum crew of five to fly it.

Meeting my compatriots, I had a feeling of *déjà vu*. When I went into the instructing game, I was aware that I was the start of a new policy of having younger QFIs. It was now evident that there was an equally new decision to recruit new blood into the transport business; this may have been driven by necessity ie the 'old blood' was running out. Whatever, a number of us on the course were a lot

164

younger than the average aircrew age evident at Lyneham. It would also emerge that most of those 'elder brethren' were experienced air transporters. One of the patterns of Service life is the dismissal of one's previous experience in other fields; so we were regarded as a very low form of life.

A surprise was that the first three months of the course would take place, not at Lyneham but at the manufacturers: Bristol Siddeley at Patchway, Bristol for the Proteus engine and The Bristol Aeroplane Company, Filton, Bristol for the Britannia's airframe. The courses were of unbelievable complexity; it did seem that we were being instructed to a sufficient level to construct our own aeroplane. With our inexperience, it was impossible to judge what was essential knowledge, consequently we absorbed very little at all and arrived back at Lyneham for the next phase of the course with a not much better level of understanding than we started. This was something of a disaster as the Britannia was a complicated aircraft and we were expected to have a good grasp of the systems. This would particularly apply to emergency situations. All could now be practised and tested in a simulator.

Aircraft simulators were just appearing on the scene; the Britannia one was amongst the first. Although an example of the white hot technology of its day, it was incredibly low key compared with later development. A huge room contained shelf upon shelf full of relays, circuit boards and old fashioned valves. The heat generated was enormous. All this just drove aircraft instrumentation and simulated control and systems operation. The 'aircraft' itself was static. For all the primitiveness, it was a very effective trainer - if it had been used as such. Unfortunately, in those early days, it largely fell into the wrong hands; the sick, lame and weary gravitated towards the supervisory staff and a session in the simulator developed into a torture. Fault upon fault was piled on the student crew until they cracked. It really was abysmal use and permanently affected my attitude towards these machines.

We settled into a pattern of simulator sorties interspersed with flying. The flying instructors were experienced transporters but, in general, whilst they could operate the aircraft extremely well themselves, they had no talent for passing that on; indeed, at times it did seem as if some of them had an opposite policy and were deliberately obstructing the progress of a student.

Remember that many of us had come from totally non-transport backgrounds and we were completing an aircraft conversion course not a full training course on the transport role. There was no instruction on the things peculiar to transport flying - airways, holding patterns, pilot interpreted letdown procedures and all the like. What is more, we copilots were required to be competent in nearly all the exercises that were required of a captain. In times gone by, the junior pilot on the flight deck was known as a second pilot and he was really only the captain's assistant; it was not anticipated that they would do much of the actual flying. The policy towards copilots was different. They were to fly their own route legs alternately with the captain. This meant that they had to be fully competent in all the flying activities. The only areas excluded to them were the handling (and practice) of the more extreme emergencies eg flight on two engines, flapless landings.

A group of us carried out the bulk of our flying at RAF Nicosia, Cyprus, to take advantage of the good weather. This was to be the first taste of the worldwide turn our lives were going to take. One day, I was struggling with the aircraft, flying circuits and landings; it did seem that things were improving with practice. Did this get up the nose of my mentor who, rather than instructing, seemed to be amusing himself at my expense? Suddenly there is a command.

'Take me to the hold at Myrtou.'

This was a flying pattern around a radio beacon situated somewhere on the island; its location, the nature of the pattern and how to fly it were unknown to me. He might as well have said, 'Fly me to the moon.'

We reached the end of the Cyprus detachment and that stage of instruction and we were returning to Lyneham. Doubts were being cast, by said instructor, about my ability to continue with my Britannia training. But can it be that this 29 year-old was beginning to think that he wasn't, constantly, the inferior one? Leaving aside psycho-analysis, on the flight back to Lyneham I sought the opinion of my fellow student, (who happened to be a Wing Commander destined to take over the Command's examining unit) on how I had been treated. I said that I thought I had grounds for complaint and should I seek an interview with the CO of the training unit?

'Yes, but don't see him first thing tomorrow,' says Wing Commander, 'I fully intended speaking up on your behalf and I shall be talking to the boss man in the morning.'

I was duly given more flying with a different instructor and passed the course. I think this was yet another one of those occasions in my life where my whole future could have been changed but for a twist of fate ... if that Wing Commander had not been my co-student ... one whose opinion had to be respected ... if ... if ...

The last component of the course was 'The Route Trainer'. This was the original, almost totally useless, instructional exercise that, in spite of this description, survived through all the Britannia years. The normal trainer circumnavigated the globe; by Day 3, the students would be flagging with the unaccustomed long flying hours, time zone changes and climatic challenges. Half way round, these effects had accumulated and little instruction was absorbed.

Our course was 'lucky', we 'only' went to Hong Kong and back! All the conditions listed above were met; it was a completely bewildering experience. My outstanding memory was the sensation on stepping out of the aircraft door in Singapore. It was just like entering a hot shower room. The body was cool from the air conditioned flight and moisture condensed on the teeth! I was required to fly the approach into Nicosia and the landing. I had the distinct feeling that the aircraft was flying me rather than being in control. It all was really too big a leap from Meteor, Provost and Anson to Britannia.

Fortunately, it was apparently seen that I would eventually get the hang of things and it was reluctantly agreed that I, along with my fellow 'low forms of life', were marginally fit enough to go to a squadron, 'But an eye would have to kept on us!'

As a postscript to this training phase, I was destined to spend many years flying the Britannia and I am pleased to report that there was an increasing improvement in instructing and examining -

indeed, I like to think that I, in time, played my part in that.

It became a feature of my life that any pressure that I was under 'at work' would be leavened by 'home life'. Just one aspect of this was that Valerie and I adopted a pattern which included an annual, family summer holiday. This was to lay the foundations of leisure life to come. So, even in our parlous state, we had 'gone away' each year. 1962 was going to be a bad year for this; the Britannia course was to run right across the summer

months. It was a good summer and we bought the kids a tent. As a tent proper, it was a pathetic thing, but they enjoyed it. I must have crawled into it one day and, for all its size - or lack of it - the smell and atmosphere obviously had an effect. I actually suggested that we go off in it! Sensibly this idea was rejected by the woman in my life. But a seed had been sown and it

168

would not be long before we were to invest in a 'proper' tent.

With the end of the course there was an allocation to be made. Whilst the aircraft were pooled, as was the servicing of them, the aircrews were split into two squadrons, Nos.99 and 511. Which was best? Well, loyalty will make me pick one over the other, but it did seem that when one was 'up', the other was 'down', the situation reversing with time and changes of personalities. I was posted to 99.

As a young lad, for some reason which I have forgotten, I visited the Plymouth Corporation bus depot. I remember all the drivers and conductors standing around in this large room; details of the allocation of the bus routes, shifts etc were displayed on blackboards; the conductors were counting their money and balancing this with their records. Supervisors would appear from back offices and mutter orders and make changes to the blackboards. The whole place had an air of scruffiness.

This obviously left an indelible impression on me, for when I walked into 99 Squadron, I was reminded of that scene from my youth. Substitute 'drivers and conductors' for aircrew, just delete 'bus' from 'details of the allocation of the bus routes, shifts etc were displayed on blackboards' and for 'blackboards' read perspex and chinagraph boards. Replace 'supervisors' with pilot/navigator etc leaders. Keep, totally unamended, 'The whole place had an air of scruffiness'.

All this appeared to be the way of life. Obviously there had to be a statement of the task ahead, hopefully for the next four weeks. But it did seem that the way of achieving this was in a constant state of flux - not that soldering variety! As one became more acquainted with the way of things, it was realised that the next month's task came to the squadron some ten days into the present month. In it would be some goodies: a group of senior officers to be taken on a European tour, support of an army exercise in the Caribbean, some special freight to the USA. This part of the commitment would all be carved up in the back offices and would be set in stone.

The 'stuff' that was being constantly amended on those chinagraph boards was the 'bread and butter' tasks: the Changi Slip (see later), exercises to, say, Norway, trooping to Malta, routine supply

169

runs to Gibraltar and other garrisons. The crews for these had been allocated in the original plan but for a number of reasons - not the least being those crews being delayed on current trips, because of unserviceability - there was this constant need for amendment.

So, like the 'drivers and conductors', one stood in front of the boards and waited for the change which would affect your life. That effect should not be underestimated. To be suddenly changed from a couple of Germany 'day' trips plus a 'three day Cyprus', say, to a Changi Slip - sorry about another 'see later' - could mean the difference between a few days away, interspersed with a lot of time at home, for the 'head of the house', Daddy, the breadwinner, the loved one - pick a suitable title - to being away for up to three weeks. All this uncertainty about one's future and what was actually happening ie that important date of return, and the effect it could have on the family, was not acknowledged in those days. There were still shades of regarding the wives as 'camp followers'.

My 'camp follower' was coping with all this change and sorting out three young children. One indication of that managing was a 'commendation' that she received from the landlady of our cottage let in Aldbourne. We had moved up the Married Quarters' list, once more, and it was time to move. When we first arrived at the cottage, I will always recall the look on the landlady's face, as she let us in and showed us around, and realised that we had three youngsters. There was clearly some concern. But, in the pre-renting I wasn't asked about, 'How many?', and didn't volunteer. When we were settled in our MQ, there was a kind letter for Val thanking her for the condition in which we had left 'Red Cottage'.

What of that pattern of all our previous moves? 'I think I'm pregnant!' I waited, in trepidation, but the words did not come - mercy!

It was around this time that I did an incredibly sensible thing - not always my strong point. I gave up smoking. I had battled with this habit, which I had taken up under peer pressure, and then become addicted. And I mean addicted. I had acquaintances who could enjoy a 'social' cigarette - and that was it. Fellow pilots would buy a packet of cigarettes for a particular, probably boozy, occasion

- and the next day not smoke one. Valerie would join me in an evening cigarette - and that was it - just one. Me, if I was running out of cigarettes, I would go to untold lengths to correct the situation - and this was someone who had to work, initially, on enjoying a cigarette. I wanted to stop, not for health reasons; that was no big deal in those days. My reason was economics; financially, we were living from month to month and at the end of each those months I would have a Mess Bill. Because I bought my cigarettes in the Mess Bar, there was no escaping how much the habit was costing.

My first approach was to emulate those of my contemporaries with just that social habit. This was when I had my second desk job at Manby. I resolved that I would only smoke when I had a social drink - well, maybe, drop the 'social' ... when I had a drink. It came about that at the stroke of 12 noon, I would beetle off, from my office, to the Mess Bar for a pint during which I would get through two or three cigarettes! After a week or so of this, I slipped back into what seemed a more sensible regime - twenty a day, with no drink.

Then came the Britannia move. Coinciding with this was my increasing pre-occupation with woodwork; what has this to do with

smoking? It would seem that my handicraft interest was so consuming that it was sufficient to beat my addiction. It might sound somewhat pathetic but the key was that I desperately wanted a small workshop - a garden shed! The only way that I was going to realise this, within our over-burdened budget, was to release funds by giving up smoking. It was

agony - I have every sympathy with those smokers who are in the grips of the nicotine habit, as I was. What I am able to appreciate, with hindsight, is that it was extremely fortuitous that I stopped when I did for I was entering a world - the Britannia one - where the majority smoked and this during the hours and hours of what could be monotonous flight. Their habit was supported by the availability of duty free cigarettes. And my motivation had been financial.

Our new address was No.115 OMQ (Officers' Married Quarter). In 1962, RAF Lyneham was not having any nonsense with fancy road names on its Married Quarter patch. It might seem that we were taking a backward step from our two previous quarters, which were detached; 115 was semi-detached - but it had four bedrooms. It was a substantial house.

Married quarters' life of that era - the early 1960s - was a strange mix of the old and the new. Doing the 'visiting card' bit remained vaguely expected; coffee mornings, amongst the wives, was still *de rigueur*. But correctness was difficult to sustain with a husband who was away more than half the time - and an amazing number of young kids about. Anyway, times were changing.

With my lowly state of Britannia ability, how was I going to survive amongst the 'big boys' on the squadron? I had double good fortune here: firstly, it was policy that a new copilot should fly with the same captain for his first six months on the squadron; the second piece of luck was that I was allocated to Graham Bayliss.

Graham was a New Zealander who had completed an engagement with the Royal New Zealand Air Force. The latter part of this had been on a Bristol Freighter squadron based in Singapore; the unit was very much involved in the Malaya Confrontation troubles, supply dropping in the most demanding situations. Graham's part in this had earned him the Distinguished Flying Cross. He was a total flying enthusiast and one of his ambitions was to fly large aircraft. The RNZAF was a bit short of these so, engagement complete, he applied to join the Royal Air Force and was speedily accepted - and posted to the new Britannia fleet. When I arrived on the scene he had completed a brief copilot tour and was now a new captain. He was extremely kind to me - and protective - which allowed me to

172

Graham and his wife, Vonnie - Valerie and some dozey bugger with his eyes closed!

build up my skill and confidence ... the latter having been badly shattered by my training experience.

So, I settled into squadron life and that of a long range RAF transport pilot. My first trip was to Larissa in Greece where an exercise of some sort was being carried out. My memory of it was that the poor guys on the detachment had been flooded out; there had been days of torrential rain. This was shortly followed by my first 'Changi Slip'.

One of the mainstays of Britannia operations was routine support of our garrisons in the Middle and Far East; people and 'things' had to be flown, to and fro. The major route operated to do this was UK to Singapore. Some of these were extended to Hong Kong. Separate flights catered for our Services' requirements in Gibraltar, Malta, Cyprus, Nairobi and Germany. These were, indeed, the heady days of our global commitment.

An aircraft left Lyneham each day for Singapore. The route changed over the years but the initial one was to El Adem, not far

This spot, alongside the Terminal Building at Lyneham, was traditionally reserved for the daily 'Changi Slip' aircraft.

174

from Tobruk, Libya, then on to RAF Khormaksar, our base in Aden. The next stop was a purpose built staging post on the island of Gan, one of the southernmost of the Maldive Islands in the Indian Ocean. The terminus was RAF Changi on the island of Singapore.

With the time and distances involved, the maximum one crew could fly, before having to rest, was two of these legs. But the aircraft had to be kept moving so a 'slip' crew would take over the aircraft at Aden. Another one would be ready at Changi for the return; 'slipping' would then take place again at Aden. Changi was the destination; slipping crews was the method ... hence the name, 'Changi Slip' ... QED, as maths teacher, 'Polly' Perkins, would have said.

My first Changi Slip was accomplished in the record time of ten days. This really was the minimum time; many of them, because of unserviceabilities, extended to three weeks. Consideration of the starting time of the crew's day was not part of the planning; you could be scheduled to depart at 11 o'clock at night - and that to start a potential 19 hour day!

Yes - that was the incredible maximum that one could go to; the original plan would not have been to those limits but if there was a delay, for some reason, then there was the real chance that one could be facing an arrival those 19 hours after reporting for the flight - and what of the amount of sleep that had been achieved whilst anticipating an 11 o'clock departure - and what of those three kids just being kids in their own home? It is quite astonishing that there was not an accident attributable to this shocking length of a crew duty day. It was subsequently reduced to 16 hours, which was still tough enough.

So, with my first Changi Slip, I faced my first long day, a double leg - Lyneham to El Adem, refuel and flight plan, then on to Khormaksar. I have to admit that the departure time was 'civilised' - 11am. Also, we were not delayed - but counting the two hours pre-flight preparation time and the 1fi hours on the ground at El Adem, it still amounted to over 15 hours from start to finish. So at midnight, UK time, we landed in Aden; there the local time was 3am. I was totally knackered, just point me to my bed. But, I was then introduced to a quaint transport flying tradition.

The venue was only a few yards from the aircraft and went by the name of 'Neddy's Bar'. Neddy Pearson, a one-time Wing Commander i/c Operations at Khormaksar decided that, no matter what the time of day or night, transport crews should have the facility to have a 'wind-down' beer after their long flight. Using the singular for 'beer' is somewhat misleading - something approaching eight cans of Amstel each certainly warrants a plural. I remember those cans ... they were decorated with elegant ladies - well, perhaps it was the increasing distance from home that made them appear elegant. When even those with maximum capacities had had their fill, we staggered from the bar, into the scorching morning Aden sun, to the crew bus which took us to our accommodation.

Khormaksar had new transit aircrew accommodation. This was perhaps a more sober consideration of our needs than Neddy's Bar. With constantly moving aircraft, our arrival and departure times were going to be all hours of the day and night - in fact, departures seemed to be inevitably at night and arrivals in the day. Sleep was required at these unnatural times so this accommodation, isolated from those with more normal routines, was purpose built. Another 'must' was air conditioning. We poured ourselves out of the bus and fell into our respective beds - I slept for 24 hours!! I didn't ever repeat this amount of time in the arms of Morpheus; sleeping was an eternal problem and I, amongst the majority, never mastered the art of being able to obtain, on demand, sleep at strange hours of the day.

Having been unconscious for that period, there was no worry about what to do when I awoke ... it was time to get back in an aircraft again. The next leg, from Aden, was to Gan, refuel and on to Singapore. The length of the day was even longer - over 16 hours.

The resting place went by the magic name of Changi Creek Hotel. This was a facility for all people in transit and we aircrew had our own section. Here, the air conditioning was basic - the rooms had the tops of the walls open to the breeze off the water. Some years later there was a custom built block. I shall return to all these places as this story continues. Sufficient to say now that the Changi stop was always a pleasant one, in spite of the humidity and downpours. We did have a good break there - three clear days off - which was a

176

The traditional buildings of Changi Creek Hotel. This was the Japanese Officers' Mess during the occupation of Singapore.

good chance to recharge the batteries before our return. Changi - Gan - Aden, 16 hour day; 15 hours on the ground at Khormaksar and then a 15 hour day going on to El Adem and Lyneham.

We had left Lyneham on 11th October 1962 and we were back on the 21st having flown some 12,000+ miles. In spite of the fact that I can reflect on many years of doing this sort of thing, it still comes as something of a surprise doing the calculation and putting it in black and white. Needless to say, in those early days, on returning home, I didn't know if I was 'punched, drawn or countersunk' - as I think the saying goes. Picture, if you will, returning in this state to the family home with three young children about - but the 'honeymoon' was wonderful!

Staying with the domestic scene, amongst the remnants of past married quarter life that still existed was that batman service. In fact, this had been transformed to 'batwoman' and even more sensibly to a domestic help recruited from the local village. Mrs T was a great help to Valerie, even though our portion of her week's effort was small. We 'shared' her with a nearby Wing Commander. Professionally, he was known for his somewhat eccentric ways; from Mrs T we learnt that this extended to the domestic scene. Wing Commander L's family were 'horsey' and in the atrocious winter of 1962/3 they had a problem. One freezing day, Mrs T discovered the solution when she opened the back door of their married quarter to find a horse in the kitchen!

So, we are settled in our new abode and I am getting myself established on the squadron. The world awaits!

Chapter 16
The World is my Oyster

This tome is intended as a personal story so I have to be careful not to turn it into a history of the Royal Air Force - and, in particular, for the times we are at, a history of the RAF Britannias. That has been amply covered in my book, '*The Whispering Giant in Uniform*', published in 1997. What I cannot resist doing is repeating some of the stories from '*Tales from the Crewroom*', an earlier book of mine which many partakers of these pages will not have read. My apologies to those who have - but I'm sure a chuckle will still be raised. These comments are prompted by the fact that I will not be describing what the Britannia force, as whole, was up to, but only my part in it - and that will not be every 'part' otherwise the forests would be out of trees.

Before continuing that narrative, I need to refer to my engagement status. As already noted, I had changed from an eight year commission to a 12 year one but that would have been running out by now. I am not sure of the time scale but, sufficient to relate, it became possible to carry on delaying having to face up to civilian life. Twelve year people were offered a new long term commission with retirement depending on rank achieved; for a Flight Lieutenant this was 43.

Later, it was decided that this would lead to an awful lot of experience being lost, so serving to age 55 was offered. This was part of a package known as Specialist Aircrew. With all pilots and navigators being commissioned, then there was no hope for many to rise above Flight Lieutenant. It was seen that if people were to be retained then some financial reward had to be offered to compensate for lack of salary increases through promotion. This was a great scheme - one's professionalism was being acknowledged. Specialist Aircrew Flight Lieutenants and Squadron Leaders were to become the respected 'Senior Citizens' of the RAF flying world.

Returning to those early Britanna days, my next trip, worthy of comment, was one to Sharjah, in the United Arab Emirate. This was another one of those exhausting days - 6fl hours to Nicosia, refuel, then 6 hours to Sharjah ... a 16+ hours duty day. The length of time is emphasised because it is my excuse for my fairly positive arrival on the Sharjah runway. It was my turn to fly the leg - unless there were some overruling circumstances, the pattern, for flying the routes, was turn and turn about between the captain and copilot. This, and observing the *modus operandi* of the various captains on the squadron, made the copilot tour an excellent training ground for captaincy - which was the intention - there was also the aspect of 'killing two birds with one stone'; two pilots were required to operate the aircraft, anyway.

Am I, purposely, digressing away from that Sharjah landing? To return ... there was a lesson to be learnt; the runway there was narrower than normal giving the perception that one was higher than was actually the case; *'the (copilot) doth protest too much, methinks.'*

I will remember that Sharjah trip for another reason, a crazy one. Appropriately it is linked with a crazy, but talented man - the comedian, Tommy Cooper. He was on an 'entertain the troops' tour which indicates that it was before his big leap to fame. I well remember that he had us all in tears but, probably because he didn't really tell jokes, I can only recall one of his 'funnies'. This was a prop he had which was an artificial sunflower growing in a pot. As his act proceeded, the flower would slowly wilt, only to be saved, at the last moment, by Tommy's watering can! He was a truly funny man and I relished all his subsequent appearances on 'the box'.

It is a bit of a big, backward step on the temperature scale to move from Sharjah to the UK winter of 1962/3. It went into the record books as the severest one since 1947. I had enjoyed a family Christmas - not something that could be assumed with the Britannia's involvement in any sort of worldly troubles. It was a large family occasion as Mother and Father came to stay. This was a most unusual event - I can only recall it happening three or four times; as a visitor, Father was like a fish out of water. This was tough on my mother who was almost entirely robbed of her grandmother years. His transport was now a motorcaravan - one of the original Dormobiles with a sideways tilting roof to give standing room inside. It was a great source of pleasure ... it was also an accident waiting to happen! Fortuitously it never did.

Peeping out of the bedroom window, in the morning, there was the gratifying sight of the snow laying inches - if not feet in some places - deep. Not having had any official notification of a delay, I felt I had to go through my preparations to leave. This included the rather bizarre donning of KD - our version of khaki drill tropical dress was long sleeved shirt with black tie, long trousers and black shoes. The policy was that one departed in the uniform appropriate to one's destination. So, snow or no snow, KD was *de rigueur*.

Ready, I sat waiting for the inevitable message that we were delayed. To my complete astonishment, the crew bus, looking more like a snow plough, pulls up outside the door. The flight was still on. We moved around the married quarters collecting the rest of the crew; the consensus of opinion was that we were just going through the motions and would be back home in a couple of hours.

Doubt was cast on this prophecy when we discovered that our

181

aircraft had been kept in a hangar all night and the intention was to load the passengers in there and then tow the aircraft out, ready to start and go. There was clearly some determination afoot and that had been applied to keeping the runway clear; this was bordering on a losing battle as, relentlessly, the snow continued to fall.

Our passengers boarded, no doubt with hearts as heavy as ours. They were fellow aircrew, as the purpose of this, the first Changi Slip after the Christmas break, was to reposition the slip crews at Aden and Singapore - it was traditional to try and get everyone home for the festive season. The hangar doors opened and the aircraft tug, attached to our nose wheel, started pulling us out into the open. As soon as it was on the snow, traction was lost - and our hopes rose. But two more tugs were summoned and they were attached, by cables, to our main wheels. A run was taken at it and, in spite of the slipping and sliding, we were outside. Engines were started in double quick time.

Sod's Law was at work and the wind dictated that we needed to use the most distant runway; the route to this was an uphill taxiway. We came to a halt. But determination was still there and the hangar despatch party appeared with shovels and dug us out. We made it to the runway; it stretched before us as a ragged line - just the centre had been cleared and dirty crooked banks of snow lay down the edges. We started to roll; the ride was bumpy as we hit uncleared lumps of ice. Take-off speed was reached and we rotated into the leaden sky. Almost immediately the aircraft entered cloud ... 10,000 feet later we burst into the sunshine with blue sky above. Not another cloud was encountered, all the way to Singapore.

The UK weather worsened and not a single aircraft departed Lyneham for ten days. Meanwhile, we sat in the Far East sunshine wondering what was happening back home. A feature of international travel is the parochial nature of the news in the country of your temporary residence. But the big Singapore daily actually mentioned the state of things back home ... so the situation must be bad. At 115 OMQ there was that young mother with her three small children - and her father and mother-in-law.

Henry was like a caged lion; visiting for the scheduled number of days was agony enough; that stay being prolonged was a torture. In spite of atrocious road condition reports, he resolved to 'have a go'. Neighbours became aware that he was digging himself out in preparation for leaving; they turned out to help dig and push. He did not get outside the married patch before he was forced to turn back. If I had known all this was going on, perhaps I would have been happier with my stay in Changi; as it was, I felt very dejected about being separated from Valerie and her problems.

Eventually, on 8th January, the first RAF Britannia flew down the Malacca Straights and into RAF Changi and within a few hours we were flying it back to Aden for one of our fellow slip crews to take it on to the UK. It was our turn to do the same, a day later, and we landed back at Lyneham on the 10th. We thought, by now, there would be nothing to see of the weather trauma - wrong! The place looked like a battlefield ... and it remained like that for many more weeks. Perhaps I am ashamed to admit that, to my intense relief, road conditions had improved sufficiently for my father to have left! Hard luck, Mum.

Ironically, my next route trip was to one of the coldest outposts in the World. The Royal Canadian Air Force Base, Churchill lay on the western shore of Hudson Bay, northern Canada. Some military equipment required cold weather testing and it needed two Britannias to convey the load.

I flew the aircraft into Churchill, experiencing for the first time one of the lots in life of an RAF transport flier - the route check. I have already commented that, as an RAF pilot, you have never totally 'passed'. Part of 'passing' in the transport world was surviving a check by an examining pilot (or other trades for other crew members) whilst operating a route leg - say A to B - or Y to Z - in fact any leg. In these bad old early days of quite tyrannical testing these route checks were a constant threat. Typically, a crew could arrive in the flight planning room to prepare themselves for the next leg when, from behind a filing cabinet, would leap a 'route checker'.

'Hello Bloggs, I'm 'doing' you on the next leg.'

Thankyou very much. These were, indeed, unfortunate years for the 'testing' fraternity; some of them were, to not put too fine a point on it, reviled. Their contribution was destructive - it took many years for this tradition to be reversed. But do you sense that it is the case that, once more, *'the (copilot) doth protest too much, methinks'*? My experiences have left a scar.

My route checker was that first instructor who had failed to recognise what a delicate creature I was, in need of special nurturing to realise my potential. Either it was a matter of no consequence to him that I had complained about my treatment at his hands or that he was prepared to give me a fair deal. Whatever, during the flight he was reasonable, apart from tripping the auto-pilot circuit breaker during the descent to 'teach me a lesson'.

'Always keep your hands on the control column when making attitude changes with the auto-pilot.'

The inevitable conclusion of a route check is the debriefing. You will have 'noted' that, during the flight, things had been 'noted' on a page of the essential equipment of the route checker - the spiral-bound note book. Out of the corner of one's eye it could be seen that your most recent action had caused a flurry of note taking; if things were really bad then the turning of fresh pages could create a breeze on the back of the neck. At the 'debrief' the pages of the note book would be turned.

'During the checks before take-off I noticed that you were engrossed in picking your nose ...'

And so it went. My debrief at Churchill was going along these lines. After some half dozen comments about my shortcomings on the flight, I blew my top.

'This is enough - I've had you up to here!!' An appropriate level of hand was displayed. 'I don't know who you guys think you are - you can do this job standing on your heads but you should now be helping and encouraging those of us new to game so that we can become as good as you ...'

Actually I didn't say that, I've just made that up. What I did was use some of the useful advice I was picking up from my new compatriots on the squadron.

'Put yourself in the route checker/tester's shoes - he's got to find something to say so, when it comes to the debrief, with each point raised, use a variation on the theme, 'I think that the comment you have just made is entirely justified and the advice that you are offering is the most incredible that I have ever received and I shall be eternally grateful to you for pointing out my shortcomings.' ...'

I followed the spirit of this advice and my 'Cat Card' - the document we all possessed to record the results of each test endured - was signed up for a pass - in fact, a step up from a 'D' to a 'C'.

Churchill was cold cold - if one was in possession of hairs in the nostrils, then they froze. We had thick plastic bags in which to carry our communications headgear. I hesitate to say 'headsets' - astonishingly we wore the blue cloth, inner helmet intended for use with a 'bone dome' - the aircrew 'crash helmet' - and the microphone in an oxygen mask. This totally unsuitable equipment, being used in the most expensive RAF aircraft to date, was endured for many years before we were provided with airline-style headsets. It was notice-able how these 'headset' bags became more pliable, the higher the temperature. At Churchill they became brittle and split!

Heated buses were waiting at the bottom of the aircraft steps and took us to the accommodation, centrally heated, in the tradition-al North American way, to the point of oppressiveness. There was no need to step outside for any of the amenities; corridors, also heated, linked all the buildings. Whilst we were being treated like hot house plants, our aircraft sat outside. In the morning we were to realise the effect of such cold; some of the equipment refused to work - that which did seemed to be going at half speed.

Our tyres were frozen to the ground and hot air had to be blasted on to them. Clearly there was a need to get out of here 'asap'. Doom and gloom had been spread by a Royal Canadian Air Force engineering officer who had demonstrated the effect of the tempera-ture on one of our hydraulic system seals as compared with one for their Yukon aircraft. Both left outside for an hour, the Yukon one remained supple - ours cracked into pieces.

With a struggle, the two aircraft started; we were first to the take-off point and rolled on to the runway; full power was applied and with the engines swallowing the freezing cold air, we leapt into the sky. Our compatriots had a problem, a particular Britannia one that only revealed itself just before take-off - they had to return to the parking area. The cold now started to bite; those seals, which had been subjected to pressure whilst the engines were running, started to leak. They were there for a week. I had a chuckle - my route checker had transferred his attentions to another 'victim' - on board the doomed aircraft!

I now settled into the real routine - Libya, Nicosia, Malta, Bahrain, Aden, Gan Island, Singapore - page after page in my log book lists the associated airfields. It did seem that I was no sooner back from one trip than it was time to start another - those words from Manby rang in our ears, 'He'll be living out of a suitcase.' It

meant lovely 'honeymoons', albeit that some of them were quite short!

If all had operated according to plan, then the time away from home would have been reasonable; but the bugbear was unserviceabilities. One aircraft with a problem on the Changi Slip, say, and there was a knock-on effect for all the slip crews. Spending longer than anticipated at a staging post was a frustration - now I would (and could) pay a lot money for a week in the Maldives! The problem was that a delay did not generally affect the major squadron plan.

'Hard luck, Bloggs, you'll still have to go out on Tuesday - there's no one else.'

But there **were** some more; they were resident, fully paid up members of 'The Country Club'. Qualification for this brotherhood was long service in the transport world and an element of pushing.

Membership gave you early access to 'next month's programme', allowing the 'cream' to be extracted before the 'skimmed milk' was allocated to the *hoi polloi*. Prime trips would really be anything away from the Mediterranean, Middle and Far East - unless it was Hong Kong. North and South America, Australasia, the Caribbean - these would all feature large on the 'Club's' menu. If any such morsels dropped our way then there was usually a catch; it would be a large exercise, perhaps, with slipping and unsociable hours. It must have been a trip like this that took me to Fredericton, New Brunswick, an airfield where it seemed that the runways had been, deliberately, built so that they did not point in the direction of any of the most likely winds.

The 'Club' did not mind us lesser mortals frequently visiting a particular North American airfield. Gander in Newfoundland was the stepping stone to all places Canada and USA. Newfoundlanders will have to forgive me for describing it as a God-forsaken place. The summers can be hot and sticky, which the mosquitoes love. The winters are atrocious - fog, snow, feet deep. There's many a crew who have spent days snowed or fogged in at Gander as the aircraft that they were supposed to be taking on, has had to divert to another airfield.

Strangely, we and the Russians were the only major users of Gander International. It had been built to cater for transatlantic USA traffic when refuelling was a necessity. With the advent of the 707 and the like, direct flights became possible. Gander was a 'white elephant'. The Russians used it as a staging post to Cuba. When an RAF aircraft and a Cubana one were on the ground at the same time, there were a lot of suspicious glances. Why do Russian uniform hats have tops the size of dustbin lids?

The terminal building had all the trappings of an international air terminal: check-in desks, fashionable but uncomfortable seating, hundreds of locked doors, escalators ... one of these leads to a story. A particular copilot compatriot of mine had an inclination to upset COs. On one occasion he was copilot to his CO captain and they were at Gander. The Wing Commander was looking his dignified best as there was a VIP due through at the same time and he knew him from the past. But his flight planning activities had to proceed and it came time to visit the Met Office, upstairs. The copilot led the way up a stationary escalator and pulled ahead, his CO was only half-way up when Dave reached the top where, for some inexplicable reason (at least it was subsequently), he pressed the escalator 'Go Down' button. His leader had a great deal of difficulty maintaining his dignified appearance whilst continuing to try to make his way upwards!

A place name leaps out of the pages of my log book; in fact it appears two days running - Bangkok! These entries have led to conversations with civilian friends, over the years, along these lines.

'Dave - we're going to spend a few days in Thailand - have you ever been there?'

'Well - yes - er, twice. But not for any length of time. Well, actually, just for an hour on two successive days!'

This is the story of much air transport life - been everywhere, seen nothing! On this particular occasion we landed, sat in the terminal building for an hour, whilst our aircraft was unloaded, and then took off to return to Singapore. In that short time two things were impressed on my memory: the beauty of young Thai ladies and the heat. Over the years I was to collect many 'heat' experiences but Bangkok retained the record.

Again, I juxtapose a hot story with a cold one. The Britannias did have a regular Arctic commitment. This was to the Specialist Navigation Course for whom we flew, annually, two polar training flights. One of these was airborne for 13 hours and 15 minutes, possibly a record for the Britannia.

The intention of the flights was to allow the students to observe navigation equipment operating in the difficult environment of extreme latitudes. Compasses are pretty useless when the Magnetic North Pole is directly below you. In the early days, the flights routed out of Lyneham to the North Pole and then to Thule AFB in Greenland. On this leg I was the copilot of the second crew, travelling as a passenger - a lowly position. On the way to the Pole the news on the Thule weather was not good and it was decided at 87° North to forsake the Pole and turn for Thule.

The subsequent approach there proved that the reports were not exaggerated - nothing was seen. The diversion airfield for Thule was Sondrestrom, holding the distinction of being particularly far away for an alternate airfield. On the overshoot a climb was made to 35,000 feet for the two hour flight. This really was on the limits of the fuel set aside for such a diversion and the height was essential to eke this out.

Communications were poor and an emergency had to be declared in order to convey the critical situation. It was a great relief as Sondrestrom hove into sight at the end of its fiord. The subsequent fuel checked revealed 3,000lbs remaining - barely enough to wet the bottoms of the Britannia's several large fuel tanks.

There is a chilling sequel to this story. The next day we, the second crew, took off for the return flight to Lyneham. Climbing through 15,000 feet there was a bang and a rush of air. The pressurisation had failed and the cabin altitude climbed rapidly. As we started an emergency descent the airquartermaster reported that the curtain over the entrance to the Gent's toilet was streaming rearwards. A valve in the toilet ground discharge mechanism had failed. With fuel jettisoned, we landed back at Sondrestrom.

Surprisingly, we were airborne again a couple of hours later with a new valve made in the USAF workshops. But why should this failure subsequent to the diversion the day before, produce a shudder? Reflect, as I have - the valve had not been touched since we left Lyneham. If it had failed on the previous pressurisation, ie on the climb out of Thule, then disaster would have resulted. The aircraft would have been forced to climb to 35,000 feet in order that the diversion could be accomplished with the fuel available. The crew had oxygen but there was none for the 40+ passengers. Man does not survive at 35,000 feet, for two hours, without oxygen!

I must have had some time at home in the midst of all this. It is said that everyone can remember where they were when they heard the news of President Kennedy's assassination; I was in 115 OMQ. My recollection is that the TV was on for kid's stuff when the news started coming through.

On a happier home note, that aforementioned tenting bug

took a big bite. We bought, I know not how, a tent. It was a new breed - a frame tent of French manufacture. This was camping on a level above the Boy Scout stuff and we thought it was magic. We packed all our gear, and the five of us into a Ford Anglia - yes, we had gone up in the world and we now had one of those, sloping forwards, back window models. We had it for a long time and I had lots of time to reflect on the colour scheme; it must have seemed a good idea at the time to choose two-tone (all the rage) white and pale lime green! I am appalled at the way that we travelled when judged by present day safety standards. An essential ingredient of squeezing us all in was that one of the boys had to sit on a cushion over the handbrake.

I bought a trailer frame and made my own box for the top - this was a cunning device that converted into shelves and cupboards when pitched. A trailer requires a tow ball and the tow ball needs to be attached to some sort of frame on the car; I made that out of the angle iron from an old bedstead and attached it to the body work with the bolts that secured the rear bumper!

After a family holiday, I found it really hard returning to work. There was the dread of finding out how your programme had been changed during the absence. Eyes anxiously scanned the boards of the 'bus depot' to see what was one's lot in life for the coming weeks. Surprise, surprise ... a Changi Slip ... tomorrow!

Chapter 17
Travels Continue

Australia did not normally feature in the lives of us lesser mortals. But there was an exercise involving the Army, so lots of slipping and night flying were involved - not the *métier* of 'The Country Club'. It was quite an arduous ten days - and that is all it took to get from Lyneham to Adelaide via Perth and back to base. From Gan to Perth took ten hours and was very marginal on fuel, given our full load of passengers. In fact the Perth airfield was a military base to the north and my abiding memory of it was the pitch blackness of the night with just the 'side of the runway' lights (no fancy lead-in illumination for the Royal Australian Air Force) and not a glimmer from the surrounding countryside.

We visited Perth and were impressed; some of the local people pointed out that they were almost not part of the rest of Australia, a fact we were able to appreciate when it took us over three hours to fly to Adelaide, with nothingness in between. As pleasant as Perth was, Adelaide was dull; the layout of the streets was a grid *à la* USA. My only other memory of the city was our navigator, in a shop, turning over skin upon skin of kangaroo looking for one without a bullet hole in it!

Mention above of army passengers reminds me of a story of a notorious Britannia captain who believed in speaking his mind. Flight Lieutenant L was mostly right to do so; it's just that many of

A superb Britannia photograph by former 99 Squadron captain, the late Bill Robinson.

us weaker souls might have let the matters pass. His reported actions were a treasure trove of stories to feed the 'folk lore' world we lived in. On this army passenger occasion, Flight Lieutenant L was making his duty visit to the passenger cabin whence he came upon a soldier, stripped to the waist, asleep in his seat. He is prodded in the chest and awakes to these words.

'Put your shirt on, sonny - some human beings have got to use that seat after you!'

After all the Polar and 'Down Under' gallivanting, it was time to return to earth. In this case, my 'driving test' was the crunch. Once every 6, 12 or 24 months, depending on the category held, we were subjected to a day and night flying test. These could be conducted in a somewhat tense atmosphere.

'Right, Bloggs, I want you to fly a circuit and do me a normal four engine landing.'

A while later.

'Well, you made a right balls of that - let's see how you get on with three engines.'

With the speed of light, a throttle would be whizzed rearwards. By some miracle, this landing is OK.

'A bit fluky that; I thought you only got the stick back just in time. Now, I want you to fly this circuit with your eyes shut and your right index finger up your ...'

Not really, but it conveys the spirit.

It was a pass or fail job, so anxiety was a natural condition; I was suitably nervous, but passed. No matter how experienced one became, this testing was a recurring strain - well, it was for me!

In October 1963, a squadron of night/all weather Javelin fighters flew to give demonstrations, advice and training to the Indian air defence formation. The Javelins flew out via Cyprus and Bahrain with in-flight refuelling being provided by Valiant tankers. In support, along the route and flying the men and materials, were the Britannias.

The airfield was Kalaikunda, near Calcutta. My log book records that I flew there via Nicosia and Bahrain in mid-October and again at the end of the month. I remember it well. Within the means available, the Indian Air Force had prepared for our coming; but those means were limited.

There was the usual bustle around the aircraft as we disembarked. With the responsibility for the aircraft handed over, it was time for bed. It had been a long day. Came the oft asked question.

'Where's the crew bus?'

A finger points, 'On its way.'

Sure enough in the distance, across the flat fields of crops could be seen the top of a coach. It was moving slowly along but did not seem to get any closer. As time went by it became clear that it was having to wend its way along the road that followed the edges of the haphazard fields. Eventually it came to a noisy, smoky standstill beside our aircraft. It was apparent that the bus, which normally conveyed the workers to the fields, had been commandeered for our use. We climbed gingerly aboard.

Firing on only three cylinders, the journey seemed endless; but eventually we came to a grinding halt outside our accommodation - TENTS!! This was not our normal style! Admittedly they were erected on concrete bases and were fully furnished. From somewhere had come proper beds - and wardrobes, for the visiting British ex-colonialists. As we walked from the bus, a gnarled, white cotton clad figure stood to attention with a shaky hand permanently at the salute. It turned out that he was the '*dhobi wallah*', no doubt with many a memory of our grander military presence in the India of the past.

It certainly was a night stop with a difference. It had amused us that part of our UK departure preparation had been the issue of snake bite kits. That amusement had continued as we examined the contents, en route:

Instructions: 1. Identify the snake ... !!!!

The smiles slowly faded when we learnt that one of our compatriots had to beat one of these reptiles to death in order to get back from the outdoor toilets!

As a wonderful relief from all this route flying 'excitement', a pattern continued to develop in my life; one that I have been eternally pleased came about. I was evolving into a serious hobby person and, at this time, woodworking was becoming a consuming

194

interest. I had my small workshop (the smoking cure had worked) and was slowly building up a set of tools. My projects became more ambitious and totally absorbing; I remember resenting being dragged away on the next mammoth trip because I had just finished an oak rocking chair. I wanted time to sit and admire it! The chair is still in the family. I have found it very satisfying having these interests; at boring times - and there are plenty of those with long range transport flying - it was great to let one's mind dwell on the latest project - or some future one.

The 'mammoth' trip was a 'Cable Route'. This route was so called because it followed, in its initial concept, the necessary path of the underwater Cable and Wireless lines of communication. It was initiated and regularly exercised in order to provide an alternative, albeit a lengthy one, to routes which required the acquiescence of countries which might not be willing to cooperate in a particular operation or exercise. This 'Cable Route' varied over the years. With ours, the first stop was Sal, Cape Verde Islands - a God-forsaken place. Ascension Island was next, then on to Luanda, Angola, then Salisbury, Rhodesia.

Next stop was Mauritius and then the Cocos Islands - this begins to sound like the programme for a cruise liner but, so far, we have only been on the move for five days! From Cocos it was a return visit to the military airfield near Perth and then one near Sydney. This seemed to be the object achieved - we had reached Australia without overflying any land except that of southern Africa - and we could have avoided that if we had flown around the Cape. Now it was time for home - back to Perth, but then Gan, where we picked up our normal route from the Far East. We had left Lyneham on 8 December - we were back on the 21st!

Perhaps it is not surprising that I do not remember anything amusing about the trip - but there was one thing! A feature of Britannia flying was that the pilots did not touch the throttles. They called for the power required, which was set by the flight engineer. This could make things interesting on the approach to land. On a really good day the call, at the start of the approach, might be, 'Torque 250', and there it would stay until, 'Flight idle,' just before touchdown. On a bad day, the power could be going up and down like - as the saying goes - a whore's drawers! Anxiety could show through as, with the increasing number of changes, the voice of the caller would be rising in pitch! A situation could be reached where the aircraft was too high. The temptation would be to bring all four engines back to their lowest setting, 'Flight Idle'. This was not a good thing as, with reduced prop wash, it removed a lot of the airflow over the tailplane and, when it came time to come back on the control column to arrest the rate of descent just before touchdown, nothing might happen - crunch!! Too high? It was OK to bring the outboard engines to flight idle. On one of our approaches - high - the call required was:

'Flight idle the outers.'

What came out was: 'Idle the flighters.'!

So, I was only back for Christmas just in time - and then was off to Cyprus on the 28th! Life was full - and before long it was 'driving test' time again and another route check. This was carried out flying into a place completely new to me - Nairobi. By some fortuitous combination of circumstance - not all of them influenced by me - the landing was a really smooth one, which was not something generally achieved in a Britannia. This was treated with complete indifference by my examiner.

'During the checks before take-off I noticed that you were engrossed in picking your nose ...'

But I was progressing up the category ladder; these went by the first five letters of the alphabet. Starting in reverse order - and skipping the special case of an 'E' cat - most people graduated from their training with a 'D' ie inexperienced. The next steps were: 'C', average; 'B', above average and 'A', exceptional. The associated testing periods were: 'D' and 'C', six months; 'B', 12 months and 'A' - holy of holies - a whole two years! That 'E' cat? If you made a complete 'horlicks' of a test then the award was an 'E', in need of further training. With that duly given, there would be a retest.

One had to obtain the required grade in five areas to upgrade e.g. to go up from 'D' to 'C'. Firstly, there was an 'Operational Assessment' given by the squadron commander before the test; this depended on 'how you had been' in the last months. Not the least factor in this was 'social behaviour'. This could definitely be a 'clash of personalities area' - or perhaps the CO, too, had noticed you picking your nose ... With an 'Operational C', the game was on; just get one for day flying, night flying, in the simulator and on a route check and a rung of the ladder was climbed. The new status was not irrevocable; like share prices, you could go down as well as up! So, I was now a precarious 'C'.

Valerie felt obliged to understand all the 'ins and outs' of this system for she had to endure the tension surrounding each test and have to listen to the outcome.

'... and then the silly bugger closed one of the throttles and tells me to fly the next circuit with ...'

We continued with our camping summer holidays and a few shorter trips in between. Inevitably we suffered the deprivations of the UK climate; on one Wales' trip it rained for a fortnight. I had to dig a trench around the tent to drain the water away! Surprisingly we persisted and had some wonderful family occasions as a result - happy memories, but I wouldn't want to do it all over again.

It was some time during my first two years at Lyneham that an event took place of the sort that is the substance of 'myth and legend' - but this is a true story - and I repeat true, because I was there. As well as being the home of the Royal Air Force's Strategic Transport Force, the Comets and the Britannias, it was also the location for a Maintenance Unit specialising in the major overhaul of aircraft and their storage. Commanding the Unit was a Wing Commander of the Technical Branch. It so happened that this Wing Commander, in his earlier years, had participated in a scheme to give young Technical Officers a wider appreciation of their engineering role by allowing them to undergo pilot training. That is all they did - the training - before returning to their normal duties. It will transpire that this is of some significance to this story.

On a sunny day at RAF Lyneham, across at the Maintenance Unit, an English Electric Lightning required engine tests. This incredible aircraft can best be described as two enormous jet engines strapped together, one on top of the other, with the pilot perched on

197

top, the whole being surrounded by aluminium - a potent piece of machinery. The aircraft was positioned for this test at the end of a disused runway. The canopy was not fitted, nor the ejector seat. A wooden box was provided for the person who was to run the engines.

For some reason that has disappeared into the mists of time, the CO, the aforementioned Wing Commander, decided that he personally would carry out these engine runs. Head down, seated on the wooden box, he started the engines and began the test routine. High power settings were called for as the test progressed.

As full power was applied, the aircraft leaned forward, straining against the brakes and the wheel chocks. Suddenly, with a bang and a roar, the Lightning leapt over the chocks and went streaking down the runway!

The Wing Commander, in the few seconds that he had as he hurtled along towards certain death, experienced an immediate recall of how to fly an aeroplane - and pulled back on the control column. Now he was airborne - alive - but with what could only be described as a deferred termination problem. To keep the Lightning airborne, he needed to remember all he could of his flying days and, more to the point, to land it in one piece. And all this, only equipped with his, long past, very basic flying experience, in an aircraft of considerable weight, performance and complexity with the 'pilot' sitting on a wooden box with no flying helmet or canopy!

A full emergency was obviously declared - and the spectators turned out! But there was little anyone could do except keep the airfield clear and wait. There was some initial relief as it became clear that the CO did have the aircraft under some reasonable control as he circled Lyneham.

Such relief returned to anxiety as he made his first tentative approach to the runway. He was much too high and fast. Now the fear was that, on his next attempt, he would go to the other extreme and be too low and slow - a not unfounded apprehension; but the Wing Commander had the good sense to abandon this approach early and overshoot. Time was now a factor, as the aircraft had only a small amount of fuel at the start of the engine runs (probably a contribution towards its chock leaping act) so now, with the circling of the airfield and the two approaches, his fuel state was critical.

The Lightning once again started an approach to the runway. It was apparent that this was probably the last possible attempt by the increase in the unsteadiness of the flight, conveying to the onlookers the even more heightened anxiety of the 'pilot'. However, in spite of the approach resembling a weaving roller coaster, the Lightning arrived on the end of the runway and landed hard, but safely!

Such a story should have a happy ending but I believe that the Wing Commander was praised and admonished simultaneously and was probably of a somewhat nervous disposition from that day on!

Back to work and, by way of a preface to the next saga, some thoughts on the matter of 'diplomatic clearance'. Although it might seem somewhat removed from the image that our Britannia generated, we were a military force and, as such, there could be some opposition to our activities. Flying personnel and equipment in support of one country's cause could 'get up the nose' of one of its enemies. We lived constantly with this. For the major Britannia years we were forbidden to overfly Egypt. I think we upset them when we decided to try and hang on to the Suez Canal. This avoidance was something of a nuisance on our regular flight, Libya to Aden - the straight line took us firmly over Egypt. We had to bend the flight around the south west boundary and this inconvenience was known as 'Nasser's Corner'.

Another example was flying from Cyprus to Bahrain; the common sense route is eastwards but, to avoid hostile countries, we had to go north first, over Turkey then east into Iran (they were on our side then), before turning south for Bahrain. Even the countries that permitted overflight could be sensitive to our activities; Turkey, for instance would only give permission for a flight for the time we requested and would only tolerate a delay of one hour on that. If the hold-up was longer then the clearance had to be re-negotiated. There were many more nuances to diplomatic clearance but it will be clear that it could be a considerable barrier to us going anywhere, if all the cards were stacked against us.

At the time of this account, we, as a country, were still trying to sort out the problems of the world. Many of our commitments were in the Far East and if a number of the Middle Eastern countries were against us then we would have been unable to reach the required destinations. One way of tackling this has been discussed: the 'Cable Route' Another solution: 'Go West, young man!' It could be safely assumed that the USA and Canada would not be hostile to our causes so a plan evolved to reach the Far East via North American and Pacific military air bases. To practise this contingency an exercise was planned, not inappropriately called 'Travelling Causeway'.

This elaborate operation took place annually. On the declared day the exercise would start, the first phase being to position the ground crews and the aircraft slip crews at each staging post. The route varied over the years but one of the first was Thule AFB Greenland, Elmendorf AFB Alaska, Midway Island and Guam in the Pacific and then Singapore. With all in position the first exercise aircraft proper would leave Lyneham and the stream would follow at four-hourly intervals, stopping for refuelling and to change crews.

This grand plan came to an untimely halt on the first run. The slip crews, with me amongst them, and ground crew had reached Greenland, some beyond, on the positioning phase when the exercise was cancelled because of a requirement to fly troops from the UK to Aden, the scene of much unrest for many years to come. Back we all trooped to the UK. Another start was made two months later. Six aircraft, on the main lift, set off at the two hourly intervals from Lyneham. Five of them made it, all that distance to Singapore, within five hours of the schedule.

That sixth aircraft, which developed a propeller fault between Alaska and Midway Island, provided me with a memorable week. Midway was manned by the US Navy - and 'officer-wife-womanned'. The commissioned lot had their wives - no such luck for the enlisted.

If one ignored the military presence, it was a paradise island. White sand, turquoise-blue sea, the assaults of the sun tempered by a gentle breeze. But civilisation was there, which provided us with three Bs, within a 100 yard radius: a Beach, a Bar and a Bed! Another essential ingredient of the almost tourist nature of our stay was the bird-life, represented primarily by the Gooney Birds.

We were there at the stage when the chicks - if you could use such a word to describe something the size of a big duck - were starting to fly. We learnt that the parent Gooney Birds returned to precisely the same spot each year to lay one egg. This was tended by the female whilst the male, on his long, thin, glider-like wings, soared many miles from the island in search of food. This was regurgitated on return to feed the chick. As it grew, Mum had to go foraging as well and if the chick moved, or was moved, from its spot in that time, the parents would be unable to find it.

It was highly amusing, come flying time. We lay in the sun watching the build-up to this. A promising sign was 'engine run-ups'. These huge offspring, with their already large wing span, would stand into wind and exercise their wings, Flap, flap, flap - a bigger flap and there would be a slight lift into the air. But the next step was a greater one - a run into wind with the wings flapping. This was the one to watch. It would most likely stop and fall over. But there was a chance that it would get airborne - and then it would be flying like a ... bird (?).

All their awkwardness on the ground was transformed into grace in the air. But wait, the ground still had to be contended with, on landing. The thing to do was to keep an eye on a particular one of these 'first soloists' and watch out for its attempt to land. It was all there; the unsteady, uncertain approach - and overshoot. Try again - better approach, some nervousness at the end - overshoot. Round again! This time, awful approach, desperate last stage, catastrophic landing - head over heels, a blur of feathers and feet! But down. If you examine a Gooney Bird, it does have a very well developed breast bone that generations of such landings have evolved.

Whilst our aircraft was being fixed (a new propeller had to be flown in first), the days drifted by. We taught the US Navy how to play darts. One afternoon an invitation came for us to go along to one of the Officer's room for a 'sundowner'. This stretched our politeness to the limit as it had been noticed that this particular host had held a couple of evening Bible classes during our stay. Although feeling that we might be a captive congregation, we politely trooped along to the room. We sat in a mannerly circle.

'I hear you guys like Dry Martinis,' says the 'God-Botherer', producing an enormous bottle of gin, ice and dry martini. Into a jug goes all the gin.

'I make them really dry, only two fingers of dry martini!' Ice is added, 'and only two stirs'.

The glasses are filled and we sit genteelly until everyone has one.

'Here's to you Brits.'

'Cheers,' say we and sip. Further conversation was difficult for a while, with our cheeks and lips locked against our teeth. The pain subsided - glasses refilled - no pain at all! The RC Padre popped in and rapidly diminished our lead on the number of glasses. He had been a noticeable character on the beach, sunbathing all day, wearing a rather stylish straw hat. I commented on the hat - he admired my Britannia tie (in true British style we were with tie and long sleeved shirt) - a swap was agreed. I gave him my tie - I never did get the hat. The chances of my conversion to Roman Catholicism had been slight before all this - now they were reduced to zero.

Long stops like this tend to heighten any tensions in a crew and some outspokenness can occur. I was the humble copilot and I don't think the captain was too impressed with my sociability. Perhaps my feelings about him showed. The outcome of this, one evening, was the statement that, when we did get going, I would do everything as if I was the captain - 'that should teach me!' When we eventually set off, it was a very glum and silent occupant of the left-hand seat. And he sat there and sat there. Eventually I had to break the 'sound' barrier and say that I needed to go down the back to answer 'a call of nature' - euphemisms still live on!

'You'll have to wait - I'm dying to go myself - but I was waiting for you to say I could!'

There were some funny, obtuse, over-inflated captains around in those days.

After musing on such esoteric travels, it is time to return to more of the 'run of the mill' stuff.

Chapter 18
Oil on Troubled Waters

News of home life has been a bit thin but this is not a reflection on its lack of importance in my life. Even though I enjoyed myself whilst away, it was always with a heavy heart that I contemplated another separation - but there were those homecomings!

There was a significant happening on the 'Home Front' - we bought our own house. The word 'bought' is used loosely; how loose can you get when the deal has been completed with a 100% mortgage? In the previous year there had been a lot of talk amongst my contemporaries about the feasibility - and good sense - of house purchase. This was something virtually unknown in past years. Postings every two to three years, the (eventual) availability of a married quarter and our impecunious state, they all militated against home ownership - it was something that did not cross people's minds. But some of my entrepreneurial compatriots began to think differently.

Our postings were getting longer - we pilots, at least, with a copilot tour followed by a captain's, were looking at six years. Specialisation was being recognised so there was a strong possibility that we would go to another air transport slot and many of them were not a million miles away from Lyneham. Set against having one's own place, the appeal of a married quarter was dimmed. Money? If the right deal could be struck - and there were a number of brokers prepared to sort something out for you - then, with the aforementioned 100% arrangement and repayments equal to married quarter rent, it did seem sensible to 'have a go'. If the postings thing didn't work out then one could sell and perhaps have something in the pocket - which is more than can be said for the married quarter rent paying scenario.

I sound convinced - and that was the way the conversations were going. So we went for it - not immediately - we blew hot and cold. We cancelled the first place we went for - an estate house, which was the standard fare to fall within the economics of married quarter (MQ) versus buying. That was it.

'We'll stick with the MQ - you would never get a house as good as this - the kids can play outside without traffic worries and ...'

But it still niggled at us and we were, subconsciously, still 'looking'. It was on a drive, 'We'll just take a look at those houses at Corston ...', that we passed a 'For Sale' bungalow in a small 'hamlet' that went by the name of Startley. On the way back we stopped and had a peer through the windows.

'It's got tiled floors!'

This was an important consideration; it meant that we would not have to buy carpets, straight away. It stood in a third of an acre - generous. The only snag was that it was £1000 more than that 'sensible' estate house buy. The next day we contacted the builder, who was selling the property. As he showed us around, we became more and more convinced - in fact, we couldn't resist, to the point of leaping in with both feet.

'We'll have it!'

Sensibly, he said, 'Well I should go home and sleep on it, if I were you.'

But I was back the next day, just in case someone else slipped in and snapped it up! As I write, I sit in that very house, much extended and improved, 35 years later!

The first couple of years were crippling. I have told a tale of how brown paper carrier bags featured in our first house move. A family groan goes up when I refer to it. A moan of equal intensity greets my repetition of the fact, in our new abode, I used to get into bed with my socks strategically positioned so that, in the morning, I could step on to them instead of the cold tiled floor!

My developing woodworking and DIY skills were much in demand - when we could afford the materials. I made an armchair and settee to match the rocking chair. The kitchen was 'unfitted' so, eventually, units were built to replace the tea chests! My small shed 'workshop' had been part of our removal load.

Alison and the front garden digging stage.

Horticultural skills were required. Fortunately the original pasture grass on the large area to the rear of the house had been preserved; the front was a builder's tip. A lot of effort was required to get this to the grass seed sowing stage. I associate one little story with this activity.

Whilst engaged in digging, raking, de-stoning, whatever, Alison, now aged three or so, comes rushing from the front of the house.

'There's a worm with a face on it!!'

By the time we investigated, the grass snake had disappeared - at least, I hope it was a grass snake and not an adder!

What of the pattern of pregnancy being associated with moving? Well, we must have had that cracked - we had moved from Manby to Aldbourne and then from there into Married Quarters without issue. Perhaps that made us overconfident! Matthew (No.4) was born six months after our arrival in Startley. It might be that some of you may see some significance in the previously reported fact that we have not moved since - we needed to see out our potential child bearing years.

Flying life continued with unremitting North Africa, Aden,

Maldives and Singapore - that 'bread and butter' route to the Far East. There was the occasional respite - Cyprus, Malta, Bahrain, Norway, Germany. If all this reads as glamourous, then words, like appearances, can be deceptive. It was hard work - long hours at 'unsociable' times - with inhospitable climates. But there was fun!

One of the greatest things about Britannia transport flying was the camaraderie that built up within a crew. This had to happen anew with each route trip, for we did not have established crews. Each section on the squadron (pilots', navigators', engineers', signallers' and airquartermasters') would nominate individuals for a particular flight. It could be that, when the trip started, with the crew bus collection, you would be with five relative strangers; by the end, perhaps some weeks later, they could be five good friends.

This crew arrangement might seem strange to those raised on the constituted crew idea, which was the WWII way and the immediate years thereafter. It was very much the original transport aircraft style - a captain had the same crew members for every flight - but was dropped soon after the introduction of the Britannia because of the administration difficulties. It meant that, to work, the whole crew needed to take leave at the same time - and coincidentally be sick, go on courses - their wives have their babies - synchronised procreation is a bit difficult to organise. It was also deemed that the performance of such a crew could become sloppy ... a 'thumbs up' could be translated the wrong way!

In the early Britannia years there were many diehards and some of them longed for the return of the constituted crew. A particular squadron commander weakened slightly and agreed that members of the squadron would be tested for their reaction. This was done by putting a notice on the board. Across the top were all the captains' names and other crew members were invited to put their names beneath the captain with whom they would like to fly. After a few days the notice had to be taken down because Captains H, D and R had no names beneath their's. Others were over-subscribed!

The 'fresh crew for each flight' also overcame another problem. With set crews, there would be a steady trickle of visitors to the CO's office.

'I cannot go on flying with Flight Lieutenant So-and-so; he's always picking ...'

This problem might resolve itself with another complainant about another captain. The simple, if possibly temporary, solution was to do a swap. This meant that there were always several crews, at the bottom of the morale pile, who were in a constant state of flux. With flexi-crews, most people suffered their fellows' shortcomings, knowing that it would only be for that trip.

My time in the copilot's seat was adding up and the prospect of being 'converted' to a captain was getting closer. The scheme was very democratic - if you exclude the fact that unsuitable candidates were 'eased out' of the system. The remainder spent something between two and three years in the right hand seat whilst their names crept up the 'time served' list.

Eventually, I was next and my period of training duly followed. This was spread over three weeks with just ten flights. This was the average and proved the value of that, almost, sub-conscious training that had gone on during one's copilot time. The ten flights were all 'local' flying: circuits and landings, instrument approaches and the like. On completion, this was tested and then you were almost ready to go - the final touch was a 'route check' with you in the left hand seat. It will perhaps only be the experienced hands who will appreciate the really outrageous thing that happened to me at this stage. My first route trip was programmed; the intended route checker rings me.

'Dave, I've got something on on Wednesday - so I can't do your check on the way to Cyprus ... but I'll see you out there and check you on the next leg.'

In later years, this route checker would have been hung by his toe nails from the flagpole outside the guard room - with me alongside, for my, albeit innocent, part. It meant that I flew the aircraft, with passengers, without a full category.

With the route check satisfactorily completed, I continued on my first 'solo' route - not one unknown to me - to Singapore and back! Now was the time to put into practice my interpretation of how an aircraft should be captained.

This would be a distillation of what I had seen of the ways of the many captains with whom I had flown; but the overriding influence was going to be one's own personality. Mine is not the most thrusting sort but it seemed that people were happy with my modest ways and I think I led happy crews. There did develop some notoriety about my 'social drinking' habits.

'Don't go on route with Dave Berry, you'll end up with a hangover to last you a fortnight!'

I have mused that the utterers of such statements really needed a peg on which to hang their own consciences!

With my style of leadership, there would be the odd occasion when someone would, well and truly, step out of line which would stir even quiet old me into action. I wished I had handled such situations with the aplomb of a young captain; I heard the story in later years. He was in the situation of leading men much older than himself. One day something arose and the captain starts giving instructions to sort out the problem when the airquartermaster launches into a five minute diatribe as to what should be their course of action. The young captain listens patiently and at the conclusion of the advice he pauses.

'Let's start this conversation again ... this time, you pretend that you're the airquartermaster and I'll pretend to be the captain!'

The months went by along the well trodden Middle and Far East tracks; perhaps not a bad thing, as confidence and experience grew in the new role.

December 1965 loomed and thoughts start turning to Christmas ... but the Rhodesian Prime Minister's thoughts had turned to declaring his country unilaterally independent. This upset the United Nations who had been insisting on racial equality before the country could be independent of the Commonwealth. This was not to the liking of Mr Ian Smith and the majority of his fellow white Rhodesians ... so he decided not to play any more - and go off with his 'bat and ball'! Not unnaturally, this further upset the UN and trade sanctions were imposed.

An unintended effect of this was to close off the normal oil supply routes to neighbouring, land-locked, Zambia. This would not do - a solution had to be found. Perhaps oil could be flown in?

Over the years, I developed a theory concerning the standby situations to which we were subjected. My imaginary scenario goes something like this:

No.10 Downing Street - The Cabinet Room: 'If something comes of Chief Okonobo's nose bleed, then it might be a good idea to have an aircraft standing by to fly out a few troops.'

Air Ministry (later MOD): 'The PM thinks that we might have a standby situation. A couple of Britannias would be the answer. Just warn Transport Command of the possibility.'

HQ Transport Command: 'The word is that there is trouble in Imbyjimbyland - there might be an air lift. Tell Lyneham to put eight aircraft on 12 hour standby.'

Lyneham Operations: 'Eng Wing - we need 16 aircraft ready to go ... 99 and 511, get 30 crews on four hour standby.'

Well, I am sure the essence of this is true. It would explain how, to cover the possibility of having to start to fly oil to Zambia, six crews and three aircraft flew out to Nairobi on 4 December to be followed by nine days of virtual inactivity. The only thing that changed was the degree of our standby. Little news filtered through to us. I swear that an expression originated from that situation which, over the years, has received more widespread application. I can picture the nav who said it, his voice muffled by his slouch in an armchair.

'We're just like bloody mushrooms ... kept in the dark and fed on horse shit.'

The year's activity that was to follow was labelled 'Mushroom Airways'.

Christmas was now getting closer and there we were stuck in the not too grand surroundings of The Spread Eagle Hotel - it was at this establishment that a naive officer placed his shoes outside his balcony room door, for cleaning. He was somewhat surprised to find that, in the morning, they had disappeared!

On Day 10, the word came: 'Return to Lyneham.' Thank God for that. It was now the 17th so all was well for the pre-Christmas preparations and celebrations ...

20 December ... 'Go back to East Africa - do not pass 'GO' - do not collect £200!'

'But it's nearly Christmas ...'

'Fly to Dar es Salam.'

And, so it was that six aircraft, 12 crews and 50 ground staff found themselves 'celebrating' the festive season in Tanzania. There must have been some legacy from my religious upbringing, now largely abandoned - on Christmas Day, I took my crew to church.

There was still some uncertainty about the 'Oil Lift' starting. Some international anxiety about the whole thing could be sensed by an instruction for us to fly in civilian clothes; that nervousness was confirmed by the order being rescinded after a short while. We waited in comfort; the newly emerging African nations were establishing their image by building status symbols. One of Tanzania's was The Hotel Kilimanjaro; we were the first customers of this five star! It was good practice for the inexperienced, locally recruited staff.

John Hunting

An 'Oil Lift' scene. The barrels are on board and some extra freight is being loaded.

The transporting of the oil started just before Christmas Day. It did seem that a pattern was established right from the start which endured for the whole ten months of the lift. Six aircraft would be loaded for an early start. These would fly the three hours or so to Lusaka or Ndola, off-load their oil drums in rapid time (20 minutes or less!) and then return with 'empties'. The aircraft would be reloaded for an afternoon departure with a fresh crew. The only change to that original pattern was that the East African launch point became Nairobi - another sign of political tension? The change came towards the end of our stint - we flew back home on 12 January - not a Christmas tree in sight!

I have to resist telling the whole story of the 'Oil Lift' - I have done that elsewhere - for it was quite a considerable achievement. It was hard work - but done in an agreeable environment. In those early days, this attracted the media's attention and a swimming pool picture was published in *The Daily Telegraph* of 4 January with the caption: 'High Life for Oil Lift Men'. This was too much for my 'flying widow', who wrote:

Dear Sir,

The Britannia captains and crews taking part in the airlift carry enormous responsibilities as well as coping with difficulties such as landing on a short runway at an airfield not really equipped to deal with aircraft of that size. For many of them it has meant spending Christmas and New Year away from their wives and families and whilst their accommodation might be costing the country an estimated £1,000 per day, the men's personal allowances are small.

Some are still away, waiting and wondering what they might be called upon to do next in the course of their duty. This time they are lucky; the waiting and wondering is being done in the sun with good accommodation. It is not always the case.

Yours truly   *Valerie Berry*

The message was so strong, they dare not publish it!

211

I was to return to Nairobi many times that year. There was a gap initially as 'The Country Club' realised that a spell in Kenya was available. But their interest waned when they discovered that it was hard work - an early or late flight each day for three weeks or more. In one 28 day period I exceeded the normal legal limit of 128 hours. The flights to Zambia did become incredibly routine; on the early morning sorties, in particular, one's brain could be on auto-pilot, as well as the aircraft. It was on just such a morning that we were an hour into the flight south. Whether the destination was Lusaka or Ndola, the initial couple of hours were over the same route. The conversation on the intercomm, to the airquartermaster (the 'Q'!) went something like this.

'Captain to Q?' 'Q here.' 'Brian ... is our load for Lusaka or Ndola?' 'Dunno - hang on Captain, I'll check the paperwork.'

Silence - a while later, a sheepish airquartermaster appears at my shoulder. 'I can't find anything that tells us!'

We did ask the oil drums but they had no idea either - so we took them to Lusaka. There was no comment, so we either guessed right or it was a matter of no consequence.

This chapter has seen my progression from copilot to captain - from the crew member who has to take the most stick to the one who 'should' be most respected! A story comes to mind of a copilot's landing at some staging post. The wind up starts as they are taxying to the aircraft apron.

'I thought that you were a bit low on that approach, Co,' is the comment from the engineer, who gradually whips up the general agreement of the rest of the crew. The copilot is puzzled - all seemed reasonable to him. In dispersal, everything shut down, the crew leave the aircraft - together. At the bottom of the steps they are greeted by the ground crew who seem somewhat agitated.

'Come and look at this!'

The crew are led to the nosewheel from which tree branches were poking. Later, during the wind down beer, the copilot is put out of his misery, being informed that he had been 'set up'. An 'arrangement' had been made with the ground crew for the nose wheel greenery when the crew had passed through on their outbound leg!

Chapter 19
Another Ground Job

An air transport squadron is atypical of RAF squadrons. Our tasks were away from base - often being the sole aircraft and crew in the area. So, not for us the '*gung-ho*' crewroom atmosphere with aircraft and crews coming and going, perhaps on an hourly basis, from outside the door. If we were in our crewroom then it meant that we were back at base - and back at base we were not doing our job.

This situation undoubtedly affected the first occupants of our, purpose-built, squadron accommodation. It has been reported that the entrance hall had a 'bus depot' atmosphere. Squadron Commanders change and 'new brooms sweep clean'. On the 99 scene arrived a particularly charismatic new leader; he too must have been struck by the lack of the right sort of character of the squadron premises. The chinagraph programme boards were banished to the 'back offices'. The DIY skills of squadron members were deployed. Flying Officer TG professed some ability with the plasterer's trowel. The squadron was covered in pink dust when a sander had to be subsequently employed to create a smooth finish. A board was constructed (by guess who?) listing the past COs. Framed, historical pictures appeared. The crewroom cum coffee bar was a rather meagre affair for the size of the squadron.

'We could knock a hole in the wall!', declares the Wing Commander.

In charge of the design was a captain with an artistic bent so the hole was not rectangular. When the, unconsulted, Air Ministry Works Department representative saw the finished result, he became very agitated muttering things about load bearing walls and other technical stuff. Things could not have been too serious as the building still stands to this day, housing one of Lyneham's Hercules squadrons.

With the atmosphere, back at base, that we were not 'working', there was the inclination, amongst most, not to hang around the squadron but to catch up on some 'home time'. This was accepted by the 'powers that be' providing, '... you have everything up-to-date.'

Books of orders had to be signed, once a month, as having been read - a particularly, meaningless, 'back covering' exercise. Flying log books needed completing; training records up-dated; headsets serviced; inoculations and vaccinations kept valid. Trying to get 150+ people, of varying degrees of self-discipline, to perform all these routine tasks was the continuing challenge of the executive element of the squadron. All manner of threats and coercion had to be used on the wayward before they departed, out of reach, to some distant part of the World.

A recurring demand for one's action was booking an appointment for 'The Annual Medical'. This was a tedious exercise for the examinee - I am sure it was equally trying for the examiners. The novelty of that cupping in the hand of testicles and saying, 'Cough please.' six times a day, must wear a bit thin after a while. In later years, my 'Senior Citizen' status prompted one Medical Officer to confide in me.

'See, on this form that we fill in - by each test item we put 'NAD'.' I noted the annotations.

'That's supposed to mean 'No Abnormality Detected' - more than likely, it stands for 'Not Actually Done'!'

One thing I find astonishing about the medicals of those years, when viewed with our present day awareness of the body damaging effects of heavy metals, is the 'Blowing Up the Mercury Test'. Metals don't come much heavier than mercury! From the rubber tube on his blood pressure machine, the doctor would remove the inflating bulb and instruct you to blow into the pipe to keep the mercury in the glass U-tube at 70, say. One was given the impression that if this could not be maintained for a set time, then this was a 'Fail'. In fact, it was just a convenient way of making the test candidate exert himself. I forget what was tested during this exercise; it must have been pulse - blood pressure would have been difficult!

In October 1966 there was trouble in Guyana. It did seem that the Britannia was attracted to the poorer countries, with little to offer the traveller. Around 9pm, we arrived at an airfield called Atkinson with our complement of soldiers. With the aircraft 'wrapped up' for the night, it was time for us to be taken to our hotel. This turned out to be an inappropriate name for the establishment at which we were deposited. Admittedly it was hot but we would have liked the option of covering ourselves when in bed. The management had decided that a bottom sheet was all that was required. Similarly it was thought that, with the dark nights, there was no need for curtains. I stood in the shower and made the mistake of looking up at the shower head which was lurking in the exposed overhead woodwork. When I saw the frayed electricity cables disappearing into it, I decided I could go dirty. Breakfast was a ghastly sight; the canteen of cutlery was plastic - and not a full set at that! Oh, the joys and magic of international military air travel!

The end of the 'Oil Lift' was in sight and I managed to be squeezed into one final trip to Nairobi and brought out the last aircraft with all the detachment personnel on board.

With East African adventures over, it meant the re-establishment of the Changi Slip routine. I note that I was on the aircraft departing Lyneham on 27 December to reposition the slip crews. At least, for this Christmas, I was at home for the day - and Boxing Day!

A couple of months later there was a nasty shock for the Berry household. A feature of Service life of those years was the 'unaccompanied tour'. Many overseas bases were not equipped for accommodating families - or perhaps it was undesirable, for military reasons, for them to be present. The island of Gan has been mentioned a number of times. It was manned by the unaccompanied for logistic reasons. Labuan, an island off the northwest coast of Borneo, was 'men only' for strategic reasons - it was 'Confrontation' time in the Far East. Out of the blue, with barely two years' captain time completed, I was told that I was posted to the latter for the standard period of one year.

As much as the 'unaccompanied tour' was a feature, so was the squirming out of it. Wives suddenly had nervous breakdowns, children developed serious disabilities; much ingenuity was used. We had witnessed the result of this - the poor sucker, last in the line, had little time to dream up an excuse and also was short of opportunity to sort out his affairs. Val and I had resolved that if the finger should point at us we would take it like a man - and a woman. Now was our chance to prove this. With the weeks remaining there were priorities. One of the major ones was to protect our 'investment'. If I was to be away for a year then the outside of the house needed paint.

Engaged in the mind numbing exercise of painting windows, I had plenty of time to think. I had found three weeks away from home emotionally painful ... how was I going to cope with a year? Think ... paint ... think ... paint ... 'Bugger, it's gone on the glass.' Val calls me.

'Bob Henderson is on the phone.'

'Hello Bob'

'Dave - you've probably heard that I'm posted to Upavon as an Ops Controller ...' The word had reached me. 'How do you fancy doing a swap?'

Can I believe my ears? I try to calm my response - obviously without much success for Bob to suggest that we immediately ask to see the squadron CO and test him on the idea. I think I did the trip from Startley to Lyneham in record time. The outcome? Bob went off to Labuan - which suited his purposes; I reported to the Transport Command Operations Centre on 1 May to start 2fi years as an Operations Controller.

Bob Henderson was another stalwart of the Specialist Aircrew contingent. Canadian born - Vancouver - Bob had joined the Royal Air Force after doing his time in the RCAF on a short service commission. We virtually arrived on the Britannia fleet together.

With the favour outlined above, it is perhaps not unnatural that we have been firm friends ever since. The basis of this was the five years we had already served on 99 together. In that time, Bob had been awarded the Air Force Cross for his part in the Oil Lift. He flew the most hours and spent the longest time on the detachments.

Bob arrived at Labuan to be greeted by the Squadron Leader Operations.

'We did think about cancelling your posting - we're closing the unit soon.'

I think that if that had been my welcome, after what would have been a stressful departure from home, then there might have been an instance of a superior officer being given a punch on the nose by a junior one.

The unit did close and Bob floated around the Far East for a few months, eventually returning to the UK convinced that he had served his ground tour time. He was a fanatical flier and part of his plot, when doing the posting swap, was that he would only be on the ground for a year. But the 'posters' weren't going to let him off the hook. He was sent to Brize Norton Operations. He escaped when he had done his 2fi years - total.

This was back to the Britannias, which were at Brize Norton, by this time. He progressed to becoming an OCU instructor. In time he went to the VC10s - moving through their hierarchy - and it was OCU instructor, again. His final move was to TriStars - and you can guess that he ended up as a Training Captain.

All this added up to him spending 26 years at Brize Norton! It also added up to his total flying hours, at the end of his service, being over 18,000! This is a record for a RAF pilot. This is REAL Specialist Aircrew!

To return to the ground and Upavon - I needed no sop to cheerfully accept this posting - but one was given. There had been a tendency for operations rooms, like simulators, to be staffed by the sick, lame and weary; but things were going to be different at Upavon. HQ Transport Command intended to exercise closer control over its fleet, one that was, at any time, scattered all over the World. To do this, more sophisticated communication and control methods were to be introduced and, dare one say, more sophisticated operations controllers! Well, at least, controllers who had current captaincy experience.

I was eagerly trained up by the guy I was replacing - well he would, wouldn't he? In what seemed a very short time, I found myself at the helm; this was a strange tiller with many other, more senior, hands influencing it between the hours of eight and five, Monday to Friday. Outside these times they were, sensibly, at home and humble Flight Lieutenant You was in charge.

Time zones of the World - or international affairs - have no respect for the normal UK working week. When Singapore, and in particular RAF Changi, is deciding, at 8.30am, how to play the rest of their day, it is 1am in TCOC (Transport Command Operations Centre). Signals would arrive for approval of plans; do not think that there was a message delay time - we had a permanently open teleprinter link with all the major staging posts. Also they, like the aircraft and Upavon itself, were equipped with the relatively new and extremely long range, Single Side Band (SSB) voice radio.

Part of the revolution in 'Control' was HQ Transport Command being registered as an airline operator (callsign ASCOT) and, with payment, being able to use the, computer controlled, virtually instantaneous, civil airlines communications system. Joining this had been a battle between the *avante-garde* and the die-hards.

'What happens when we are at war?'

'Is that a real reason for denying ourselves good communications and control for 99.9% of the time?'

Another element of control introduced at this stage was

'Flow'. Mention 'Flow Control' to one of the guys 'down the route', at the time, and you would stand a good chance of getting a poke in the eye. Imagine his situation where he has been unserviceable - and now the snag, with a big effort all round, has been fixed.

'We're ready to go,' Bloggs tells Upavon.

'Standby,' is the reply, followed by, 'Make your departure time 0300 hours.'

This is several hours hence - how can this be true?!! What everyone has slowly realised, well nearly everyone - Bloggs, down the route, has clearly not been looking about - was that we were now operating a very large fleet of long range transport aircraft: 23 Britannias, 14 VC10s, 5 Comet 4s, 10 Belfasts, the strategic transport share of the 60+ Hercules and the odd Argosy and Andover thrown in. Many of these aircraft would be operating up and down the prime route - to and from Singapore.

We had some wonderful ground crew but coping, at the same time, with a full passenger-loaded VC10, a Britannia and a Hercules, all on a 1fi hour refuel and fault fixing turnround could provide too much of a challenge. At the planning stage of the flights, some weeks, if not a couple of months before, such clashes would be avoided. This involved a special planning staff using a lot of graph paper, pencils and erasers. But, come the actual events, all this effort could be 'turned to worms' by an aircraft going unserviceable and then being injected, when ready to go again, back into the system without any thought as to those possible clashes.

It was initially declared that the Duty Ops Controller would get the graph paper, pencils and erasers out and redo the plan. This meant he was trying to repeat a process, singlehanded, that was previously carried out by a team ... and under pressure, time-wise. The impossibility was realised and a 'Flow Cell' was established with its own 24 hour controller coverage. Also, some clever bugger built

what amounted to a wooden analogue computer to replace the graph paper activity. These were heady control days, justified by the fact that we were handling a very large fleet of aircraft.

With our shift system we worked long hours for four days/nights but with a healthy bit of time off in between, in order to recover. The nights and weekends could seem the longest with all the decision making and problem solving down to lonely old you. The power that one had and the facilities to dispense it were really pretty awesome.

* * * *

This occurred to me when I discovered (for my ears only) that I was going to be on duty the night that, in anticipation of our imminent withdrawal from Aden, all the currency, bullion etc from its bank vaults was going to be flown to the UK in a RAF Britannia. I had a number of days to think about this and realised that I had the power and the means of communication to order this aircraft to divert to an airfield of my choice and ... 'The Great Train Robbery' had been all the headlines some years before. This could be 'The Great Plane Robbery'.

The night of the flight was here. I climbed the stairs of the headquarters building to the operations centre with my mind in a turmoil - which I calmed by going over the plans that I had made in the preceding days.

Firstly, I would release as many as possible of the operations clerks; this would not be difficult - it was something always hoped for on the evening of a quiet night. Luckily the Corporal on duty, who would have to remain, was one of an unquestioning nature. When the aircraft was over France, destination Lyneham, I would pass a message to the captain that he was to divert to Fairford, a fully operational, but little used Gloucestershire airfield. He would be advised that:

'This is for last minute security reasons. Let London Radar bring you off the airway, as normal, but then become radio silent and fly to Fairford. Also, for security reasons, the airfield will be in darkness and you will have to land without runway lights. You will be met by, what appears to be, three commercial haulage lorries and a team of civilian unloaders. The SAS is at work! On completion of the off-load, you and your crew are to remain on board the aircraft until the morning. A team will be along then to congratulate you - if all goes well - and release you back to Lyneham. Is all this clearly understood - over.'

It had taken me a remarkably short time to alert the criminal fraternity to the potential of this heist. One of my early Service compatriots had been 'eased out' of the RAF for unapproved entrepreneurial activities. He had regularly sent me a 'Change of Address' card with the annotation: 'If there is ever anything I can do.' He must have been clairvoyant.

I took over from the day shift controller; he went through our standard litany, going over the flights displayed on the boards with details of their latest position; any difficulties; any 'special requirements' from the HQ staff for the night. He didn't mention the Aden operation ... it was strictly 'need to know'. I knew - he didn't. With him and his team departed, we, the night shift, settled down for our vigil: coffee ... correct the perceived mistakes of our predecessors ... tidy the files and various bits of paper to our liking ... act on the latest information on the teleprinters ... and some which the outgoing shift had been slow to clear ... more coffee.

'I think it's going to be a quiet night - me and Corporal Bloggs will look after things for a few hours - eh, before you rush off ... one word ... keep the noise down on your way back from the NAAFI!'

Things were working to plan ... I already knew, from the day shift, that the aircraft, callsign Ascot 6534, had departed Aden on time and had completed its refuel in Cyprus. It would now be coming up the west coast of Italy. I went into our SSB radio room.

'Evening Eddie - all OK? Give Ascot 6534 a test call.'

'OK Sir,'

'Ascot 6534, Ascot 6534, this is Upavon, Upavon on nines upper, do you read, over.'

Magic - back came the reply.

'Upavon, Upavon, this is Ascot 6534 ... reading you loud and clear. Request selcal check Charlie Delta Alpha Mike.'

'Roger 6534 ... Charlie Delta Alpha Mike coming up.'

The chimes of that aircraft's unique calling code go out.

'Upavon, 6534, selcal received OK, maintaining selcal watch.'

My hand signals indicate to the radio operator that we have more to say.

'6534, standby for a further message.'

'6534 standing by.'

I scribble on a note pad: 'We will call you again when you pass Nice. For security reasons, this will be on frequency 7453.'

The message goes to the aircraft ... I return to the Ops Room and Corporal Bloggs.

'A Mr Al Capone - funny sounding geezer - has been on the line - says that everything is set.'

*   *   *   *

I must stop this fantasising! Please excuse this lapse from a life's true narrative. Actually, amongst the lies above, there is one more. The Corporal was not Bloggs but a very attractive WRAF lady of that rank ... blonde ... very ..... That night, when the rest of the team had gone to the NAAFI, Corporal Jane and I retired to the office of the Squadron Leader Ops and ...

There I go - lying again. It was a quiet night. 6534 landed safely at Lyneham; I drove home to my lonely daytime bed - and more fantasies!

Amongst the above nonsense, there is a picture of life in the Ops Centre. The constant challenge was to keep an up-to-date picture of the location of each aircraft. By each captain advising us of with his time of arrival, a communications link would be established - not always a straightforward matter at some of the remoter airfields in strange parts of the World. If there was a change to our plans then the captain could be instructed. It might be that the aircraft was unserviceable ... it was down to us to initiate the provision of the necessary spares and, possibly, extra technical help. Emergencies could arise - a seriously ill Army wife in some remote garrison - a local uprising by some dissidents - you would be the first link in the chain of reaction and then would play a part in its implementation.

Part of the team for all this were the operations clerks - airmen and airwomen drawn from the Air Traffic Control branch. A feature of commissioned aircrew life is that one is rather isolated from 'The Men'. This is not by choice but circumstance; squadrons no longer had their own technicians - servicing was centralised. There were the administrators, air traffic control, catering, medical - but the contacts were fleeting, more so with our periods away from base. So, an interesting part of life at Upavon was the closer association with a group of 'The Men' - and Women. The realisation did come that we were missing out on a lot by not having closer links and that morale could possibly be improved with better acquaintance.

It was interesting to build up a picture of individuals from the

223

guarded conversations in one's presence: the tearaway, the womaniser, the surprising hobbies and interests. One Corporal intrigued me - extremely studious, serious and well spoken, he seemed completely out of place. Half the complement were female - tall, short, fat, thin, good looking, ugly. There was one young lady who had a pretty enough face and manner but was rather large. It used to intrigue me to be aware that, in the quiet hours, she would be earnestly engaged in telephone conversation with some equally bored young man in an air traffic tower somewhere. The conversations seemed to be pretty 'hot'! I would wonder at the young man's reaction if they ever met.

We had an ever increasing array of equipment to help us with our task. The whole of one wall was covered in a perforated plastic board. Into the holes could be pressed letters; thus details of every flight were displayed, with their latest position. Teleprinters clattered away beneath, only partially effective, soundproof, transparent covers. An air delivery tube connected to the communications centre on the ground floor ... message containers would regularly thump into the delivery box. Loudspeaker phones were a novelty, as was the link to the Meteorological Office. Apart from a CCTV, there was a device where the forecaster wrote on a pad using a special pen, the movements of which were slaved to a pen and pad in the Ops Centre. Rather weird to watch ...

> '*The moving finger writes; and, having writ,*
> *Moves on: nor all thy piety nor wit*
> *Shall lure it back to cancel half a line,*
> *Nor all thy tears wash out a word of it.*'
>
> Omar Khayyám

... thought that these pages were a bit short on culture!

On one pretty average morning, all the above equipment in full swing, phones ringing, the clerks updating the boards, outgoing signals being written, incoming ones being actioned and filed in flight folders, someone noticed that they could not dial any extension number that contained a nine. Others checked this out and found it to be true. Then the Met Office CCTV screen went blank; one by one a red failure light came up on each teleprinter ... some stopped in the middle of receiving a signal. All the phones were now 'down' ... and finally, the 'moving finger' became motionless. The Ops Centre had died. A panic investigation discovered the cause. A workman, engaged in the construction of an extension to the headquarters, had sawn through what he thought was an obsolete cable. The one by one failures had occurred as his hacksaw blade severed the strands. Panic investigation was followed by panic repair.

Pilots do not like doing 'ground tours' but if you have to do one then this Ops job was very satisfying - and it, sure as hell, beat being on my own in Labuan!

I am quite proud of the fact that my service was rewarded in two ways. Firstly I received a MoD (financial) Award to Inventors - yes, I was the 'clever bugger' employing my woodwork skills to construct the 'wooden computer'! I also received the Commander-in-Chief's Commendation for 'Meritorious Service' - cor!!

I did not exhaust my craft enthusiasms with the computer construction. I now had a woodworking machine which sped up production; the controlling influence was finance for materials. One Sunday I

It does look rather as if I am presenting something to the gentleman in the grey suit. In fact, it is the C-in-C, Air Chief Marshal Sir Andrew Humphrey giving me my commendation certificate.

225

My own design and manufacture of a cart cum baby walker.

saw an article in '*The Sunday Times*': two brothers, who had been in advertising and tired of it, decided on a new venture. As fathers of young children, they were disappointed with the quality and style of the toys available - 'Lot of garish plastic ... no traditional use of wood ... no character ...' They decided to set up their own business in Bath, '... and we will get local craftsmen to make the toys for us.'

I wrote to them.

'I could be one of the 'local craftsmen' you need. Can I show you a couple of toys I have made?'

There was an enthusiastic response and I went to their Bath shop with a wooden trike and a large sit-on train that I had constructed for my own children. They looked interested. In a short time there was a reaction.

'We'll have a dozen of the trikes and six trains.'

I tried not to look completely gob-smacked! I was used to 'one at a time' manufacture. I started developing a lot of production

The workshop - it kept me off the streets!

line techniques and investing in more power machinery to keep up with the pattern that followed where I would deliver one order and receive another. I fed in some more samples and they had ideas that they wanted me to produce.

This went on for the last two years of my Ops Controller tour. It fitted in with this extremely well; I could reliably forecast the time I was to have free and this was generous because of the long hours which we worked when it was our duty spell. But there were signs of it getting out of control. One Sunday I opened the pages of '*The Observer*'. On a 'What to Buy for Christmas' page was a pen and ink drawing of one of my wooden scooters. I knew that the shop only had half a dozen of these. Sure enough the call came, 'Make more - fast!' Valerie became very skilful at varnishing and some of the assembly!

The death knell of this business enterprise was another Upavon 'reward' ... the welcome news was that I was to return to the Britannia fleet - and my old squadron - No.99. Making two dozen wooden scooters was not going to fit in with the uncertain and 'away from home' life of a route flier. There were no regrets; it had been a good experience and I had built up an excellent workshop. I had also learnt that I was no businessman!

Any ideas on what to do with £1 million worth of Aden dinars?

Chapter 20
Back to Britannias

The start of 1970 found me cheerfully back in the left hand seat of a Britannia, at Lyneham, undergoing what was called 'Retread Training'. It was to be hoped that using this term, borrowed from the car tyre trade, was not a reflection on our perceived subsequent reliability. Twenty two hours of flying, which included a route trip to Malta and return, saw me considered 'retreaded' to sufficient quality to return to 99 Squadron. My first trip? Well, not a full Changi Slip, but half way there and return - and I was pleased to be back, doing just that.

It might be considered that my recent Britannia experience was pretty humble ... but on my next trip I had royalty on board. We were due to fly an aircraft out of Cyprus to Lyneham. When reporting to Akrotiri Ops, the word was:

'Your passengers are all Army - they've been on exercise here. Perhaps you should know that the Major in charge is HRH The Duke of Kent ... but he wants to be treated as a normal passenger.'

Well, that made life easy.

Off we set from Akrotiri, westwards over the various Greek islands: Rodos, Milos, Araxos, turning north west at Caraffa, on the toe of Italy to fly up its the west coast, then heading for Nice. As was routine, we were listening to the hourly broadcasts of the latest weather at the UK airfields. Lyneham was fine but when we were passed the latest forecast, things did not look good; early morning fog was due to creep over the Lyneham Bank and sit over the airfield. We started making plans for a possible diversion airfield. At this stage, I decided that HRH could not be treated 'as a normal passenger'. Hat on, I retired to the passenger cabin.

'It does look, Sir, as if we might not be able to land at Lyneham ... Manchester looks like a strong bet. Is there anyone you would like us to inform?'

It seemed not, he was quite happy to continue 'as a normal passenger'. As we approached the Channel, the Met Men continued with their threat of fog at any moment, although the current visibility was good. We passed over London, turning west for Wiltshire and reducing height. Swindon came into sight and there, eight miles to the west, was the Lyneham runway, loud and clear. This was the way of things - more often than not.

As we settled on the final approach, I happened to glance over my shoulder and there was His Royal Highness, standing in the doorway, with a headset on, listening to all that was going on. The airquartermaster had thought it would be a good idea, '... to keep him in the picture.' I pointed out to this young man, later, that it would have also have been a good idea to have let us know what was happening. There could have been a lot of inappropriate flight deck banter - not an uncommon practice - perhaps on the topic of the reuniting of our 'normal passenger' and Her Royal Highness. Such reunion matters always weighed heavily on our minds for those last few hours before homecoming!

I have alluded to the 'new mix', crew-wise, with which one started each trip. This could produce interest, amusement, tension, irritation. It would put a newcomer to test as he demonstrated his abilities, both professional and social, to a critical audience - and also adjusted himself to all his new compatriots. For a trip to Cyprus, this April, my navigator was a recently arrived flight commander. These people had a double burden - settling in as a proficient crew member and establishing themselves in their executive role. My Squadron Leader navigator was trying very hard in all directions.

We had hired Akrotiri's recreational mini-bus for a tour of the island. Lunch at the Paphos harbour-side, with its pelican, was a starting point. Moving on, we spotted a motor club hill climb competition and decided to view it from the terrace of a convenient tavern. The navigator had done a tour in Cyprus and there had been several occasions already where, for our benefit, he had aired his local knowledge. Now the recommendation was:

'Try Ouzo - it's the Cyprus version of Pernod - yeh, goes cloudy when you add water ... I'll get them!'

The wizened, clad in black, landlady approaches.

'Six Ouzos, please.'

There is a look of disbelief on the old woman's face:

'Seecks?!!'

Navigator waves six fingers in the air and adopts the traditional English course of action when a foreigner doesn't understand ... say the same thing again ... but louder:

'SIX OUZOS, PLEASE.'

The landlady shrugs her shoulders and shuffles off. We settle on the terrace chairs. The old lady reappears with a tray holding six glasses, a jug of water and six BOTTLES of Ouzo. With a fixed grin, the navigator had to put on the appearance of 'that is what he had meant'. It now fell to us to back that by getting on and consuming same!

It has to be admitted that the bottles were only 35cl size but the contents were sufficient to upset the judgement of my crew; the engineer persuaded a local to lend him his rather decrepit looking horse to ride around the village square; the copilot fell in love with a Cypriot lady almost as old as the provider of our libation; our lady airquartermaster managed to lock herself in the toilet. I've never fancied that aniseed flavoured drink since.

It did seem as if we spent half our lives in Cyprus. If you were *en route* for Bahrain, Gan, Singapore, Hong Kong, a westbound global trip, Nairobi, Australia - in fact, all points west, then in this era, the first stop was Akrotiri. Cyprus itself generated flights with the large military presence on the island requiring support - and it was used as an exercise area. So, a trip to Akrotiri was a very familiar one and one that could be flown in an autonomic way. From

Lyneham, the routing over London, down over France, the west coast of Italy and then over the Greek Islands was always the same. Leaving Athens control, the handover was to Nicosia Centre:

'Nicosia Centre, this is Ascot 6543 on handover from Athene, at flight level 230.'

'Ascot 6543, Nicosia, roger. You are clear to descend to flight level 130,'

'Nicosia, 6543, leaving 230 for 130.'

The height lock on the autopilot disengaged and the pitch control switch lowered the nose slightly. The speed increased from the 240 knots, cruising, to the maximum permitted of 258 knots. At that speed the airspeed lock engaged. The outboard throttles moved to the back stop, followed by the inboards. The needle on the altimeter wound rapidly, anticlockwise, as the height decreased.

'Nicosia, Ascot 6543, passing 150 for 130.'

'Roger 6543, contact Akrotiri Approach on two three fife decimal three. Good day, Sir,'

'6543, Good day,'

The frequency dial on the UHF set clicked around to the pre-selected frequency for Approach. The UHF buttons on the communications boxes at crew members stationed popped in. The autopilot airspeed lock went in and the pitch control switch flicked back in blips to level the aircraft. On reaching flight level 130, the height lock came out and, as the speed dropped, the throttles moved forward to give sufficient power to maintain 200 knots.

'Akrotiri Approach this is Ascot 6543, level flight level 130. Request further descent.'

'Ascot 6543, Akrotiri, you're loud and clear, continue descent to two thousand feet, QFE one zero one zero.'

'Roger, 6543 re-cleared to two thousand, one zero one zero is set, leaving 130.'

The height knob lock clicks in, twists through 180° and comes out to engage the airspeed lock. In pairs, the throttles come back to 'Flight Idle'. On the Tacan, the range from Akrotiri clicks down. It is a mid-summer night, clear, but with the lights on the ground shimmering in the remains of the daytime heat. From a range of ten miles, it is the lights of Akrotiri that are flickering in the distance.

'Akrotiri Approach, 6543, airfield in sight, request join downwind for a visual circuit.'

'6543, clear join, call Tower on two three two decimal one.'

The aircraft is now passing 2000 feet and once again the airspeed/height lock clicks in and the pitch control blips back to slow the rate of descent. The airspeed is allowed to decay.

'Akrotiri Tower, Ascot 6543 is downwind to land.'

'Roger 6543, call turning finals, the wind two nina zero at fife knots.'

Time for the auto-pilot to disengage. A perfect night, made more so with a gentle wind right down the runway. Approaching 1000 feet, there is a whine as the flaps run to the 15° position. The throttles advance to give 250lbs torque. The speed stabilises at 160 knots as the aircraft gently banks to the left to take up the downwind heading of 110°.

There is an increase in the roar from the airflow noise as the undercarriage starts to lower; two powerful clunks and one lesser one signal that the main and nose wheels are down and locked. The three undercarriage indicator lights have gone from off to shine red then green to indicate this. A little more power is needed to maintain 150 knots. Opposite the upwind of the runway the aircraft banks to the left and the nose drops. The throttles come back to give 200lbs of torque. There is that whine once more as the flaps move to the 30° position. The speed falls off to 140 knots.

'Tower, 6543 is turning finals with three greens to land.'

'6543 is clear to land, wind still two nina zero at fife knots.'

'6543.'

The turn continues; bank is adjusted as the runway comes into sight ahead. Two beams of light appear below the wing and rotate upwards to shine ahead; the landing lamp switch had moved to the 'on' position. The power setting is spot on; the angle of approach indicators on either side of the runway show green/red - also spot on. At 400 feet the speed is 130 knots; the whine again as the flaps lower to 45°. The nose has to be lowered to prevent the speed falling too low; it settles at 120 knots, 5 knots above the threshold speed - once again, spot on. The trim wheels are rotating forward to adjust for the lowering of full flap.

The approach lights are now glaring up on the underside of the aircraft and the red lights marking the runway threshold are crossed. The ground looms but the control column moves back to hold the aircraft level just above the ground; the throttles retract to the flight idle position. As the speed falls off, the control column comes back and back and then the main wheels kiss the runway surface. (This didn't always happen with a Britannia landing!)

The noise level increases with the rumble of the tyres; the control column moves gently forward to place the nose wheel on the ground. There is a sound of a hammer blow - that is 'Superfine' being engaged. This reduces the angle of the propeller blades, below that used in flight, to allow the propellers to run fast enough, on the ground, to keep the alternators 'on line'.

A lever to the left of the throttles moves back and this lifts a plate behind the throttle levers which allows them to be further retarded - they move back an inch and there is an increase in engine/propeller noise. The propeller blade angle has been further reduced, to the point of being negative. This is the start of the slowing down, reverse power application. Before more reverse power is applied, four green lights confirm that the propellers are, indeed, in reverse pitch. There is a much bigger roar as the throttles move back even further applying more engine power to the reversed propellers. There is a mark deceleration of the aircraft speed.

The foot brakes on the rudder pedals depress and the slight jerk on the aircraft confirms that the brakes are working. With that, the throttles move forward to the position they were in for the touchdown. This will now give 'ground idle' power from the engines.

A lever to the right of the throttles moves rearwards and five red lights illuminate on the centre of the instrument panel coaming - the controls are locked. And, once more there is the distinctive noise of the flap motors as the flaps are raised, fully up. The aircraft trundles to the end of the runway and turns left. The intensity of the landing lights is reduced as the landing lamp switch moves to the taxy lamp position. The taxyway curves round to the left and then there is a sharp right turn into the parking area.

Ahead the illuminated wands of the ground marshaller beckon. The taxy lamp switch goes to off. As the aircraft reaches the required spot. The marshaller crosses his wands over his head. The brakes go fully on and the parking brake lever clicks on its ratchet.

Switches now move rapidly; there is a clunk as the superfine switch moves; the four high pressure cock switches go to off; the engine noise immediately dies. As the rpm falls away, more switches move to close the low pressure fuel and the oil cocks. Brakes to the propellers go on and as they come to a standstill, the underside flashing red light extinguishes, indicating to the ground crew that it is safe to approach the aircraft. The noise outside is the ground power unit starting up. A green light on the electrical panel indicates that it is ready to supply current to the aircraft.

The Movements Staff, who will be attending to the load, push a set of steps to the rear door of the aircraft. Tradition dictates that they do not mount these yet. They wait for the airquartermaster to open the door, from inside the aircraft, and descend the steps to hand over the necessary paper work and brief the Movements Officer on the requirements.

With the engines stopped, aircraft exterior lights extinguished, the steps in position, the scene is calmer now - though the grinding of the ground power unit does not allow complete peace.

The 'movers' wait for the door to open ... it stays shut. They wait patiently. Minutes tick by ... something is clearly wrong. The officer leads the way up the steps and the door is opened from the outside. The ground team step into the aircraft ... no airquartermaster ... the passenger/freight cabin is deserted.

'He must be on the flight deck,' volunteers the officer.

He moves up the cabin, past the lashed down freight and opens the flight deck door. No one ... all five crew seats are empty. There is a double click to his right ... he looks down ... it is the electrical panel and he sees two switches rotating, unaided, from the 'Flight' position to 'Ground'.

It is the '*Marie Celeste*' revisited - the aircraft has flown to

Akrotiri so many times that, on this occasion, it has got there all by itself!

The Movements Officer rushes down the cabin and the steps and grabs the radio telephone in his Land Rover. He struggles to control his voice as he calls his superior, the Senior Air Movements Officer.

'6543 - just landed - taxied in - but there's no one on board!!'

'Well, there wouldn't be - the crew are up here in the Transit Lounge bar having their wind-down beers ...'

*   *   *   *

I didn't want this story to appear too ridiculous - a crew would never miss their relaxing beverages! Sorry about another 'Flight of Fancy' but, it is hoped that this bit of nonsense painted a picture of the latter part of a Britannia flight.

*   *   *   *

Was it Frank Sinatra who sang '*I left my heart in San Francisco*'? Perhaps it was Andy Williams - perhaps neither. One thing for sure, it is only Yours Truly who can claim:

'I left my appendix in Jamaica'!

With hindsight, I can identify that all was not well with my stomach system several weeks before I flew to that island in the sun. On our family holiday in Scotland - we had graduated from the tent to a caravan - I had felt queasy a couple of times. Must be the Scottish beer!

Off we went, taking a load of RN personnel to Kingston via Newfoundland and Bermuda. I was 'route checked' on the first leg. The rest of the itinerary seemed attractive to my route checker so he stayed on the aircraft as a passenger - jammy old life those instructor/examiners led! Passengers off-loaded, aircraft put to bed, we made our way to our hotel in downtown Kingston - and, as was our wont, sampled the local evening cultural scene.

In bed that night - well more often out of it than in it - my body suffered every form of ... I'll spare you the details.

Sitting on the edge of the bed, head in hands, eyes watering,

236

I muttered to myself:

'Dave, you really overdid it this time.'

The sun rose, the phone went:

'This is your early call, Sir.'

When I realised that I was having to hang on to the washbasin to shave, it did occur to me that I was actually ill - and not the self-inflicted sort. I rang the copilot; when he came to my room, just one look was enough to convince him that I needed a doctor. That afternoon I was on the operating table.

The aircraft? It flew off without me. How? Not another 'Marie Celeste' story! No, the route checker took my place. This he did, with some eagerness; the copilot had to restrain him from going off at the scheduled time before I had been sorted out. It was a whole 16 days before I followed, courtesy of Air Jamaica and RAF VC10.

Next month I was back in harness - on the Changi Slip! There was something different the month after - a States Trainer. A myth had been sustained, over the years, that flying in the USA was difficult and needed to be practised. This was not so, but the belief was supported, otherwise we would lose some good trips.

This one took us to Toronto, Chicago, and military bases in Washington State, California and North Carolina. Over the years, so far, I'd had a number of lesser trips to the States. Initially I was not won over to the USA way of life; but as I became more acquainted, then this all changed - changed to the extent that I am now a positive enthusiast about a lot of things Americana. This took a fairly positive form in later life.

Returning to this particular trip, like so many of our flights, it was completed in such a short time - five days - that memories are a blur - and tiredness limited full appreciation. I often say - and I have said it here, already - 'Been everywhere ... seen nothing!' So, my only real memory is of our arrival at Chicago O'Hare airport.

We were psyched up for this; it was the busiest airfield in the World and we had been briefed on the congested approach - radar controlled to parallel runways - one aircraft every minute - or something like that. No room for error and, 'Keep your speed up, Ascot.' What happens? We are on this busy approach, the runway is only a couple of miles away:

'Ascot aircraft - overshoot and do a visual circuit.'

This might seem like saying:

'Go and play in the paddling pool whilst these big boys use the high dive board.'

But I am sure that it wasn't like that. Perhaps the air traffic controller was under a bit of pressure. Which reminds me of a (true) story:

Scene: A new airport in a 'developing' country.

1st character: Royal Air Force Britannia signaller.

2nd character: ATC controller (of local origins).

Britannia signaller: 'Ascot 6543, turning finals, request clear to land.'

ATC controller: 'Ascot 6543, you are clear to land.'

Britannia signaller, now nearer the runway threshold:

'Tower, 6543, you have cleared me to land but there is an aircraft on the runway.'

ATC controller: 'Oh dear ... another day like yesterday.'

The old jokes are the best!

In my log book a Changi Slip in June 1970 reads **Lyneham** - Akrotiri - Muharraq - Gan - Changi - Gan - Muharraq - Akrotiri - **Brize Norton**. Brize Norton? Yes, we had moved!

It had been decided that Lyneham should be given over to the Hercules fleet and that the Britannias should share Brize Norton, near Witney in Oxfordshire, with the VC10s and Belfasts. It was appropriate that all the strategic transport aircraft were together. Did this mean that I had to pull up my Wiltshire roots? No! It seemed sensible for us to stay put in Startley; the journey to Brize was 'only' 40 miles. But I wasn't doing it every day.

One compelling reason for not moving was that Val was now a working woman. Whilst I was at Upavon, she completed a two year teachers' training course and she was now established as the reception class teacher in the large village school at Crudwell, north of Malmesbury. This meant a busy life - a full time job and four kids to look after, with me away, as often as not. She deserved the C-in-C's Commendation!

The year following our move to Brize Norton, the station was honoured with a visit by Her Majesty The Queen. I found myself very involved in the preparations. I built a display to show Her Majesty the role of the Britannia fleet. A crew stood by this and I had the privilege of leading this band. There was much activity smartening the station up; it has been said that The Queen must think that the majority of the country's establishments must always smell of fresh paint!

On the day, she entered the room (recently decorated) and examined our display. The Station Commander introduced me and, by way of illustrating the international nature of our job, said to Her Majesty:

'Flight Lieutenant Berry had his appendix out in Jamaica!'

Well, it's one way to make a mark with one's Sovereign!

It was around this time that we started using Masirah, an island off the coast of Oman, as our staging post instead of RAF Muharraq, Bahrain. Masirah had little to recommend it ... hot, barren. Our accommodation was somewhat primitive - prefabricated huts for ten beds. Some attempt at privacy was made with the arrangement of the furniture. One huge air conditioner roared in the corner.

All of this was not conducive to sleep, particularly if that had to be attempted during the day, in preparation for the inevitable night departure. It also did not help if the curtains are of similar substance to a dress where you notice, in the sunlight, that the wearer should be wearing an underslip!

The crews passing through, politely suggested that something be done about this! The solution sums up the time and the situation. One day a 'local' appeared with a pot of paint and painted the glass of the sleeping accommodation windows black! Now there could be no complaints! It was dark!

That was by way of setting the scene: 'The Darkened Room' - but now, 'The Characters'. Captain Couth is a quiet, serious minded person, with no time for the 'frivolity' of route life. A measure of this is a particular afternoon, where, with no sense of occasion, he chooses to go to bed in the 'darkened room'.

239

This is partly induced by his desire to isolate himself from the 'rat bags', his navigator and copilot who, perhaps, again with no sense of occasion, decide to spend the lunchtime in the bar. You now have 'The Scene' - 'The Darkened Room' - and 'The Characters'.

The navigator and copilot now return to the communal room, with much play on keeping the noise down and other well intentioned resolves of the inebriated, which are a total failure. Captain Couth is determined to ignore all this, in his bed in the dark. 'They will calm down in a while'.

And they do; copilot and navigator, with much accidental noise, do eventually settle on their beds to slip away into their, 'six-pints-at-lunchtime', afternoon siesta.

The only noise is the purr, nay roar, of the air conditioner, but that was something you came to accept as normal in those climes. But, after a short while, there is a stir and a 'stage whisper' from the navigator.

'The trouble with these rooms is that if you want a pee, you have to walk miles to the loo.'

'Got a problem there, Nav', murmurs the copilot.

The captain silently stirs, and buries his head under the pillow. There is silence, but the air is electric with the anticipated problem of the navigator's bladder! A solution is at hand, which is announced, in another stage whisper, by the nav.

'They've got those metal waste bins in here - I'll use one of those.'

In the dark could be heard the unmistakable sound of a jet of water impinging on a metal surface! This was too much for our tolerant captain. Leaping out of his feigned sleep, with one sweep of the hand, he put all the lights on - to reveal, Fred Moffitt, the navigator standing there with a jug of water poised over the metal bin!

This is just one story about Fred. More are repeated here as he was one of the colourful characters of that 'Specialist Aircrew', breed. A Geordie, he still had that distinctive dialect - and the forthright nature of people from those parts. Although there are these many stories about him, he was totally a professional when it came to his job.

Personalities, like Fred, are known by everyone. It was thus that his name was chosen for a 'protest'. It was decreed that we were all to wear name tags.

Although these became common-place in later years, there was a good deal of resistance to this introduction, especially as we were expected to provide them at our own expense. Changi was the place to have them made. Many people had two made - one with their own name and the other bearing 'F. Moffitt'. The latter would be worn when it

You might have guessed that Fred Moffitt is on the right!

would cause maximum irritation of the hierarchy!

When the following story, which I will slightly sanitise for this family reading matter, is told, then there is a 'leaping to conclusions' as to who the 'Fred' was.

A crew found themselves accommodated in a not too luxurious hotel; one of its features was very thin walls. As they attempted to settle down for the night there were distracting 'noises', but they did eventually subside. Then there was the young lady's voice:

'Oh, Fred, Fred, do it to me again ... do it again ...'

A dark brown voice comes from one of the other rooms:

'For God's sake, Fred, do it to her again and then we can all get some sleep!'

He had an occasion, in later years when writing a magazine article, to list some of his 'accomplishments':

1. I once jumped over a six feet gap on the roof of the aircrew accommodation in Bahrain, Brit House, with four gaping storeys below me.

2. I almost beat the satay eating record at Lim's stall in Changi village - I would have cracked it but I threw up and was disqualified.

3. I once took an urn containing the ashes of a very senior officer for a crew kebab night out in Cyprus. He had a really good time and by way of thanks donated his duty free to the crew.

4. When they cancelled the 'B' promotion exam, all long term Flying Officers were promoted to Flight Lieutenant except me. Apparently I had committed some minor infraction of social etiquette and received six months' suspension of promotion for my trouble; therefore for a short time I was the most senior Flying Officer in the Air Force List.

5. I sat on Dave Bridger's knee whilst he sang 'Sonny Boy' and I provided the appropriate responses in an effort to entertain the passengers of a u/s VC10 in the transit lounge at Gan.

The world needs people like Fred Moffitt!

*   *   *   *

In 1972 I was elevated to the peerage. From a cast of thousands - well, a handful of captains with the appropriate amount of experience, I was selected to become one of those instructor/examiners on the staff of the Britannia's training establishment, No.241 Operational Conversion Unit. A comment has been made a number of pages back that, as an RAF flier, one has never actually passed; there are constant tests and checks. To be accepted into this new role, there were more. Those passed, I settled into the routine of said instructor/examiner.

I entered this scene a couple of years after there had been quite radical reform of the training/examining organisation. The old way has been described: monthly training sorties on the squadron with a periodic pass or fail test. The frequency of this depended on the category held and for pilots it would include demonstrating one's ability with circuit and instrument flying by day and circuit flying by night. There would also be a test on emergencies in the simulator and an examination on technical and related matters.

This system, although long established, was seen as lacking. The main failing was there was no instructional element so after one's initial training there was no 'refreshment'. Also the 'instant death' nature of the testing might not be a true measure of ability - one might be having a bad day ... or a lucky one.

In a brave move this all was swept away. Monthly continuation training was abolished. In its place, on expiry of category, the candidate would attend a fortnight's supervised instruction at the OCU. His ability would be assessed over this whole period. This was, indeed, a bold move as it could be said that the old method had sustained an excellent safety record ... 'If it ain't broke, don't fix it!' But it worked.

I now became part of this Periodic Refresher Training (PRT) scheme. A crew would be allocated to me for that fortnight and we would work together for that time. It could be something of a 'sausage machine' routine but there was plenty of relief with other tasks.

There were regular courses for students new to the aircraft and one would have a share of this instructing. Copilots required converting to captain and then there were 'route checks'. The 'jewel in the crown' of an OCU instructor was the global trainers. Those new students were taken around the world, literally, as the final part of their course. Comment has been made on how this was really too much for an *ab initio* but now one was on the other side of the fence, this was put to one side ... a Global trainer was a fantastic trip. So, all this added up to a very satisfying job.

I have been very critical of the way I was treated over the years by some of those old examiners. I carried those memories with me as a constant reminder not to be tyrannical but to try to help those in my charge. A sense of humour helped. During the fortnight's PRT, idle moments eg sitting in the crew bus waiting to take-over an aircraft from another crew, could be filled with a few questions:

Me: 'Well, Bill Bloggs, what do you think is the longest piece of continuous metal in a Britannia?'

The question would be accompanied by a spread of the arms.

'And I mean continuous, no rivets, welding etc.'

The arms and the bit about joins are intended to mislead ... which they usually do ... viz:

Bloggs: Well, I might think it's the main spar - but that can't be one piece ... er ... what about the steel planking of the cabin floor?

'Nope!'

'Is it one of the rods to the flying controls?'

'Nope!'

'Sorry ... can't think.'

'Well, I think it could be the windings of the alternator!'

Luckily hitting an instructor was not allowed.

'I'll give you an easy one now. You're standing outside one of our Britannias ... how can you tell whether it's a Mk1 or a Mk2?'

The two different types were a legacy from the aircraft's acquisition days. The three Mk2s had civilian origins; the 20 Mk1s were totally military. Bloggs mind roams over thoughts of windows and toilets.

'Doesn't the Mk2 have an extra window forward of the freight door?'

'Not the last time I counted them.'

'There must be some waste water drain tubes part way down the fuselage.'

The Mk2s did have toilets mid-ships, Mk1s didn't. Bloggs is getting a bit smart - he'll have to be damped down.

'There's a much easier way than that.'

'Er ... no ... can't think.'

'Well, look at the number on the tail - the Mk2s are 392, 398 and 404!'

It might be as well to duck at this stage and not put too much trust in the 'no striking' rule!

Chapter 21
A Little Difficulty

For 18 months I continued with the training and examining tasks with little excitement. This was being saved up for me. In May and July 1973, I was engaged in two, three week long, hot weather trials, along the Changi route, to establish whether the performance of the Britannia was falling off with age. On each of these I experienced two major mechanical failures. These have been documented in '*Tales from the Crewroom*' but as they were significant events in my flying life, the account is repeated here.

Whether it was in the mind or was a fact, it did appear that the performance of the Britannia was deteriorating as the years rolled by. Alongside dull evidence of increased 'times to height' and cruising speeds below the targets proclaimed by the performance manuals, would be set vivid tales, from 'tired and emotional' crews, of 'hairy' take-offs. Whether you were influenced by one or the other (or both) there was a general discomfort.

Then, one hot, sultry day at the airport of Mombasa, on the coast of Kenya, a Britannia started its take-off run down a fairly critical runway, lengthwise, given the take-off factors of temperature, wind, height and weight. All these had, routinely, been considered before departure as part of the pre-flight planning and all, in theory, was well for the necessary weight at take-off. Full power was set, with the added amount given by 'water injection' - demineralised water was sprayed into the engines during the take-off and initial climb-out.

The engines looked good, brakes off and the aircraft started its trundle down the runway. Trundle is an apt word, for the Britannia was always particularly slow to accelerate in these tropical conditions. It was not unusual, therefore, for the level of anxiety on the flight deck to rise as the runway length was gradually being eaten up. It was unusual, indeed unheard of, for events to progress as they did.

The captain began to express doubts about the aircraft being able to get airborne in the amount of runway remaining. The pitch of his voice rose as that doubt increased and that uncertainty reached a point for him to decide to abandon the take-off. What had happened was a first because never before had a Britannia captain had sufficient doubt of his calculated take-off performance to take this dramatic step.

Now here was a puzzle; the weather conditions that would affect the take-off agreed with those forecast and on which the calculations had been based. Was the aircraft heavier than stated? Off came all the freight and it was check-weighed. The recalculation agreed with the first. This only left mechanical fault - were the brakes binding? They would have to be checked. The problem was now taking on great proportions - and it was only a few days before Christmas - and amongst those on board were *Pam's People*. Are you old enough to remember them?

An aircraft was diverted from the Singapore route to replace the lame one and the load transferred. It took off uneventfully at a weight and in similar conditions to the abandoned take-off.

The technical investigation of the lame duck continued. The brakes were not binding. Were the engines suspect? Were they developing full power? Engine No.1 was started and the routine for ground runs commenced. The target power figure had been determined back at base and was recorded on a placard on the flight deck.

The throttle was slowly advanced and the power check parameters set - but the engine was 'down'! The torque developed did not come up to the target figure. So the problem had been isolated. But wait - No.2 engine was tested - 'down'! No.3 - 'down' - and you've already guessed that No.4 followed suit. By standards normally applied, all four engines were unserviceable.

I will not dwell on this Mombasa situation any longer. It was concluded that all four engines could not be suspect. There must be something wrong with the run-up procedures in hot and humid conditions. So, with the aircraft now empty and with minimum fuel, it was decided all would be well. The aircraft took off safely and returned to the UK.

Back at Brize Norton the engines were tested. They were all normal and on target! So now there is a problem.

Out of all this came a decision to arrange a special flight to examine engine running techniques in the tropics and to check aircraft performance. A well worn route was chosen - one with which you are now familiar - to Singapore and return. The flying performance of the aircraft was to be checked by measuring the height to which it climbed in the configuration it would be in if an engine failed on the runway at too high a speed for the aircraft to be stopped in the remaining length. The 'decision speed' is calculated for each take-off - below it, if an engine fails, the aircraft is stopped - above it the take-off continues, the engine is shut down and the propeller feathered and the undercarriage retracted. The aircraft is then climbed at a calculated speed which ensures maximum terrain clearance. All this can be calculated and this is done if the take-off path is over rising ground and the aircraft weight is high. Because the graphs are available to do this, it is a useful datum for assessing the performance of a multi-engined aircraft.

I was nominated as aircraft captain for this trip which promised to be different - but the difference went beyond that anticipated. The route was to be Brize Norton to Akrotiri, Cyprus and then, instead of our normal, for those times, staging post of Masirah, we were to use the recently constructed Seeb International on the North East coast of Muscat and Oman. Gan was the next stop then on to Singapore, where we were now using RAF Tengah in place of Changi. It was then about turn for the reverse route.

Our instructions were that, after take-off at all these places, we were to set ourselves up with our No.4 engine shut down, propeller feathered, undercarriage up, flaps at 15° and then climb with full power for five minutes and record the height gain achieved. This would then be compared with a figure obtained from the appropriate performance graph. On the ground the two technicians we had on board - having, incidentally, true Service names: Chalky White and Spud Murphy - were to carry out engine ground runs using post-Mombasa parameters.

So off from Brize Norton we set - a motley crew. The copilot was Flying Officer Dick King, on his first operational flying tour and, like so many of his ilk, a sharp, sensible and extremely competent young man. The navigator could give him a year or two! Flight Lieutenant 'Rev' Wilkins, very experienced and an OCU instructor. Master Engineer Paddy Tranter was the air engineer, again a wise old hand with many years of flying experience. Down the back were two equally 'hairy' airloadmasters, Paddy Harper and Sam Justin. Out of place in this crew was a young WRAF Sergeant, Janet Robinson. She was awaiting her airloadmaster course and had been put on the flight for 'experience'!

We proceeded to Cyprus and braced ourselves for the first of our unusual departures. Airborne from Akrotiri, heading out to sea, 1,000 feet, shut down No.4, check undercarriage up, 15° flap set. Ready? Full power, climbing and timing. Five minutes later we were at 5,000 feet - there were sighs of relief. We were not used to such goings-on!

Now we were back to normal and proceeding to Seeb. This was one of a number of new airports being built to international standards by the rich oil states. But we were not to have long to wonder at it. This was a double-leg day. Akrotiri to Seeb - 90 minute refuel - Seeb to Gan. We had arrived at Seeb in the cool of the evening - a mere 30°C. Refuelling proceeded, flight planning calculations complete, time to go.

We were heavy - it was hot - the Britannia was in 'trundle' mode, but the new runway was good and long and after what seemed an age we clawed our way into the pitch black, desert sky. Not for us the settling down into the normal route flying routine. There was our performance check to be carried out.

It seemed a foolish thing to be doing, shutting an engine down in this hot and hostile environment, but that was our job and these were just the conditions for which figures were needed. So once again 5, 4, - full power - 3, 2, 1, go! The Britannia wallowed upwards with the three engines gulping the hot night air. The rate of climb was poor - time seemed to stand still. Four of the five planned minutes had elapsed, the flight deck had a somewhat anxious air. Then there was what seemed like an explosion of lights - red ones!

On each of the pilot's instrument panels was a central red light which indicated that there was a fault on the electrical panel located, rather obscurely, behind the copilot's seat. These two lights were ON! Eyes sped to the electrical panel - three red lights ON! And, what is more they indicated the most serious fault that could occur on that panel - alternator overheat - (or should it be alternator overheats?). Three lights showed Nos.1, 2 and 3 alternators over-heating. The only reason for No.4 not being on was, remember, that No.4 engine was shut down!

The alternators of the Britannia were permanently connected to the engine so the only way of stopping them was to stop the engine. The drill then for an overheating alternator was to shut down the associated engine - with No.4 already shut down, at least things would be symmetrical!

Clearly something less drastic had to be done. Power was reduced to a minimum and Paddy qualified for an entry in '*The Guinness Book of Records*' for the quickest engine relight drill ever carried out - No.4 was up and running and giving valuable full power. With the lower power setting, No.1 overheat had cancelled so that throttle was advanced to allow Nos.2 and 3 to be completely closed. This had half the desired effect - No.2 light went out. No.3 persisted so that engine was shut down and feathered. All this took place very quickly - perhaps only slightly longer than it has taken you to read about it!

While the engineer's hands had been rippling over the switches, buttons and throttles, the navigator had determined the best way to turn for Seeb for maximum terrain clearance and the copilot declared our emergency on the radios. It is not recorded what the loadmasters were doing!

But now a relative calm had returned. Albeit that we had one engine shut-down, the aircraft was flying safely and the fault with the alternators unlikely to return - unless we were foolish enough to try full power for five minutes at low speed again! In this situation, Seeb did not seem a sensible place to go, with Masirah just down the road with all its servicing facilities. So, to Masirah we headed. A lot of beer was consumed that night in the specially opened Sergeants' Mess bar. Perhaps that is really why landing at Seeb did not seem a good idea!

The ground engineers were examining the aircraft. The alternators did not look too bad but they were changed so that they could be examined in the UK. The heat sensing devices which were linked to the overheat warning lights were also changed. The aircraft was declared serviceable and we were cleared to go. But our instructions were to proceed normally. No more performance testing for the time being!

So we settled to a gentle, normal route flight to Singapore. By the time we arrived there the matter had been considered by our masters and it had been decided that we could resume the trial at Gan - in fact we were to stay at Gan for several days and fly special flights out of there. All went well - no overheats.

We, as a crew, became overheated one day. We were getting tired and we had just done our fourth or fifth trip, climbing on three engines, trying not to stare at the overheat warning lights. We were asked if, on our return to Gan, we would simulate an emergency situation for the Fire Service and, after landing, turn off the runway and shut-down. The emergency vehicles would then surround us and do their bit. I reluctantly agreed on condition that the fatigued crew would not be involved.

We duly landed and turned into the loop at the end of the runway, a piece of concrete, by the way, so close to the water's edge you felt you could reach out of the window and dapple your hand in the turquoise water. We did join in a bit by deploying one of our escape chutes, down which the crew slid. This was somewhat devious though - we thought we would get to the bar quicker that way! At the bottom we were greeted by the Warrant Officer Fire Chief:

'The aircrew resuscitation equipment is on the back of the Land Rover, Sir.'

I inwardly groaned, my message about our non-involvement had obviously not got through. But it would have been wrong to argue so we meekly trooped to our fate at the Land Rover - to be greeted by a case of cold beer!

From Gan we continued home. There we were quizzed on our 'goings-on' and awaited the decision of where we were to go from there. The answer came a month later - we were to go to Singapore and back, repeating the trial. An additional feature was the fitting of heat-sensitive strips to the alternator ducting to investigate the temperatures therein. This was to be the start of more trouble!

With the benefit of two months' healing of the memory wound left by all those red lights, we set off once again with our own aircraft to Singapore. With us came an engineering officer whose particular concern, being in charge of Brize Norton's Electrical Section, was the validity of the warnings that we had previously received. With no signs of damage to the alternators, the integrity of the overheat warning system was put in doubt.

Our plan therefore was to repeat the 'second segment' climbs at each staging post. Whilst the aircraft was on the ground heat sensitive strips in various parts of the alternator ducting would be removed, examined and renewed. So we would be building up additional performance data and information on the alternators' temperature behaviour in these adverse conditions of low speed at high power in hot climes.

Lest it be thought that we were allowed to take our time about all this, it is interesting to note that my log book records that we flew Brize Norton, Malta, Cyprus, Masirah, Karachi, Gan, Colombo, Singapore, Colombo, Gan, Karachi, Masirah in eight days! But we were to have an enforced rest at that last stop.

On the morning of 20 July 1973, Masirah was its normal unexciting self - hot, in spite of a steady breeze. Britannia XL635 was being prepared for our departure. This included filling the engines' water tanks with demineralized water. We were to use 'water injection' for take off which would give us the extra engine power necessary at our weight and the airfield temperature.

Six sticky crew members climbed on board the aircraft at eight o'clock and started the preparations. The engineering officer reported that the temperature recorders had been renewed. At ten to nine we were on the runway ready to go. There was always a slight anxiety about a 'wet' take-off in the Britannia. One did not know whether the water was actually going to flow until full power had been applied. Today we were OK - four green lights, water flowing, extra power being given by the engines. As we climbed away and began a lazy turn back over the airfield, to set course for Cyprus, many of our cares should have been over. But not for this crew - we were still doing our engine shut-down and five minute climb.

Preparations for this were slick - this was our eleventh in eight days. All is set, No.4 shut down, 15° of flap - just full power to set. Suddenly there is an unmistakeable lurch of the aircraft. All eyes flash to the engine instruments - the lurch is in sequence with the needles associated with No.1 engine. The aircraft swung left in sympathy with those needles rotating anti-clockwise. The sway to the right came as they reversed their rotation. The engine flame was being extinguished and relit just as it would be in icing conditions. But the only ice you were likely to experience in the Masirah area, upwards as well as along, for many a mile, was that in your gin and tonic! No, there was something radically wrong with that No.1 engine and the device for ultimate defence against ice - a continually glowing plug in one of the combustion chambers - was the only thing preventing a complete shut-down.

The flight engineer, Eddy Godwin, obviously came from the same stable as Paddy Tranter, whose record he equalled for re-starting No.4 engine. This done, No.1 was put out of its spasm by being shut-down. So it was, 'Masirah, we're coming back'. Such a return in a large transport aircraft is not entirely straightforward. There is a landing weight restriction and, at take-off and for a number of hours afterwards, until fuel is used up, the aircraft will be above that limit. For this reason a fuel jettison system is standard and we were now to utilise it. This is never done lightly - one always has in mind the potential fireball to be created as fuel is discharged from pipes in the wings and atomises as it meets the high speed airflow. All was well, check list followed, the necessary amount of fuel had been dumped.

Hindsight would have shaken what complacency we had as we sprayed the desert with our inflammable load. Firstly, the engineer observed that the engine parameters of our relit No.4 engine were not compatible with 2 and 3, a clear indication of some incipient failure. Normal operating procedures called for it to be shut down but with No.1 in that condition already this seemed injudicious and so it was throttled back to the idle position and left there for the rest of the flight. Next, and of some significance to our only just past 'fireball condition', when we came to retract the throttles of our only two serviceable engines, the inboards, they displayed the same symptoms as No.1, which had started this whole drama off. They were 'autorelighting' - the business where the flame was going out and being re-ignited by the glow plug. But now we had some 'very aware of predicament' people down the back of the aircraft. Air Loadmaster Howard Tonks told us that with each 'autorelight' there

was a huge tongue of flame from the engine jet pipe as unspent fuel was ignited. What if that had happened during our fuel jettison!

A haze had settled over Masirah during our absence and with one engine shut-down, one throttled back and two only giving intermittent power, we completed a very uneasy radar approach and landed - thankfully! All this must have made us very thirsty because we drank a lot of beer that lunchtime!

The next ten days were unique in Britannia history. It was decided that we needed three of our engines changed and whilst preparations for this were afoot the aircraft was moved to a more convenient location. When it was being manoeuvred, by tractor, a huge casting in the undercarriage cracked - a crack wide enough to take a fist! Never was a Britannia so sick.

I will never forget the feeling of possible guilt as to whose fault this whole thing was as a Belfast aircraft lumbered in with our three engines and undercarriage leg to be followed by a re-routed VC10 with all the necessary ground crew. They set to work in the boiling sun and, to their credit, completed the task in just over a week. It was time for the air test to check their work out and all went remarkably well. At the end of the morning we were able to declare the aircraft serviceable and fit to depart the next day for the UK.

It must have been the relief that caused me, completely out of character(!), to over-indulge that lunch-time - and through the afternoon, with my equally relieved ground and aircrew. As the sun went down, but the party showed no signs of abating, I decided enough was enough and headed towards what was now a well known refuge, the Visiting Aircraft Servicing Flight, for a cup of black coffee.

Although it was well after normal working hours, the place was not deserted and I was greeted by:

'Hello Sir, you're the first - make a cup of coffee and have a seat.'

In my befuddled condition it took a long time for me to realise what was going on. A bed sheet was being pinned to the wall, cables unwound across the room - the assembly of equipment - with knobs and switches, two circular objects on arms, a glass eye. Ah - a film projector! And the room was now filling up. I had stumbled on my first (and last) blue movie show!

Curiosity overcame the remnants of conscience I had left and as the film rolled, I concentrated. I was reminded of the instructions that went with those incredibly clever and complex plastic aircraft construction kits which were then just establishing themselves. The first directive, always, was to 'identify the parts'. With the bad quality of the film and my disabled vision, I failed to single out any 'parts' and my inquisitiveness about things indecent portrayed on the silver screen remained unassuaged.

Four engined aircraft are safe on the premise that it is virtually impossible for coincident faults to strike all the engines at the same time. The one weak link is the communal fuel and for that reason stringent precautions are taken with its purity. Checks showed the Masirah fuel to be uncontaminated. But subsequent examination of our engines in the UK led to doubts abut the purity of that demineralized water used during the take-off. Valves that are closed when at full power, have to open at lower power settings to maintain the balance of air to fuel in the engine. The signs were that these could not open, when they should, due to contamination. The water, which came from a special point in Masirah's desalinisation plant, was found to be impure. The cause of much anxiety had been found.

There were two outcomes of all this - three if you include the way they aged me - firstly, I think that the way it was perceived that I handled the situations smoothed a path towards me gaining an 'A', 'Exceptional' category. Secondly, I am proud of the fact that, in the 1974 New Year's Honours List I was awarded The Queen's Commendation for Valuable Service in the Air - a great moment.

Just to compensate for this 'glory news' I will reveal, at this stage, that the award of the 'A' meant that, in my time, I held every transport flying category ... A, B, C, D, and yes, the dreaded 'E'!

A number of pages back, these categories were defined and it was said that 'E' was, basically, a 'Fail' - 'in need of further training'. What wasn't revealed, 'a number of pages back', was that I was awarded the 'E' on one of my early, copilot categorisation tests. Basically, I decided to overshoot from a three engined approach with which I wasn't happy. The examiner wasn't happy with my late

255

decision. I think mine was a bold one and was better than pressing on 'living in hope' ... like that low flying incident, once again - the squeezing together of the cheeks of the ass, this time to assist the aircraft reach the runway threshold ... but (again) I *would* say that, wouldn't I!

So 'E' it was but, like the Phœnix, I rose from the ashes ...

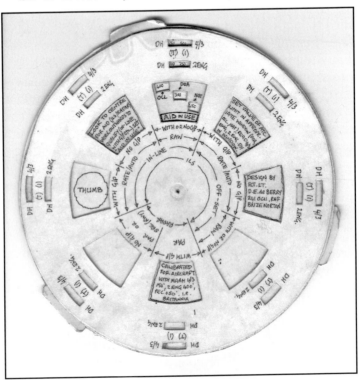

Whilst I was instructing on the OCU, an amazingly complex system was introduced for calculating the lowest height to which a pilot could fly when making an instrument approach to a runway/airfield in conditions of low cloud and/or poor visibility. I designed this device to help with the calculation. The words of the AOC, Air Marshal Neil Cameron, sum up the outcome: '*Although it rather looks as though production costs and possible future modification to the overall concept will preclude the adoption of your idea, nonetheless, I would like to congratulate you on your initiative and thank you for the painstaking effort which I know went into the design of your calculator.*' Oh well ... back to obscurity!

Chapter 22
Very Mature Student

Service life is always rife with rumours. Some piece of news, of doubtful veracity, is launched and spreads, like wild fire. The ones of 1974/75 concerned the scrapping of the Britannia fleet. Rumours reached us from above but, at our level, it was difficult to believe them. Life continued apace; our training commitment for newcomers did not falter; the squadrons were as busy as ever; there were several emergency situations where the Britannia played its full part. How could there be any substance in stories of 'scrapping'? But when the Commander-in-Chief visited Brize Norton to deliver the news, personally, then there was no doubt.

I, like all my compatriots, wondered what it would mean, individually. One thing, for your sure, there were going to be an awful lot of people on the RAF's labour market. When this happens, some end up with rubbishy jobs. This uncertainty made me realise that I had, to some extent, been the controller of my own destiny for a number of years - 13 to be exact - and I didn't fancy the idea of taking pot luck. Perhaps not altogether coincidentally, a redundancy scheme was in the air; two in fact to reduce the numbers in particular age brackets. I decided that if I fitted one of these, I would apply.

But what would I do in civilian life? I have related that Valerie was established in the teaching business; she had moved up the ladder and was now the deputy head teacher of that school at

Crudwell. With the years I had spent in the training role in the Royal Air Force, I felt that I had potential as a teacher, myself - and I had enjoyed my time as an instructor. So, I started enquiring about teacher courses.

Bath seemed a natural choice and I attended an interview cum consultation. My mentor was the senior Mathematics tutor, (mathematics was, potentially, my 'main' subject), and I remember him revealing his disbelief that I was leaving flying for teaching with the question:

'Are you really sure you are doing the right thing?'

But, I was sure. I'd had a good time with the Britannias, but that was coming to the end. I didn't relish starting afresh on another aircraft - that's if I was given a flying job - or the prospect of having to move - and I'm the one who commented on my father's disinclination to be mobile. But - he says, in mitigation - our children were settled in local schools - and there was Val's job. I also thought that husband/wife teacher would be quite a good leisure combination - don't mention the long holidays!.

On 6th January 1976, after I had left, a joint disbandment parade was held for Nos.99 and 511 Squadrons ... a sad occasion.

The result of the interview was that I would be welcome at Bath, if I decided to leave. I awaited the redundancy news - here it is! I was too young for one scheme and too old for the other! 'Rats', say I, 'I've gone a long way along the 'Leaving Road' - I'm going to continue with it!' So I PVRed - RAF-speak for premature voluntary retirement.

Valerie checks out Newton Park. This is a trip down 'Memory Lane'. Her education course was based there although most of the lectures etc, for the convenience of the mature lady students, were held in Swindon.

On 26 September 1975, at the age of 42, I found myself a mature student on a Bachelor of Education degree course at Bath College of Further Education, Newton Park. Detail of the following three years would not be appropriate in this, hopefully, aviation oriented book, but here is a brief report. I am pleased that I did the course but whilst I was doing it, surrounded by fellow students more than 20 years younger, there were moments of doubt.

I remember one 'Music and Movement', or some similar

session, where I didn't actually have to pretend I was a tree, but it was pretty close! I elected to train for junior school - the top juniors, in particular. That decided the slant of my education studies. Alongside these, one was obliged to study a subject at post-VIth Form cum 1st/2nd Year university standard. I chose Mathematics.

In the New Year, 1976, Val and I made a dramatic move towards that mutual 'leisure' aspect of a teacher's lot. We bought a cottage in Wales. Clear from your minds a picture of a stone built dwelling with a slate roof ... ours was constructed of corrugated iron! But it was, or perhaps I should say became, magic inside. It was entirely lined with tongued and grooved boarding.

Summer vacation, some nine weeks long, came along. With the considerable help of Tim, No.2 son, who had developed some building skills as a schoolboy part-timer with a local builder, I set to on bringing the 'amenities' up to scratch - like converting one of the rooms to a bathroom. The 'facility' on purchase was a 'Privy' at the bottom of the garden - a genuine earth closet!

Staying on the RAF track, there was a significant moment in the September of that vacation. Val had returned to Startley; school holidays were not so long as college vacations! I stayed on to work on my summer assignments.

Late one afternoon I decided to walk a bit of the Pembrokeshire Coast Path, arranging my route to take in The Swan Inn at Little Haven, a favourite pub with us. The landlord was a retired Wing Commander. Various pieces of RAF memorabilia decorated the walls. One was a framed portion of what I recognised as a RAF map ... and I knew the locale ... it was down the coast of Oman, south west of our latter day staging post, Masirah. In the centre of the piece of map was a place called 'The Swan Inn'! I was an early customer and chatted with the landlord for some time. Not surprisingly, the main topic was our RAF days.

I moved away from the bar as the place began to fill up. There was a sudden surge in numbers as 20 or so came in together. I rapidly realised that they were from RAF Brawdy. I sat, alone, in a corner observing the camaraderie and jokiness of the group ... a relationship that I remembered so well and had given up. I missed it.

I left them to their jolly evening and returned to my lonely cottage. Out came pen and paper and a letter was composed to the Ministry of Defence asking if I might rejoin the Royal Air Force. I did not post it straight away, whilst I agonised whether I should. I decided, in the end, that I ought to really give civilian life a proper crack - but I carried that letter in my brief case for the rest of the course.

The three years passed and I put real effort into it. The mathematics was a total challenge. I have made the comment that you have to have a talent for maths to keep up with an advancing complexity. I thought, with my maturer years and second time around, I would be able to 'keep up'. Wrong! I floundered further and further out my depth.

What I was prepared to do was spend hours and hours on my assignments, which went towards our final result - in the text books I found 'similar examples'. I felt that Father was looking over my shoulder! As a result of these efforts I went into the final written exams with enough marks, already, to pass. With the effort I had put into the other areas as well, my result was assured.

As the course had progressed, it became clear that the job situation in teaching was changing. The pattern for many teachers had been to move on every several years, perhaps to more senior posts - or to build up experience to obtain such posts - or perhaps some were, simply, unhappy with their current situation. For whatever reason, it certainly was a fairly mobile scene.

All this changed with the economic straits of 1977/78. Also the number of children in school was falling. The result? Jobs were short. I did have one interview where my 'scientific' and 'manly' skills were in competition with a piano playing, corn dolly making fellow candidate ... she got the job!

This was the excuse I needed:

```
Your Majesty. I would very much appreciate being
able to rejoin your Royal Air Force. I have missed
the way of life enormously and would love to be back.
                          Your humble servant ...
```

Well, something like that. In a remarkably short time, the telephone rang:

'Yes, Your Majesty ...'

No, I discovered that there was a civil servant whose sole job was to look after people like myself and he set to with arrangements for me to rejoin as Specialist Aircrew, again, and with my old rank and seniority. I could not believe my good fortune!

A post-mortem: what of that three years? Was it all a waste of time? I don't feel that. When I was 'back in' I became convinced that every long term serviceman should have a break in a different environment, preferably a stimulating one. On return to normal Service life, one has re-adjusted one's values. I became very aware of 'the moaners' who really did not have anything to complain about. I also became very aware of the good salary and, with advancing years, the pension arrangements.

I think the academics of the education course were refreshingly

BATH COLLEGE OF HIGHER EDUCATION

Newton Park,
Bath BA2 9BN
Saltford (02217) 2681

Sion Hill Place,
Lansdown,
Bath BA1 5SJ
Bath (0225) 25264

NORMAN PAYNE, M.Sc.
PRINCIPAL

Please reply to   Newton Park

Mr. de Berry was a student at this college from September 1975 to July 1978.   He followed a three-year B.Ed. Degree course and his studies included professional training directed towards Junior/ Secondary teaching with Mathematics as his other academic study and appropriate elective courses.

Mr. de Berry was a very able and intelligent mature student who set standards well above the ordinary in the organisation of his studies and the care and application with which he pursued them.   As a mature student he found some early difficulty in recovering his mathematical skills, but by dint of intelligent hard work he achieved a standard which would have been adequate to proceed to the Honours degree had he wished to do so.   His work in the Education course and in Professional Studies courses in college was well above average, and he graduated successfully with a B.Ed. Ordinary degree of Bath University.

In school Mr. de Berry proved to be an outstanding teacher. The same qualities of thoughtfulness, care and organisation which he brought to his academic studies were evident in the classroom, and to these were added a calm, firm but friendly approach to the children and a concern for their individual needs.   He took infinite care over all preparation and everything was meticulously presented and carefully thought out.   He was always prepared to change his plans midstream if necessary and this made his teaching effective.   He had experience with children from 6-11 years during his college course and in each case his work was of a very high calibre.

As a family man of mature years he was not a participant in Student Union activities, but he is a first-rate recruit to the teaching profession.

Personal Tutor

Principal

taxing - a three-year work-out for the brain. I would not have developed my interest in computers if they had not been an element of the course. Finally, and most importantly, it started me in this writing business. Having to sit down, at the age of 42, and write an essay for the first time for 26 years is a demanding experience ... and that's only the first one. Many more followed over the three years. With such practice, the words flowed.

When the requirement ceased, there was a void - so I kept finding reasons to write. The result is four books published, with this one the fifth, numerous magazine articles, editorship of magazines, a video script, a history of a nearby village ... I am sure none of this would have been accomplished if I had not been that mature student.

I will record, without comment, my very last college commitment ... as the finale of an environmental course unit we visited a sewage treatment works!

Chapter 23
Back In!

M y civil servant coordinator advised me that there would not be an immediate vacancy on the flying refresher course that I would require. But he suggested that I rejoined, anyway, and a temporary job would be found. I could see the £ signs flashing and instantly agreed. The 'temporary job' could have been in the 'back of beyond' ... but it was seven miles up the road! There was a short term requirement for an Operations Officer at RAF ... yes, Lyneham! So, I couldn't be more back home than that.

An Operations Officer, at station level, is a very tedious job, with unsociable hours, but I was as happy as a pig in ... well, very happy. It was useful to have three months of this which gave an opportunity for readjustment and getting various matters sorted out before I started my refresher course.

In the November I drove to RAF Leeming, North Yorkshire to start the course on the Multi-Engine Training Squadron. The air-

craft was the twin turbo-prop JetStream.

I did not find the flying easy; the aircraft felt cramped and I realised that I was much happier with something bigger and heavier to handle. I also felt

Pleased to be back in a Course photograph!

266

that the three year break from flying and my 46 years were handicaps to overcome. But I did ... and a bad Yorkshire winter ... to be considered refreshed and ready to start a course on the aircraft I was to fly. What would that be? The Hercules! Where are they based? Lyneham!

I considered myself to be a very fortunate individual. I really would confine the allocation of that good fortune to the domestic, financial, social front. I wasn't desperately happy being a 46 year-old copilot amongst a, mainly, much younger element. I tried to fit in ... but it was difficult.

But the World opened up to me, once more ... first trip, Decimomannu in Sardinia, next, Washington DC ... Patrick Air Force Base, Florida. Less exotic routes followed. The scrapping of the Britannias had marked the reduction in our country's global commitment and a concentration on a European one. So, Germany featured a lot as a destination. But there were many jewels: one seven day trip took in New Orleans, Washington again and Bermuda. This

was followed rapidly with one to Belize, Central America.

A completely new aspect of transport flying became my lot ... tactical work ie parachute delivery of men and stores preceded by a low level routing to avoid radar detection. All this did not make me feel any more comfortable with my situation ... all a bit gung-ho ... and there were the difficulties associated with teaching an old dog new tricks.

I felt more at home on the next big route trip which needs the whole route outlining, for impact! Lyneham, Athens, Bahrain, Colombo, Butterworth (Malaya), Hong Kong, Port Moresby (Papua New Guinea), Darwin, Nandi (Fiji), Honolulu, Sacramento (California), Ottawa, Gander (Newfoundland), Lyneham. Only a week after getting back from this two week epic, I was in Nairobi and Rhodesia! But for the fickle finger of fate I could have been spending all those days in the primary school of Upper Seagry!

My three years on Hercules proceeded thus. An awful lot of low level parachuting work and European trips punctuated by the goodies. There is one more outstanding example of the latter. We took a helicopter to Belize. To get a helicopter into a Hercules requires quite a bit of dismantling and it was declared that we should remain at Belize until the aircraft had been re-assembled and the one we were bringing back prepared for carriage. It was anticipated that this would take seven or eight days. Now, downtown Belize is not the most exciting or salubrious place in the World. One picture I have is of a dog scratching at a rubbish tip, looking for food ... and, along-side, a man doing the same.

We decided to accommodate ourselves in an hotel on one of the cays, of which there are many, off-shore. We were flown, in a light aircraft, to the small airstrip very adjacent to the hotel - every-thing was 'very adjacent'; it was a very small island. The stay was incredible - tropical bliss. Liking fish was an essential; that's all there was each day - but cooked in such a variety of magical ways.

We did some of our own fishing, hiring an expert, his boat and equipment. Using his immense local knowledge, he took us to a likely area. Before long, my compatriots were hauling in barracuda ... yes, huge, navy blue barracuda. They are described as 'a large and voracious tropical marine fish'. That was demonstrated to me as I only pulled in barracuda heads. I was clearly a bit slow with the winding in and barracuda obviously like, well, barracuda!

I find myself a little short of amusing incidents during this Hercules tour; perhaps this is a psychological block. An occasion that I do recall is when the squadron was due to be presented with a trophy. The 'big boys' had done well with their parachuting accuracy and the like and the Air Officer Commanding was going to present the trophy. A parade rehearsal was called for and this would be led by the CO, Wing Commander NH. He was a likeable man, perhaps a little older than his 'whizz kid' fellow Wing Commanders; this showed with his demeanour being, shall I say, 'straight laced'.

For the rehearsal, it was decided that Yours Truly would play the part of the Air Vice Marshal - it was the looks and silver hair! The pattern for the actual day was to be played out to the full, so, as my squadron assembled themselves in the hangar, which was to be the parade ground, I reported to the Station Commander's office. I was surprised that the 'play acting' extended to me being offered a cup of tea!

With that consumed, accompanied by social chat, we boarded the CO's car and proceeded to the hangar. The Station Commander ushered me to the small rostrum and the parade gave the 'General Salute'. Wing Commander NH marched towards me, halted and smartly saluted:

'No 70 Squadron ready for your inspection, Sir.'

I return the salute and replied:

'Thankyou, Norman.'

My Squadron Commander's face is a picture illustrating an inward torment. Should he stop the charade and give this Flight Lieutenant a 'bollocking' for addressing his Wing Commander by his first name ... in front of the Station Commander ... or would it be best to carry on. He decided on the latter course! Nice chap, Norman.

It might not come as a surprise, after this rather sparse account of three year's worth of Hercules flying, that I did not regard it as the zenith of my flying career. Similarly, you can imagine my joy at being summoned to the CO's office for this piece of news:

'There is a personal request from the Commandant of A&AEE, Boscombe Down that you go there to fly the Britannia!'

The Aeroplane and Armament Experimental Establishment, on its Salisbury Plain airfield, still had a Britannia. A civilian one had been purchased some years before.

Probably totally unsuccessfully, I put on a show of some regret at having to forego my conversion to Hercules captain. I was like a dog with two tails. Boscombe Down here I come.

Ingenuity was not completely dampened by my copilot role. Numerous Hercules graphs and tables required consultation prior to take-off and landing to determine various facts and figures. I devised this calculator to, more easily and efficiently, accomplish the task.

270

Chapter 24
Britannia Magic - Once More!

The Aeroplane and Armament Experimental Establishment (A&AEE) was a long estab-
lished ... establishment. Its title reflected more its history rather than the role in 1982. This had developed, over the years, into what could be considered 'consumer testing'. The Services wanted equipment from the manufacturers; the manufacturers wanted to provide it. There might be unbridled enthusiasm on the part of both parties to, respectively, receive and give. Some monitoring of this was required and this was the role of Boscombe Down. A 'Service Requirement' had been laid down and an order placed with a manufacturer who had declared themselves capable of meeting that requirement. A&AEE checked they had done

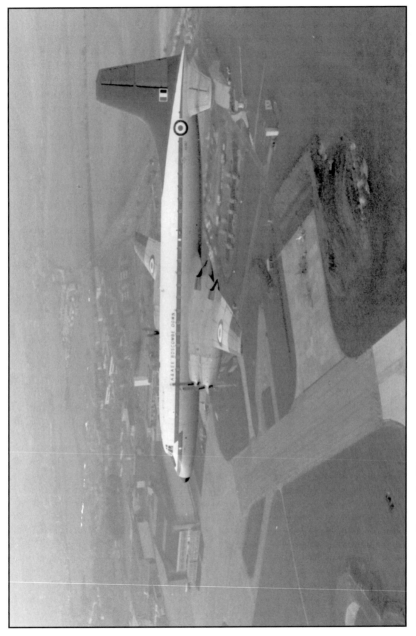

XX367 overflying Boscombe Down.

so before the equipment was delivered to the Service customer. This involved extensive trials of aircraft and associated equipment, some of them abroad in order to obtain the needed heat - or cold. Such trials required the movement of personnel and equipment and this was the role of the Britannia. The aircraft was operated by the Air Transport Flight (ATF). Two Bassett aircraft were the rest of the complement. ATF was one flight on 'B' Squadron. The major flight was manned by test pilots and their lot was the testing of large, multi-engined aircraft - 'A' Squadron tested the fast jets and the like.

I am amazed, when I examine my log book for those early days as Boscombe Down, how quickly I was absorbed into the system. A few days after arrival I went on a Britannia route trip, the first two legs as an observer and then in the left hand seat under the supervision of the resident captain, who I was to join. That trip took us to Ottawa and the Gulf Coast of Florida.

The next entries in the log book are flying the Argosy and Hercules! The pilots of ATF also flew some of the sorties of the Test Flight. In the Argosy I was the copilot for parachuting trials. In the Hercules I was put in the left hand seat and, after a check-out, made an instant captain! Eat your hearts out you guys at Lyneham who gave me a hard time!

The next two Britannia trips, which continued my refresher training, were familiar ones to me - those flights over the North Pole for the benefit of the Spec N Course were now an A&AEE responsibility. Back at Boscombe it was time for me to do some local training, practising asymmetric flying and the like. This was shortly followed by one of those good, old fashioned day and night categorisation tests - we kept up the same standards as those of the RAF transport force. To see that this was so, our checks were carried out by the CO of their Examining Unit. On the next overseas flight I was route checked. So, in a remarkably short time, I was fully qualified to captain the Britannia. I was very happy about all this.

My training had been supervised by an old friend, Squadron Leader Dave Bridger - a larger than life personality with a tremendous sense of humour. He was a solid member of the 'Specialist Aircrew' brigade so it is appropriate to have a few words about him in this tome.

Dave Bridger, on the right, in 'full flow' at a Britannia Association reunion. With him are another two ex-members of the RAF Britannia fleet, Joan Edwards (née Hisbent), AQM, and Gerry Taylor, navigator.

Dave joined the RAF in 1946 as a trainee engine fitter. Being too young, he lied about his age. This had an after effect in that, in later years, he tried to recover the 'lost year' to discover that the rule is that, regardless of proof otherwise, your 'Service age' remains the one declared at attestation - the 'swearing in' ceremony. So, Dave retired at 54, not 55! This unorthodox start to his Service career laid the pattern for the next 37 years. He retired, at that age 54, to take up a 'Retired Officer' post at RAF Henlow. This was not his first time there. As a young Leading Aircraftsman he was posted to Henlow along with a hairy old hand of the same rank. On their way, Dave heard all his companion's troubles with his wife and many children. It was suggested to Dave that they split their journey and have a long weekend at home, his cooperation being needed as they were travelling on a joint railway warrant and were really expected at Henlow straight away. Dave, with his warm hearted nature, agreed. When the pair eventually arrived at Henlow, they discovered that they *had* been missed and were duly charged with being 'absent without leave'! Dave adds a detail.

'When we were charged, the old lag spun such a convincing tale about his domestic difficulties, he was granted seven days compassionate leave. I was awarded 14 days 'Confined to Barracks'!'

After two years as an 'engines man', he 'went' aircrew, and trained as a Flight Engineer. His first posting was to a Hastings transport squadron and he took part in the Berlin Airlift. This could not have been quite as time consuming as we have been led to believe for Dave had time to court a young German lady, so successfully that she decided to come to England. However, he did not rush things and it was six years before he was 'cornered' and he and Ann were wed.

'She is still 'serving' having never been given a release date.'

Squadron Leader Bridger seized an opportunity to be retrained as a pilot in 1952. During training his soberness and calmness were obviously recognised for he was streamed into the multi-engined world and did his first squadron tour on Canberras. Steeliness continued with his conversion to one of the V-Bombers - the Valiant.

Then other talents were recognised with a posting to the Central Flying School (CFS), followed by a flying instructor's tour with Cambridge University Air Squadron. Meeting David Bridger must have been a considerable lesson in life for some of the sons of gentlefolk that populated the university at that time. One young man, who was obviously being a bit superior in his form of address to David, had to be reminded: 'You're not talking to your Father's groom!'

Doom and gloom then struck the Bridger household for he was posted on one of those unaccompanied tours to Kuching, Borneo. This was in Indonesia/Malaya confrontation times and he was 'Mentioned in Despatches'. The first part of the golden chapter of his life now starts, for on his return from Kuching, he is posted to Britannias. He progressed through the ranks of copilot, captain, training captain and VIP pilot. He played a large part in establishing Britannia operations in and out of Kathmandu for the commitment to routinely transport the Ghurkhas and their families to and from Hong

Kong. This chapter was closed with the scrapping of the aircraft. Dave flew the last RAF Britannia route schedule, which was from Cyprus to the UK.

In a short return visit to CFS, he quite conclusively demonstrated the fact that he had protested loudly before he went there - being a Jet Provost flying instructor at his time of life was not a good idea. He moved on to flying the Dominie aircraft at Finningley for navigator training. Then came a long sought after goal - the posting to the Boscombe Down Britannia. It was from this job that he retired.

The following are snippets from Squadron Leader Bridger's chequered career which clearly illustrate his 'likeable rogue' nature; how things have not always gone his way but how, in the end, life did

David receives a farewell gift from the Commandant of A&AEE, Air Commodore Reggie Spiers (who was on 64 Squadron at Duxford when the author was on 65!). Members of the Britannia crew are in attendance.

return to him the humour and friendliness that he exuded:

- His promotion from Engineer 2 Star to 3 was held up because of some matters on his 'Conduct Sheet' relating to a much earlier life. When he went to complain, as part of the interview, the subject of pilot training was raised by his flight commander. That's how his retraining came about!

- After the six year courtship, referred to above, the fires of passion were obviously not cooled for, on return to the squadron after the honeymoon, Dave decided to demonstrate his flying prowess to his new bride. He was court-martialled for the low flying offence!

- He learnt the responsibilities of captaincy - and a distrust of navigators - over a practice bomb which missed its target by some considerable margin and blew a local inhabitant off his bicycle. Dave was interviewed by his Air Officer Commanding - the navigator wasn't!

- Whilst in Germany, on a Canberra squadron, he flew under a Kiel Canal bridge, much to the surprise of a German policeman standing on it at the time! He was not too startled to get the aircraft number. A summary of evidence (the preliminary to a court martial) was taken but, through the generosity of his Station Commander who decided there were some 'grey areas', no further action was taken.

- When he was 'removed' from the Jet Provost CFS course, he was waiting at home, expecting the worse, when an official letter came through the letter box. It was his promotion to Squadron Leader!

The undying memory of Dave, for many, from his Britannia route flying days has been referred to in connection with Fred Moffitt - the rendition of 'Sonny Boy', with some 'stooge' sitting on his knee. He had the knack of getting a crowd in a bar, in some God-forsaken hole, into a happy-go-lucky mood. An impromptu band would be formed with percussion provided by table tops and bottles, paper and comb were the woodwind, voices made up the rest of the ensemble. He, as the conductor, led on his pair of spoons.

Squadron Leader David Bridger was quite a character; as has been seen, he had his ups and downs, but he didn't bring anyone down with him. I was pleased to be working with him again.

In between the Britannia trips and back at base, Hercules and Argosy continue to feature, and then there is the first appearance of the Bassett - I am being checked out in this. The Bassett was the less glamourous part of ATF life. If the Britannia was the overseas 'bus and lorry' of A&AEE, then the Bassetts were the UK 'limousines'; though perhaps that term paints too rich a picture. If a member of staff needed to visit a UK airfield or a manufacturer's factory then the Bassett took them - and waited to bring them back, at the conclusion of their business. This was somewhat painful - one was a glorified chauffeur. But it was the price to be paid for the privilege of flying the Britannia.

The Bassett was one of the RAF's less than successful purchases of the 1960s. Developed from the civilian Beagle, this twin engined aircraft, operated by a pilot and navigator, could carry five passengers. They were purchased to carry V-Bomber crews to their dispersed airfields. They were also intended for use in the communications flights, replacing the ancient Anson. In this role, it might have had to carry an Air Officer Commanding on his annual inspection of

Members of the Air Transport Flight in front of the dreaded Bassett. L to R: Ted Hilton, Clive Osborne, Ken Newman, the author, Eric Heaton and Mick Bowden.

278

one of his stations. This would be a full regalia affair - sword and all. It was felt inappropriate for the, thus attired AOC, to descend from the aircraft via the, rear of the wing, stirrup - which was the standard Beagle fitting. The RAF Bassett was equipped with a set of hydraulically operated, folding steps. They weighed a ton - as did the standard Service radios that were fitted.

Consequently, the Bassett's performance was less than sparkling - and that was on two engines. An engine failure, in certain conditions, meant 'look for the most suitable grass field ahead'. I thought that the Bassett was, essentially, a single engine aircraft but the power had been divided between two engines for cosmetic reasons.

I didn't feel that comfortable in the Bassett; it was too small! But it had to be mastered. One bonus was that the flying was relatively low level. On a fine day we would fly, say, all the way to West Freugh, Dumfries and Galloway at 2,000 feet. With my interest in travel and finding out about different parts of the UK, this was a real pleasure. On a bad winter's day, with rain, snow, ice, things weren't so hot!

The 'type' column in my log book switches between Britannia and Bassett with fairly frequent appearances of Hercules and Argosy. This was the pattern for a magic year; Britannia trips included Washington DC, Ottawa, Florida, Calgary, many times over. One of these trips I shared with Dave Bridger. His prowess with 'spoons' has been mentioned but now he was the proud possessor of a genuine set of 'bones' to perform his music hall, clackety-clack routine. He had these made in Hong Kong at a shop specialising in ivory products. Dave had taken some drawings along and, in true HK style, the shop came up with the goods. Dave went to collect:

'Vwat awe faw?' enquired the puzzled proprietor.

Dave gave an impromptu demonstration with 'My Old Man Said Follow the Van', or something similar.

'Oh - yah - yah.'

The Hong Kong Chinese gentleman was jumping up and down and is highly amused. He runs to the back of the shop and calls to the workers. Four emerge and Dave continues with his inexhaustable reportoire. More 'Yah - yah - yah!' and excited clapping. More workers are called from the floor above and soon the shop is filled with happy, smiling Chinese and this mad Englishman!

To return to that shared route trip. After a 'session', USA downtown somewhere, we retire to our beds. Shortly there is a knock on my door:

'Dave, I've lost my bones. I must have left them at that last bar - will you come and help me find them?'

I get dressed. It is very, very late and when we get to the bar, all the lights are on and the chairs are on the tables. We explain to the staff the purpose of our mission. We are searching the area where we were sitting. Dave is on his hands and knees under the seats by the wall. He's found something.

'What is it?' I enquire.

'It's my wallet!'

Happily, the bones were also found.

Florida was a regular because 'B' Squadron was often engaged in Nimrod aircraft trials there. The visits of some crew members was so regular that a pair of them, finding themselves, at the end of a stay, with bottles of the hard stuff still two thirds full, buried them in the motel garden, to be recovered on their next visit!

One Florida requirement was to take freight to Andros Island. This was a very small island with an exceedingly short runway. The Britannia was the largest aircraft that had landed there.

An excellent feature of Boscombe Down Britannia flying, compared with Lyneham/Brize Norton, is that we were given the requirement and then worked out our own itineraries. Needless to say, we stuck to gentlemanly hours. To emphasise how we were not 'mainstream Air Force', I mention the fact that on one Florida visit we were obliged to stay there a week and in that time I visited my eldest son, working in the Dominican Republic at the time.

All this seemed too good to be true - which it turned out to be. The economic axe was poised above the Britannia. As in the RAF fleet case, we were busy and could not believe that the aircraft would go - but go it did.

It was decided that future overseas trials would be conducted more as a joint enterprise with the manufacturers - and civilian air transport would be utilised. The aircraft's departure was agonisingly

There was just time, before the scrapping, to fit in a 25th anniversary flight. On 29th April 1983, XX367 was 'author landed' at Filton on that 25 years later, to the day, of its maiden flight.

slow. We stopped flying but it sat in the hangar whilst the Civil Service wheels ground slowly towards a sale. Three months later, because the hangar space was required, we taxied the aircraft to the southern side of the airfield which, in parts, had an appropriate graveyard feel. But the sale proceeded and six months later a very rusty Britannia crew delivered the aircraft to Cranfield for its purchasers. This gave me a 'Claim to Fame'! I was the very last RAF pilot to fly a Britannia!

It would be natural to think that, with the reason for me being at Boscombe Down gone, I would now be returned to the mainstream RAF. But, no. I became increasingly involved in the trials work. A major factor in this was the Falklands War.

One requirement for the operation was the conversion of some Hercules to the air-to-air refuelling tanker role and all the Hercules to be air-to-air refuelling receivers. I flew an enormous number of the trial flights for the former. My abiding memory of this was the moment of disengagement of the receiver aircraft from our hose. Because of some refining required, the force needed was enormous and, with yet another 'yank', I would have this picture of a

Hercules being turned inside out with all the bits that hung on the inside walls, on the outside.

An interlude is taken from this 'Boscombe Down Life' narrative to muse on the title of this book: *'Specialist Aircrew'*. This was chosen to draw attention on two counts. RAF people, familiar with the term, might be attracted; others would see it as an apt description of someone whose working life was devoted to the expertise of flying. These two aspects do have common ground.

It has been outlined that 'Specialist Aircrew' terms of service were introduced to encourage experienced aircrew to remain in the Service. Obviously this was only offered to the deserving who accepted the fact that they were not in the promotion race but, nevertheless were being respected - and rewarded - for their flying skills. All this is by way of introduction to what follows, which occurred in my Boscombe Down, age 50, days.

'Air Clues' is a RAF magazine with a long history. It had developed into a fairly serious publication for the dissemination of topics associated with flying and in particular, flight safety and RAF matters, in general. There would be accounts of notable exercises, expeditions and the like. In the edition of October 1981 there was an article by a Group Captain entitled, *'How Not to be Promoted'*. The Group Captain had spent some time as President of a Promotion Board and the title indicated that he was going to give some positive promotion advice in a negative way.

'A lot of time and effort is spent advising those who wish to be promoted. There are those, however, who are fully satisfied with their present rank and would not relish the responsibility, prestige, money and reserved car parking spaces that go with promotion - or so they say. Assuming, however, that they genuinely wish to be not promoted, then surely they deserve counselling just as much as those who seek success at Promotion Boards ... How best, then, to make sure these (Board) officers don't select you for advancement against your wishes? The first thing the Board members see is your photograph and many who aspire to remain in their present rank make fatal errors even at this preliminary stage. A reasonably smart photograph of an apparently intelligent and alert individual is bound to

impress the Board members. If you want to be sure of getting off to a bad start then perhaps I could suggest the 'shades'? Wearing a pair of these eye-concealing mechanisms is a most effective way of hiding your personality from those who see your photo ... have you thought of a straggly Viva-Zapata moustache? The 'non-military' impression which it adds to a photo is quite considerable.

'The main area of interest for Promotion Board members is, naturally, your set of Forms 1369 (Annual Confidential Reports). What you do and how you do it. You do, of course, do your basic job pretty well ... Let's look at the basic job for a moment, though. Is it the exact job you wanted in the ideal location for you and your family? If not, moan loud and long - so loud and long in fact that one of the officers in the reporting chain gets so fed up with your moaning that he comments on the fact in your Form 1369. If, however, you do like the job, there are plenty of opportunities to slip and inadvertently give the Promotion Board the idea that you seek advancement. It would possibly be fatal to display some enthusiasm for your work and you really would be asking to be seriously considered if you thought of fresh approaches to problems and suggested innovative ideas. Many an officer who may not have wished for promotion has gone wrong in these areas. A simple counter-measure, however, is to direct all your enthusiasm and effort to the parts of the job you like and - whilst being careful to make it obvious - ignore, as far as possible, the parts of the job you don't like ...

'It would perhaps surprise you to know that many officers volunteer for secondary duties - and some even carry out enthusiastically secondary duties which they would rather not have! That's clearly no way to be not promoted and I doubt whether you'd fall into that sort of trap. If, despite all your pleas about living in your own house over four miles away from the station, your evening classes and your wife's job, you nevertheless get a secondary duty, try not to improve the club or society placed in your care ...

'It'll help considerably in your quest for non-advancement if you can avoid, as far as possible, section, squadron, wing and station social events. Only go to the Summer Ball and Christmas Draw if it's impossible to avoid them ...

283

'What about your wife? Here we must tread delicately for there are those who think that an officer's wife has no part to play in his ability to avoid promotion. But this is not so. Those officers who allow their wives to actively support unit social and charitable work and to take an active part in things such as station Girl Guide Companies and Thrift Shops, have only themselves to blame if such matters are commented on favourably in Annual Reports. The problems of home ownership are well understood but what hope of furthering his chances of non-selection can the officer have of whom it has been written, 'Although his wife lives some 180 miles from the station in their own home, she attends all major station, social and other events!' There is far more chance of being not selected if the fact that you live 23 miles from the station is used as a regular excuse for avoiding as much unit life as possible ...

'There are many other ways, of course, to be not promoted but space precludes going into them in great detail You could always keep your golden (or bronze) locks just short enough to ward off your master's immediate wrath whilst being just long enough to give him something to write about in the larger space provided for his words of wisdom on the new Forms 1369. There will always be officers who wish to be promoted and who are working hard towards that end but without apparent success. Perhaps, if they have read this far, they may have - in some curious negative sort of way - recognised some aspect of their own performance which could perhaps be improved upon. who knows - perhaps then those who do not wish advancement go to the photographer with their 'shades' on they might see some of the others facing the camera with clear glass in their spectacles?'

As I read this *'Air Clues'* article, I could feel myself getting hotter and hotter under the collar. I saw this as a direct slur on the likes of me who, for one reason or another, rightly or wrongly, have been denied promotion, but nevertheless try to give the best service we can in the rank that we hold. A riposte was required! This was published in a subsequent edition of the magazine and is reproduced in full below as it, perhaps, neatly sums up the lives and motivations of many 'Specialist Aircrew'.

From: Flight Lieutenant D. E. de Berry, BEd
(A&AEE Boscombe Down)

There must be many officers who were offended by the article, 'How Not to be Promoted' in the October 1981 edition. Perhaps I, as an 'unpromoted' officer can speak on their behalf and further enhance my prospects of not being promoted in a way not covered in the Group Captain's advice - by countering, publicly, the opinion of a senior officer! This is perhaps best done by presenting, in a different light, the picture of the officer that one could imagine from the article.

The picture painted there might be epitomised by, say, a thirty year old Flight Lieutenant, married, two or more children, with his own house located, say, 20 miles from the unit on which he serves. His wife works. He flies, supplies, administrates, 'air traffics', or whatever, 'pretty well' but is not over-enthusiastic about secondary duties, only attends a few social events and thus spends little of his spare time on the station. He has done the minimum to qualify for promotion by passing his 'C' examination but has shown no interest in ISS. Perhaps the only colourful thing about this 'grey' serviceman is his slightly non-military appearance and his somewhat bizarre habit of wearing sunglasses when he is having his photograph taken to accompany his F1369!

Now let the years roll by and, let us say, he is now an 'unpromoted' Specialist Aircrew Flight Lieutenant who is able to reflect on his lack of success in the promotion stakes.

The hypothetical gentleman in question, being an honest individual, does admit that the facts represent his situation but would very much dispute the interpretation that could be put upon it if the criteria in the Group Captain's article are applied. He is indeed still married and happily. He has discovered the pleasure and satisfaction that comes from a strong family nucleus and also realises that such a situation is not created without effort from both partners in the marriage. This was the emotional base, on which to grow, that he and his wife provided for their four children. The physical one was the security of their own family home, purchased, as it now transpires, at an opportune moment which hindsight has revealed would have been foolhardy to let pass by.

He has stayed in the locality through doing his 'basic job pretty well' and thus being 'promoted' in the hierarchy that exists with most flying roles - junior squadron pilot, experienced pilot, senior pilot, OCU instructor/examiner - a progress acknowledged ultimately, let us say, with the award of The Queen's Commendation for Valuable Service in the Air. He does admit, however, to some lack of enthusiasm for secondary duties, for so often he has found that they are in conflict with his primary task and he has only been able to fulfil a token role as Officer i/c or whatever - a situation which must have been acknowledged by his superiors, who knew of his commitments. Furthermore, he sees many of these duties as archaic and not in the spirit of modern living. This would explain his distinct lack of interest in being, say, Officer i/c a barrack block. But then, no one is perfect.

Imperfection shows again in that he admits to the human weakness of directing 'all his enthusiasm and effort' to challenges that appeal to him. On a number of occasions he has been called upon to use that enthusiasm stemming from hobby interests and indeed, on one project it was with such success that he was, let us say, commended by his Commander-in-Chief.

But this failed Flight Lieutenant is further flawed in his off-duty activities; he has indeed not attended too many social functions over the years for he has, fairly in his own mind, divided his attention between the Service and his family and as a result feels some just pride in their achievements. His wife still works and he considers this the most dramatic contribution to the success of his children. He encouraged and helped her to gain further academic qualifications whilst the children were still of pre-school age and then took his full share of domestic activities in order that she might study, as a full time student, to be a teacher. This course of action has reached the ultimate in that she is now, let us say, the headteacher of a large village school.

The effect of all this on the independence of the children was dramatic and their success can be measured by one Master of Science son, now an agricultural adviser in the Caribbean, another who gave four years 'exemplary service' to the Metropolitan Police and is now undergoing training as a RAF pilot, a daughter at University with the chance of a promising career in Food Technology and a youngest son who has just obtained seven Grade 'A' and two Grade 'B' passes at 'O' Level. In addition to his family activities, this imaginary Flight Lieutenant's interests were broad with a taste for academic pursuits, a variety of hobbies and an involvement with local affairs by being, say, a school governor.

So, as was initially stated, this feckless officer who seemed to be deliberately not seeking promotion was married, with children, with his own house. His wife worked. He did his basic job 'pretty well' but was not over enthusiastic about secondary duties or many social events . . .

The original statement was that many unpromoted officers might have been offended by the points made by the Group Captain. But why should they be, if like this mythical person, they have found such contentment in life? I feel that the offence is in the implication that if one is not seen to be doing all the right things, as judged by the standards outlined in the article, then one is not being totally professional, even though carrying out one's basic commitment as completely and expertly as possible, at the rank level held and possibly with which one is quite content in that it allows a balance to be maintained between Service and family life. This could be seen as most unmilitary and not 'fighting talk' but then neither are Summer Balls, Thrift Shops etc.

A broader issue is that the Service could be the loser. I recall from my Education training a piece of jargon - 'The Self Fulfilling Prophecy'; the child only achieves what is expected of it and thus, if labelled 'low achiever', is likely to be just that. I think that, using the criteria in the article, many officers could be similarly dismissively labelled and thus develop the attitude that if little is sought of them then little will be given.

I cannot, for the life of me, remember wearing 'shades' to have my photograph taken ... it must have been after some lunchtime comradeship ... and that's another way of not seeking promotion! Oh, and I must have my, once 'golden', now sadly, white 'locks' cut - that 'curious negative advice' is hitting home!

I felt better after writing that! It produced two curious reactions. Firstly, there was some considerable surprise expressed by my immediate superiors - they were in the promotion race and could not believe that anyone would stick their neck out so far! The second effect was that I had numerous phone calls and letters from fellow officers who were in complete agreement with the opinions that I had expressed. I was slightly concerned that this 'ground swell' would get out of hand and I would find myself leading some Flight Lieutenant's 'Solidarity' movement! I wonder what effect the letter had on my very slim promotion prospects?

Parachuting trials were very much part of the Hercules scene and I constantly flew sorties despatching members of the Parachute Test Team, dummies, ejector seats, one ton containers, huge self-extracting loads, semi-rigid boats ... The idea with the boat was that it would be dropped, followed immediately by the clandestine, raiding party or whatever. I did suggest that if they went out of the aircraft, sitting in the boat, then this would save on parachutes.

This trials work meant a close cooperation with the Parachute Test Team. With the subsequent insight into their work, one could admire the courage that they displayed. One example was the testing of reserve parachutes and those fitted to ejector seats. Because they were only a standby and space/weight being at a premium, they were smaller than a normal parachute, with a consequent higher rate of descent; the philosophy was that a life would be saved but there might be some injury. Testing these on a routine basis could seriously damage the health. When a trial was required, the jumper would leave the aircraft with *three* parachutes. The first was the small one under test. This would be deployed and its behaviour observed - and recorded on video by the cameraman in the photo-chase Harvard. At a specified height, this parachute would be 'cut away' and the second parachute, a normal one, deployed for the landing. The third parachute was the normal reserve!

Dummies were used for some trials. It can be imagined that their 'touchdowns' were not elegant. One day there was some wind misjudgement and the dummy landed on one of the small Salisbury Plain roads causing a passing motorist to stop. It was with some

288

trepidation and a strong hold on his stomach contents that he got out of his car to inspect the 'dead man'.

The Hercules was used as a platform for other trials. One was a test of nerves; we had to fly a very accurate circular pattern over a firing range off the west coast of Wales. At a pre-determined point, an air-to-air missile was fired at us. We had the pre-flight briefing reassurance that there was insufficient fuel in the rocket for it to reach us; we kept our fingers crossed that the trials people had got their sums right! After these sorties, I could do a slight diversion to circle over our Pembrokeshire cottage, which was still going strong and provided Val and I with a wonderful refuge from our busy lives.

It is strange how, what seems a meaningless phrase, can come to play a large part in one's life. The phrase: static line square. When paratroopers, using those standard round parachutes, are despatched from an aircraft, they do not pull their own rip cords. If they did, chaos could ensue with some pulling early, some late ... some not at all! A 25 metre, or so, line attaches their parachute release to the aircraft; when they jumped (or were some pushed?) the line became taut and the parachute would open. This use of a 'static line' had been the way for many years but now a new parachute shape was on the scene; this was rectangular and inflated in the air flow of the descent and took up the shape of a wing. The parachutist could now steer himself and control his point of landing, within the range of the descent. Featuring large in the sports parachuting world, it was seen that this type of canopy could have military applications. There was one snag with this; those 'square' parachutes were released by the parachutist when in stabilised free fall ie with him 'laying', face down, in the airflow, with legs and arms splayed. As outlined above, this would go against military ways. It would also require considerable 'free fall' training.

The decision was to try and develop a system whereby the 'square' parachute was released by a static line. The paratrooper would jump and, with no further action on his part, find himself beneath a deployed canopy. There was an enormous amount of trials work required to develop this system: start with dummies, then with members of the Test Team; five thousand feet, ten, twenty five ...

Having despatched a 'static line square', the Hercules would make sure that there was a safe landing.

Despatch one at a time, a pair, pairs following pairs, a whole aircraft full ... This kept me occupied for many a year. It was great flying as it had an interest. Most of it had the immediacy of being done on our Boscombe Down threshold; from take-off, we could be over the dropping zone, on Salisbury Plain, in a few minutes. We regularly used to drop, return to BD and fly a couple of practice circuits to keep up our training and land, by which time the parachutists would have landed on the dropping zone, boarded the waiting transport and be back for a further drop!

When it came to testing the system with larger numbers and greater heights then there was not enough dropping zone space available in the UK. So, off we would go, for three weeks at a time, to El Centro in the Californian desert. Though not your California of the coastal attraction, these were great times - and there were opportunities to visit the better known parts of CA.

Valerie flew out to join me on one of these detachments and it was absolute magic. One weekend we stayed on the Queen Mary, moored at Long Island as a floating hotel. San Diego was another memorable couple of days. Val came on a few of the parachuting sorties. I am very grateful to the 'static line square'!

Earlier, the use of dummies for tests was discussed and now that the use of a 'static line' has been outlined, the trial of the HUPRA can be described. This piece of equipment is better known for its absence than presence. There's many a parachuting sortie at Lyneham that has been delayed by the question, 'Where's the HUPRA?' If it had been forgotten then the flight would have to wait until it was found. It is a piece of equipment that, to my knowledge, has only been used once in anger, no doubt by a grateful parachutist.

HUPRA stands for Hung Up Parachutist Rescue Assembly. It was seen that it might be possible for a parachutist to exit the aircraft and when the point was reached for the ripcord to be pulled by the taut static line, it did not pull out and he would be dangling on the end of the line - 'hung up'! The HUPRA would be brought into action. This was another parachute with fittings that would allow it to be looped through the shackles on the aircraft end of the static lines which ran along a substantial, fore and aft, cable.

With all secure, an enormous pair of cable cropping shears (they too should be on the aircraft for parachuting sorties) came into play. With them, the cable would be cut and the dangling parachutist would be set free, to descend on the HUPRA parachute. I remember times, at Lyneham, when this drill was briefed or discussed and cable

292

cutting would be described in the terms above:

'When all is set, take the shears and cut the cable.'

On the trials, with a 'no panic', anticipated situation, it took a superhuman, pumped up, effort, by a very fit Test Team member, to sever the cable. I can picture that parachutist being trailed through the air for a very long time whilst some, less than muscular, airloadmaster nibbled away at the half inch thick cable.

Comet now entered that 'Type' column. Boscombe had its own Comet 4, specially fitted out for navigation and radio trials. I started playing a part in these. The flying required was quite exacting. One aspect of this trials flying is again the interest. My knowledge was expanded by one trial where we were told that there is a particular area of the sea off the west coast of Scotland where, because of the rock formation beneath the waves, the earth's gravity is higher than normal. For a week we were required to fly, daily, over this area, on a very precise pattern, which had to arrive back at the starting point at an exact time, the whole to be repeated a number of times. All this was carried out 100 feet above the sea!

Argosy disappeared from my 'Types' column - it had to do a landing with one wheel unlocked. This is not good for aircraft health; this patient did not recover. So, now, Andover appeared. We used to 'borrow' a Hercules from Lyneham for various trials. If one was not currently at Boscombe then the Andover was used for parachuting. I cannot say that I was over enamoured with the Andover; like the Argosy before, it made me realise that I was lucky to have had so long on Britannias!

Passing reference has been made to the manning of The Aeroplane and Armament Experimental Establishment. It was almost total Civil Service - the only RAF element was the aircrew and a few trials officers. This definitely put us outside the mainstream Royal Air Force - which had its advantages! There were a few smaller RAF units 'lodging' at Boscombe Down; one of these was the RAF Handling Squadron. In grander days it had its own fleet of aircraft and its job was to write the Pilots' Notes for these ... the aircraft handbook. In these more stringent times the aircraft had gone but the task continued, the staff liaising with the manufacturers, test

Andover tailgating! The author with Ron Hendrick, flight engineer and Bob Tuxford, test pilot.

establishments and operational units to obtain information for the 'Notes'. In these days when 'sloppy' titles were not allowed to survive, 'Pilots' Notes' had been renamed 'The Aircrew Manual'.

Lunch was always a pleasant social occasion in the small, traditional Officers' Mess and companions at the table were often Handling Squadron people. One sometimes became aware that one of them had had a bad morning. This would be the time when his latest manual amendment list had arrived at the units operating the aircraft. The phone would ring,

'Do you realise that you've said ... and it should really be ...'

'Oh, no!!'

The Britannia notes had a misprint: '... then return the lover to normal ...' The romantic interest was removed by an amendment. It might be thought that just *one* sentence on *one* the amendment list would be sufficient:

'Delete 'lover'; substitute 'lever'.'

A writer of a helicopter amendment list had no such luck:

Part 3, chapter 5, paragraph 10, line 4: delete 'hecilpleters' and substitute 'hepilocters'.

A couple of months later:

Part 3, chapter 5, paragraph 10, line 4: delete 'hepilocters' and substitute 'helipocters'.

Attempt No.3 got it right!

Staying with the whirly birds, there was a lovely story about a time when one type was modified with floats to enable it to operate on and off water. A chapter for the 'Notes' was written to cover this. It contained the instruction:

'*When taxying on water, the speed is to kept to walking pace.*'

In a short space of time, a signal arrived from the unit operating the aircraft:

'*For RAF Handling Squadron ... request further guidance on taxying speed on water as last exponent of walking on it has been dead for nearly 2,000 years.*'

The years roll by at A&AEE; I well and truly pass the traditional 2fi cum 3 year posting point. A factor in this 'leaving well alone' could be my efforts in the non-flying area. A feature of Boscombe Down was that it was, with its 99% civilian manning, definitely Monday to Friday and 8 to 5. This was great for Val and I after years of there being no regard for nights, weekends, public holidays ... Christmas? With the Lyneham/Brize Norton routine, time not flying was time not to be hanging about the squadron. The pattern at Boscombe demanded, really, that one should be 'around' in those normal working hours, just in case something cropped up. This did mean that there could be an awful lot of idle hours. This particularly

applied to those of us tied up with the parachuting business, which is very weather dependent.

I do not like inactivity and had to find a solution. This came in the form of repaying a 'debt'. I have said a number of times that fate can change one's life. If I had not had the opportunity of being an ATC cadet and then enjoying the perks on offer, I would not have joined the Royal Air Force ... and if I hadn't done that? Well, who knows? I can make a good guess that I would not have had such an enjoyable and satisfying working life - or social one. So, I volunteered to become the station's Air Cadet Liaison Officer. This meant that I looked after any ATC cadets that visited. This would be day visits by squadrons. where I would show them around the establishment, and the summer camps where those squadrons would spend a week with us. If done conscientiously, this was quite a commitment, requiring a lot of time and effort - but I found it very satisfying.

There is an old Service adage, 'Never volunteer!' Now I was to do it again! In the past, there had been an A&AEE magazine, but it had become defunct. Obviously, all that writing that I had done at college had created an 'urge'! So, I volunteered to resurrect the publication. There was a learning curve with this, each edition improving with the last. It was all quite an effort; strangely this wasn't my part - the collection of material, the editing, the writing of my 'bits'.

Production was the bugbear. This was done from the Establishment's resources and required an awful lot of cajoling of the reluctant. Then, out of the blue, there came an unbelievable offer. A company had established itself to specialise in the production of these 'Station Magazines'. Their success depended on advertising; we, the amateurs, would collect the material; they, the experts, would assemble it, create a cover and internal layout - and persuade, mainly local, businesses etc to advertise. I believe this was done pretty ruthlessly! It worked. We had a professional looking magazine and this went on for the rest of my days at Boscombe - and, I believe, is still going strong.

I didn't volunteer for my next non-flying job - I was volunteered into it. The Establishment's, Civil Servant, Public Relations Officer had a stroke. The Commandant decided that the replacement should be a Service officer. Look no further than the Air Cadet Liaison Officer, who had experience of presenting the Establishment image, albeit to a lowly audience. It was a mistake ... I did it, but it was hard work. There were constant phone calls and correspondence, the basic principle with many being, 'If you're not sure how to deal with a query, direct it to the PRO.'

If it could be kept under control, there was a party once a week to be shown around - out of control there were two or more. There are times, now, when I find myself, with a group, being guided around a stately home, a power station, whatever. I recognise the guide's style ... the same joke, told many times before, at the same spot! With the repetition, one did develop quite a style.

If I hadn't been in my fifties, compatriots would have commented that I was obviously going for the Air Marshal rank. But, even at my time of life, there was an important outcome of all this extra-curricular activity. One day I was accompanying yet another group around the Establishment.

At one port of call I had one of the welcome breaks where a member of that staff took over. There was a phone call for me. For a number of years, to improve man management, the Air Secretary's branch had been established. Within it were 'Desk Officers' with the responsibility for caring for the affairs of an allocated group of officers. It was my Desk Officer on the line,

'Have you thought about applying for service beyond 55?'

The age of 55 years was less than three years away and I had been giving some thought to asking to stay to age 58 as I felt that 55 was too young to stop work and I had no inclination to start into something new. I replied:

'I thought it was perhaps time to make a few enquiries.'

'Well, I'd write your letter now.'

This was very odd. There was no need to recruit people for the extra service; there were more applicants than vacancies.

'Is there any reason why you are telling me this?' I asked.

'Keep it under your hat, but your name is going before the promotions board and your chances are almost 100% but we wouldn't be able to promote you because of the three year rule. You haven't that much time left to do.'

It was a really pleasant surprise to receive such acknowledgement so late in life - especially as such promotions for Specialist Aircrew were as rare as rocking horse ... well, there weren't that many.

Come 1st July 1986, I duly rose to the rank of Squadron Leader - Biggles had made it! I must have been the oldest and most senior Flight Lieutenant ever to have been promoted. It was important to me as it endorsed my 'Senior Citizen' status for those remaining years.

One thing perhaps to feel cynical about is that you might be the best pilot in the Royal Air Force and be a total expert in a particular area, flying hundreds of hours in a year. But you might not get promoted. If one distinguishes oneself in other fields, then that might be recognised. I had been that Air Cadet Liaison Officer, Editor and PRO! But what about 'that' letter?

A couple more years of that varied flying at Boscombe took me up to that age 55. Even VC10, Nimrod and TriStar appeared in my log book. In all I completed seven years at A&AEE.

What would that Air Secretary's branch find for my extra three years in the Service?

Chapter 25

Those that can, do - those that can't, teach.

Such were the advances in 'Man Management' that my posting was discussed with me. There was a vacancy - the pilot instructor - in the Hercules Ground School at ... Lyneham! Would I care to fill that post? I was only too pleased! Back to a seven mile drive to work - it had been 40 miles each way to Boscombe. But that was the least factor. I thought I would find the job most satisfying. I was, after all, a fully trained teacher who had never exercised that skill in anger!

So, farewell Boscombe Down and hello, once again, Lyneham. Not a lot had changed except that many of the aircrew seemed younger than ever. This particularly applied to my students. My job was to teach the pilots, new to the aircraft, 'pilot things'. This included Aircraft Performance and the associated calculations and route flying matters. Other members of staff covered technical and navigation subjects. The ten week course preceded the students' flying phase.

I did find it challenging, as much of what I taught were things that one should know but did not have to use very often; so there was a lot of DIY refresher training. I gradually sorted my own notes out - I did not exactly inherit a sparkling collection. The overhead projector was much in evidence and I produced my own set of slides. In time, I wrote notes for each subject for the students and developed work sheets which aided them in the take-off and landing performance calculations they were obliged to carry out. I was greatly assisted in this with my computer abilities which had developed since my college days.

Shortly after my arrival, the Ground School was presented with a computer. My fellow instructors, mostly on the mature side, said:

'Great - we can produce our own notes, OHP slides and all that stuff!'

Their belief was that computers were extremely clever and if they stretched their hands out above the keyboard and said, 'Make me some notes on ...' the requirement would be, miraculously, realised. I assembled the computer and installed the software.

Instructor No.1 sits down. The instruction on the screen is: 'Press return to continue.' 'Where's return?' Before long, disillusionment sets in and I had the machine to myself. There really is a long apprenticeship to serve in the computer game ... particularly if you are of those maturer years.

A computer spin-off came for me around this time. When I had been editing that Boscombe Down magazine I discovered that 'editing' means providing a lot of the material oneself. I wrote a series of articles, under a pseudonym, entitled 'Tales from the Crewroom'. This was, literally, what they were, a collection of some of the stories which used to be told wherever aircrew gathered together. My hypothesis was that such 'Tales' are the folklore of today. Like folklore, the stories change, are rounded, with telling and retelling until exaggeration is present. With the magic of the computer, I had saved my series and I now proceeded to assemble it into book form. I sounded out a few publishers and I had the incredible good fortune, which I increasingly realised in subsequent years, to have it accepted by a highly reputable one. This launched my 'writing career'!

I had also been working on a history of the RAF Britannia, on and off, for several years and I started to put out feelers for the publication of this but without success, 'Great idea, great book - but in a very small interest area.' Times were tough in the book business and the publishers were now quite hard nosed.

Time rolled by in the Ground School and it might seem a bit of a treadmill as course after course passed through our hands. But there could be good breaks in between which gave the opportunity to improve one's material. There was certainly a lot of 'learning as one went along'. In our classroom each student was allocated a shelf in a cupboard to hold all the necessary publications etc required for lectures. I followed the style of my predecessor and would write a list on the blackboard:

> *The books required for this lecture:*
> *AP1234*
> *The Flight Planning Document*
> *The UK En Route Supplement*
> *RTOGs.*

Inevitably, when the point was reached, in the lecture, to refer to a particular book, there would be:
'Oh, I haven't got that one.'
This would be followed by the disturbance and delay as the miscreant retrieved the missing book from the cupboard. Some alternative scheme was required. At this stage I remembered part of my teacher training. With very young children, 'Matching' is a good exercise. Give them five different buttons and a tin of assorted ones

and ask them to find as many as they can of the same. I abandoned the list on the board and laid my copies of the required books on a table by the door. As they came in they could see that they wanted the 'yellow book', the 'big thick one' and the one with the 'green cover with red writing'. Success!

With course dates plotted well in advance, it was possible to make holiday plans. We had been urged for many years by my long standing compatriot and friend, Bob Henderson, to visit his home country, Canada. We went for it, flying to Vancouver and hiring a car for three weeks.

The flight was a cheap one and it was awful. At Gatwick, it was only revealed to us at the last moment that the aircraft had to land at Prestwick to pick up fuel. We stayed on the aircraft during that refuel. Headwinds were obviously a problem and part way across Canada the captain announced that we would have to stop at Edmonton for more fuel. We stayed on board once more.

We arrived at Vancouver totally knackered! But the hotel was good and our room was a fantastic one overlooking the harbour. It was evening and we had a room service meal all laid up at a table by the window. The wounds of the ghastly flight were healing.

A few days later we set off north east by way of Ashcroft, Kamloops and Revelstoke, eventually reaching The Rockies. We found these absolute magic for five or six days. We then drove west, through rather dull countryside, but with the aim of reaching Prince Rupert. There we caught the car ferry for the 16 hour journey south through The Inner Passage. Landfall was the northern tip of Vancouver Island. We then drove the length of the island to reach Victoria - with its Victorian air. Then it was back to Vancouver for the flight home. This was a great three week trip and whetted our appetite for more of this sort of travel.

Back to the Ground School and another succession of courses. Same lessons, same problems with particular students, same jokes at the same points in a lesson! The age of 58 was approaching remarkably quickly. Perhaps because I saw it as a last opportunity, I applied for an 'indulgence flight'. These were open to all military personnel and their dependents and was a seat on a transport aircraft on an opportunity basis. Apply for a seat and have the application approved and forwarded to the movements authority ... and wait for the phone to ring. Our bid was for Canada; we wanted to return to The Rockies and spend more time there. Our number came up:

'Report to Brize Norton for a VC10 flight to Edmonton.'

This was going to be a 'significant time' in our lives that would shape our leisure time for years to come. On arrival at Edmonton, we checked into an hotel and went straight to the Yellow Pages to look for motorhome hire companies. We decided this was the way to see the area. Very quickly we were in a taxi visiting a firm and being shown a very smart vehicle that was available. The next day we were in it and on our way west. That was the best fortnight's holiday I have ever had and it convinced Valerie and I that we should take up motorcaravanning. A couple of months after our return we bought our first and have not been without one since. There was a further significance to The Rockies trip. I wrote an article on our experience, illustrated with my photographs. This was accepted by the premier motorcaravanning magazine and was the start of me being a regular contributor.

Only a couple of months to go to 'the big five eight' and I had no misgivings about leaving the Service. At 55, I wasn't ready - now I was ... totally.

Chapter 26
The Sword is Hung Up

I have never really got used to the magic of retirement - each day like a weekend ... leave ... public holiday. I have to remind myself that it this going to last for the rest of my days. I think I am totally cut out for this way of life!

I severed all but one of my links with the Service - some retired officers become honorary members of the Officers' Mess. I think this is a mistake; once you are not part of the working scene, the common ground is lost. I had witnessed others in this situation. The one link is that I play my part in The Britannia Association, an organisation for past members of the RAF Britannia fleet.

Part of the magic of my way of life is that I like to think I am only semi-retired; the writing business has grown. I mentioned articles for motorcaravanning magazines. These were fed by our increasing activity in the pastime. Not a month passes by without us going away - perhaps just for a week. Twice a year we take major breaks of five weeks or more. These have taken us to France several times, Spain, Germany and Austria ... and many, many parts of the UK, which we 'discover'.

Our first motorcaravan was a German one, secondhand but hardly used. A year with this gave us a greater appreciation of internal layouts and we bought the one of our dreams - a new French model. Interspersed with our European and UK travels, we visited the USA a number of times. On three of these occasions we hired an American motorhome.

These were great trips. Leisure is so big in the USA; on one trip we drove, over several weeks, the length of a road totally dedicated to recreation - speed limit 35 mph. The Blue Ridge Highway is 469 miles long! We found the State Parks totally to our liking.

These hirings gave us a taste for the style, size and luxury of American motorhomes. As a 60th birthday treat, daughter Alison (now the mother of four!) took us to a, near to her home, motorcaravan dealer who stocked American motorhomes. That was our downfall - we bought a Winnebago, which we had for four years. We then made the mistake of visiting another dealer and 'fell' for the latest 28 foot model.

All this is spelt out to illustrate how Valerie and I occupy a lot of our time. But it also explains my progress with writing. With my motorcaravanning experience, I felt I was qualified to write a

The 28 foot Winnebago - quite a toy!

handbook. This I did, illustrated with my own photographs and drawings ... and it was accepted by a publisher! I was, naturally, very pleased to have a second book taken up - but there was a disappoint-ment; I could not persuade the publisher to produce the book in the style I had in mind.

The consequence was a very for-mal-looking book with an informal title: '*The Motorcaravan Handbook*'. But it *was* another book in the market place - very popular with libraries! My thanks to the people who established Public Lending Right payments!

I was getting 'The Taste' - what could I write next? But it was already written ... 100,000 words worth of RAF Britannia history - with over 180

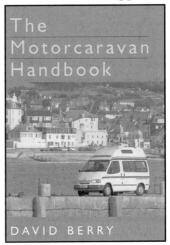

The
Motorcaravan
Handbook

DAVID BERRY

photographs (thanks to the many ex-compatriots who supported my project). With the lack of publishing house takers, I started looking at 'Self Publishing' - mistakenly called, by some, DIY publishing.

Have you often seen adverts with the wording '*Authors Wanted*' or something similar? These may cause you to muse on the, often proclaimed, difficulty of budding authors wanting to be published - '*Manuscripts Wanted*', scream the ads. 'Everyone has one book in them' - go ahead and write it and then try to find a recognised publisher. Sadly, the substantial odds are that you will be disappointed; you need an enormous amount of talent - and luck - to break into this market.

The obvious thing to do, then, is to turn to these 'author hungry' establishments. Contact them and you will find that they are not what they seem. They will, indeed, publish your book - at a price - a price that you pay. The spectrum of this market is that, at one end, with a good company playing things very fair, you will receive advice and the employment of professional skills to produce an, appearance-wise, sellable book. There will then follow some degree of help with marketing.

It is this factor which is the potential disaster area for the self-publisher. Professional publishing houses have their armies of representatives pressuring booksellers. Alongside these, the loner stands little chance. Also, there is a need to be brutally frank at this stage - you will be trying to sell a book that was not thought to be commercially viable. This is quite a barrier for even the best marketing organisation to overcome.

That was the brighter end of the spectrum. Hand your money over to a company at the darker end and you might not see any books at all for your outlay. If you do, then they will be of poor quality and perhaps only provided in dribs and drabs to, so say, match your sales progress. You will hear this, 'Print my book at all costs' referred to as vanity publishing. It really is the book world equivalent of pouring money down the drain.

But my point is not to highlight these realities of 'self-publishing' but to argue that it is misleading to call it DIY. In the home improvement scene, DIY involves gathering ideas, plans etc, purchasing tools and materials and then getting stuck into the job yourself. I did this, in the end, with the Britannia history.

As endeared as I and my ex-compatriots are to this aircraft, it was not in the Spitfire league and, with the typescript written and photographs gathered, I was unable to interest a publisher - and I tried something like 40! But I was sure that there was some sort of market - I personally knew 600 people sufficiently interested in the aircraft to belong to an association that revelled in reminiscences. Then there is a huge number of aviation enthusiasts and, as this was to be the only book on this particular aircraft, it only needed a very small percentage interest for more sales.

Convinced of all this I started investigating self-publishers. For 1,000 copies of a 250 page, A4 softback format book I received quotes varying between £9,000 and £12,000. My calculations told me that, at its best, this would make it a profitless labour of love - at the worst, a financial disaster.

My enthusiasm was waning when one of the self-publishers invited me, as we lived fairly close together, to visit him to discuss the project. It will turn out that he did not do himself a favour. He showed me his computer set-up and the software he used. Having been a computer user for many years, I had a machine as good as, if not better than, his. I needed a scanner and a removable hard disk to totally match his equipment. I also needed to purchase the profes-sional piece of software - QuarkXpress.

With all this sitting on my desk it was time to take the plunge - my learning curve had to be quite steep. I am sure that my use of the software would give the professionals the shudders - but 'there are more ways ...' I am also sure that I had a lot of good luck on my side.

Not unnaturally, I used samples of professionally produced books as examples. It was clear I needed an ISBN but, having obtained the appropriate address from the 'Writers and Artists Yearbook', this proved remarkably straightforward. The layout of the title page normally has the publishing house's imprint. I decided to create 'Keyham Books' (Keyham is the name of my house) to give the book and marketing a professional air. I determined that one can quite legally just create such a 'company', the only proviso being that one's own name must appear on business stationery.

After many weeks of effort - and it is amazing how long the closing stages take - indexing, in particular, comes to mind - I had the complete book on my internal hard disk; I had not indulged in a removable one at this stage.

Now was the time to emerge from the amateurism of my study into the professional world of the printers. I consulted the Yellow Pages for the ones that proclaimed that they worked directly from hard disk on to their printing machines. I was pleasantly surprised that my clearly novice status did not discourage replies. One large firm was particularly helpful and offered to send a representative to discuss my requirements. It turned out that their direct use of hard disk was not that advanced. This was fortunate as my efforts were not sufficiently sophisticated to employ this method anyway.

It was suggested that my material should be put to the test by their studio which produces the negatives for the printing plates. This required a removable hard disk and it was agreed that I would be loaned one! How helpful can you get! I was shown around the printing works to give me a better appreciation of the processes involved.

That level of assistance continued; my scanning of the photographs was too dark - some darkening occurs during the printing

The Whispering Giant
in Uniform

The story of the Bristol Britannia in Royal Air Force service
1959 - 1975
Told by Squadron Leader David Berry

process so this has to be taken into account at the scanning stage. I redid the photographs. I found it difficult to produce the cover as one item ie front, spine and back; my, provided, separate components were assembled into one. Bromide proofs of the pages arrived, followed by a full colour one of the cover. Thrilling moments.

A more sombre one was handing over money - 50% was required with the order, the balance prior to delivery. I was pretty confident that I could sell 500 copies - my order for 1,000 was being speculative. The cost of printing - £4,000. A sobering moment was when the pile stood in my garage.

Marketing was now the big challenge. Fortunately I received good commercial advice on an RRP - I have learnt a lot in the process on a reasonable price to charge bookshops - talk of them wanting 40% discount might apply to bulk orders - much less appears acceptable when supplying single copies to meet individual customer orders.

My shop window was aviation magazine reviewers. I bombarded every possibility with a review copy. I interested local radios in being interviewed; from my correspondence files I concocted a mail shot list. I made the book available by mail order and I managed, with a touch of good fortune, to get it on the booksellers' CD-ROM catalogue.

The result? All 1,000 copies sold in just over a year! Profit? Immense satisfaction and a 'wave of the hand figure' of some thousands of pounds - this does not bear

RV in UK

A guide to the British operation of an American motorhome
by David Berry

close scrutiny, which would reveal many 'incidentals'!

With this success, I decided to try another niche in the book market. I now had considerable experience of operating an American motorhome in this country and there are some 'ins and outs' to this. '*RV in UK*', a guide to the British operation of an American motorhome, was the result. This, again, was a DIY production. As I write, it is selling well enough.

So, I think I can claim to be only semi-retired. What next? You've read it!

Tailpipe

You have had the full treatment: the boyhood and the man's life. You can do a bit of psychoanalysis: what counts most - Nature or Nurture?

The title of this book is very significant to me - I wasn't cut out to be an Air Marshal but I hope that I matched up to the category of 'Specialist Aircrew'; I certainly tried to. But what you have read may have left you with the impression that I feel, whatever one is doing, life is to be enjoyed. Look for humour, particularly in demanding, uncomfortable or unpleasant situations.

Books of this nature are usually full of derring-do. This account has been a bit short on bullets, bombs and the like. But we were playing our part, in those 1950s, 60s, 70s and 80s, in maintaining a fragile peace - one based on the potential for action rather than action itself. Perhaps the former needs as much dedication and professionalism as the latter - a lot of self-motivation is required.

I have tried to make this an aviator's book - but a woman has kept creeping into the account. Perhaps it is a measure of how I feel about her and how my 'Life and Times' would not have been the same without ... Valerie.

The Britannia Association exists for the benefit
of members and ex-members of the
Royal Air Force and Women's Royal Air Force
whose service was associated with
the Bristol Britannia.
An annual reunion is held and there is a
magazine twice a year.

If you are qualified to join then details can be
obtained from the publishers of this book :

Keyham Books, Startley, Chippenham SN15 5HG